Adventures in
Sustainable Urbanism

D1528652

Adventures in Sustainable Urbanism

Edited by

Robert Krueger, Tim Freytag,
and Samuel Mössner

Cover art: Jane McNeil-McKeag, *Christchurch Redux*, mixed media on plastic paper, 12" × 9", 2015. Collection of Robert Krueger, Tim Freytag, and Samuel Mössner.

Published by State University of New York Press, Albany

© 2019 State University of New York

All rights reserved

Printed in the United States of America

No part of this book may be used or reproduced in any manner whatsoever without written permission. No part of this book may be stored in a retrieval system or transmitted in any form or by any means including electronic, electrostatic, magnetic tape, mechanical, photocopying, recording, or otherwise without the prior permission in writing of the publisher.

For information, contact State University of New York Press, Albany, NY
www.sunypress.edu

Library of Congress Cataloging-in-Publication Data

Names: Krueger, Robert, 1968– editor.
Title: Adventures in sustainable urbanism / edited by Robert Krueger,
    Tim Freytag, and Samuel Mössner.
Description: Albany : State University of New York, [2019] | Includes
    bibliographical references and index.
Identifiers: LCCN 2018054676 | ISBN 9781438476490 (hardcover : alk. paper) |
    ISBN 9781438476483 (pbk. : alk. paper) | ISBN 9781438476506 (ebook)
Subjects: LCSH: Urban ecology (Sociology) | City planning—Environmental
    aspects.
Classification: LCC HT241 .A38 2019 | DDC 307.1/216—dc23
LC record available at https://lccn.loc.gov/2018054676

10 9 8 7 6 5 4 3 2 1

Contents

Illustrations

Figures

Tables

Preface

Initially, our plan was to publish a book focusing on the social dimension of sustainable urban development. We wanted to present a series of models from the world over to show that many projects—although promoted as promising contributions to sustainable urban development—can be questioned and contested in terms of social equity and social justice. During the process of composing the book, we became increasingly aware that we should not limit ourselves to one way of looking at sustainable urban development, but to open ourselves to a broad range of perspectives. We thus decided to present the series of models in a "field trip" format in order to provide readers with firsthand experience of places as "raw materials" that must be actively assembled to produce meaning.

Adventures in Sustainable Urbanism is not just a book, but a starting point, an invitation, an open project to examine sustainable urban development in novel and exciting ways. Our aim is to involve students, scholars, and decision makers in many parts of the world. From this point on, you can be part of this exciting and interactive proposition. It is in your hands to explore the following pages as a living book and to activate connections with your real-life experiences. Thus, the book is what you will make of it; you are entitled not only to produce and to share, but also to critically reflect on knowledge of sustainable urban development.

As editors, we are happy and grateful to have received such good responses and excellent field trips from our contributors. Now we're excited at the prospect of putting the book into practice. We plan to use the text in teaching classes at our universities and to share it with practitioners. We hope it will be seen as a valuable resource for teaching and thinking. It is our plan to establish an interactive website that allows our readers to share their own adventures in sustainable urbanism, with an aim of representing many countries and regions not included in this initial project due to space constraints. We are looking forward to learning from your experiences.

Rob Krueger
Tim Freytag
Samuel Mössner

Introduction

Global Transformations, Cities, and the New Sustainability Consensus

ROBERT KRUEGER, TIM FREYTAG, AND SAMUEL MÖSSNER

The end of the twentieth century marked a profound transformation of the Earth's natural and social systems. For example, some geologists postulate that the Earth, for the first time in human existence, is in a geological epoch where the influence and transformative power of human beings has become the *de facto* dominant force in nature; indeed, the very layers of the Earth show the profound effects of human activities. This new era is often referred to as the "Anthropocene." And it's not evidenced only in the Earth's crust, as *The Economist* (2011) has poignantly claimed something even more extraordinary: "Humans have changed the way the world works." Following on, we, the editors, soberly call for a fundamental change in how we think about the Earth and its systems. To be sure, the search for new modes of managing global change and consequent transformations is *the* major global task of today.

Some have tried to extend the concept of the Anthropocene to cities. The Population Division of the United Nations Department of Economic and Social Affairs, for example, has reported in the World Urbanization Prospect that by 2050 two-thirds of the world population will live in urban areas (UNDES, 2014: 7). Consequently, the Intergovernmental Panel on Climate Change considers urban adaptation an opportunity "for incremental and transformative adjustments to development trajectories toward resilience and sustainable development" (IPCC, 2014: 538). At the same time, however, this observation is disrupting our traditional and somehow romanticized imaginary of cities, with some authors arguing that we all live in a moment of planetary urbanization (Brenner, 2014). These two big transformations can be merged into one term—"Urban Anthropocene"—establishing urban areas and processes of urbanization as the focal points for sustainable interventions.

Today, you would be hard pressed to find anyone opposed to sustainability. This is not to say that everyone agrees with what it means to be sustainable, but perhaps it *does* mean the concept should be addressed, no matter how we choose to define it. For example, in a recent radio report, the executive director of the Heartland Foundation, based in Alberta, Canada, claimed that constructing a pipeline for that province's oil shale is "more sustainable" than trucking the fossil fuels to refineries in the United States. "Sustainability" is thus a concept that means everything and nothing, which is not to suggest the concept lacks social importance. Indeed, there are significant material implications when the concept is invoked in whatever form. There may be a new sustainability consensus, and this makes things more complicated.

Before going further, let us explore *sustainability* as a word, or a set of words, that are common in our vocabulary. In its most basic form, sustainability can be thought of as a three-legged stool, with the legs representing social, economic, and environmental domains. At an urban scale, one manifestation of sustainability could be thought of as the locus where economic security, ecological integrity, and social well-being are linked in a complementary fashion. In the following sections we will develop our argument as to why transforming sustainability from theory to practice is not so simple. Further, we will help you think transformatively about sustainable urban development.

Sustainability: Simply from Theory to Practice?

There are dozens of definitions of sustainability. However, the challenge of sustainable development does not lie here; rather, it is in the details. Indeed, over twenty years ago, academic planner Scott Campbell made the bold statement that "in the battle of big public ideas, sustainability has won: the task of the coming years is simply to work out the details and to narrow the gap between its theory and practice" (Campbell, 1996: 301). We believe the first clause of this statement is accurate, and it has stood the test of time. It is true that sustainability, and its various synonyms (e.g., green, renewable, smart), have become household terms. But if the second clause in Campbell's statement were true, we would not have needed to write this book. While you can hardly find anyone in the world who is against the idea of sustainability, narrowing the gap between theory and practice has hardly been simple.

Forming, Norming, and Performing Sustainability

Sustainability is a long-established concept that means many different things depending on who you ask. For people in the global north, the meaning of sustainability is quite different from that held in the global south—the meanings can even seem contradictory. The concept is defined differently by people living in the countryside from those living in the city. It can be a very narrow term, such as sustainable economic growth, or very broad, as conceptualized by the World Commission on Environment and Development in 1987. No matter how its meaning is understood, sustainability, both conceptually and in practice, is imbued with various politics and influenced by various political forces in different places and times. Sometimes it is mobilized as a concept to influence policymakers and to get "buy-in" from stakeholders. Sustainability is thus both a *word*, often used in adjective form—*sustainable*—to describe behaviors and conditions, as well as a *concept* that implies a set of principles for how the economy, environment, and society interface should function. This book explores many of the different influences and forces that act on sustainability concerns as they have been understood in the conceptual academic literature as well as in practice, primarily in urban contexts, which we will henceforth term as "sustainable urban development."

Sustainability, only a generation old as a discrete concept, has a long historical legacy. In terms of practice, it has been implemented differently in different places. Indeed, many policies and practices go by the same names. Local Agenda 21, a process for envisioning sustainable urban futures conceived in Rio de Janeiro in 1992, has been implemented thousands of times around the globe. However, no two processes or their respective outcomes have been identical. These differences can largely be attributed to the material needs of the cities and the perceptions of various stakeholders where they were conceived. Phoenix differs from Boston;

Paris differs from Rome; Berlin differs from London; and Johannesburg differs from Rio. The institutions and agencies that develop sustainability programs also differ. Sustainable urban development can be initiated by local NGOs, local economic development agencies, planning organizations, or politicians.

Finally, perhaps the most difficult to understand are the forces that act on practice of sustainability. These practices, as well as the concepts from which they come, are not created in a vacuum, but have complex social histories attached to them and norms—agreed upon ways of doing things—that preceded them. These histories and norms do not go away with each new generation of policymaking or conceptual understanding of a problem; the "old" and the "new" get braided together in new and unpredictable ways. Thus, there is not a single idea shaping practices out there that doesn't have a complex and diverse social history. What makes these histories even more challenging to comprehend is that they represent norms. If norms are the established ways of doing things, this means that actors involved in these processes don't think about these histories; they merely act in accordance with the past, as a perceived matter of course. The point we are making here is that ideas are *socially constructed*. In procedural terms, scholars call the process of braiding new conceptual and programmatic ideas with existing and preexisting notions *social construction*. This means that despite having a *normative* conceptual status, actors and institutions will privilege different aspects of a new idea and bring their own particular context to bear on it without thinking about these details. Social norms exist, but they are not consistent across space, even when they look exactly alike.

The Power of Words: Sustainability as Text

Thinking sustainably takes a number of forms. It's theoretical—about how the economy functions and people's role in shaping it. Thinking sustainably is a conceptual act in that it requires us to consider explicitly, but more often implicitly, the connections between the three domains of sustainability. Above all else, sustainability is a word. Even with its diverse and variegated meanings, the *word* has become part of our common parlance—"my hybrid car is sustainable," "my organic food is a sustainable form of agriculture," "my city buys sustainable energy," "I live in a green building," and so on. The last example, green building, shows the common connection people make between sustainability and greenness, and in popular usage the terms are synonymous. We could just as easily substitute "green" as a descriptor in each of the examples above ("my city buys green energy," etc.). Philosophers and social theorists have noted for some time the power of words. Rorty, for example, argues that language is "interposed, like a cushion between us and the real world" (1991: 81). A simple example illustrating this viewpoint comes from the current environmental condition under global debate: is it "climate change" or "global warming"? Just a generation ago, global warming was the phrase of choice for scientists, policymakers, and the public, as far as global warming figured in the public debate—in the United States, at least. As research evolved on this issue, it turned out that global warming was only one factor of climate change, which seemed to have regional and annual variations. Other factors include acidification of the oceans and extreme weather events, such as rain, snow, drought, and superstorm cells. Yet, despite this conceptual change, the phrase "global warming," the words "global" and "warming" together, are sometimes used as a foil to action on climate change because in many places the weather is not warmer. Words, then, can be more than just combinations of letters that have meaning; they are employed instrumentally to harness power.

"Green," a popular synonym for sustainability does not come without rhetorical consequences. Think for a moment about the rhetorical difference between the words "green" and "sustainable." Being green implies environmental consciousness, but are all green acts sustainable? For us, the answer is no. What is beneficial to the environment does not always bring broader social benefits. Sustainability scholar Julian Agyeman has argued "a truly sustainable society is one where wider questions of social needs and welfare, and economic opportunity, are *integrally* connected to environmental concerns" (2013: 5). For him, the power of the word *green* obscures the wider question of social needs and welfare. Thus, what is green for one social group may have a negative social impact or affect the welfare of another. This is different—albeit similar—from the concept of "green washing," which refers to practices used by organizations to create the perception that they are good, assuming green equals good or desirable, when in reality they are going about business as usual. "Green" as it is used here is a powerful social construct that has made being green popularly synonymous with sustainability. To do so, it uses real—and perceived—green benefits to suggest that social welfare and needs are being incorporated into policy and practice.

Sustainable Development? No. Yes. It Depends . . .

In the previous section, we described how words are used instrumentally to create the illusion of certain outcomes while obscuring the undesirable consequences. Let us illustrate this point through a few examples.

The Green Economy

Local Agenda 21 was developed as Chapter 21 of Agenda 21, which came out of the United Nations Sustainable Development Conference in 1992. Twenty years later, in June of 2012, leaders from around the world again gathered in Rio de Janeiro at the "Rio +20" Conference. On the agenda at the conference was the "green economy." A generation ago, having a green economy on the agenda would have seemed anathema to a high-level conference on development. However, the world had only a few years prior experienced the worst economic downturn since the Great Depression, and there was a need for alternatives. Just as the Welfare State in the United States, led by Franklin D. Roosevelt, was an alternative to laissez faire capitalism of the 1920s and early '30s, the global "green economy" discourse embodied an antidote for the corrupt economy that brought derivatives, toxic debt, and a minimally regulated US banking industry.

Going green had been sought in earnest by some national governments for some time, such as in Scandinavia and Germany, which was essentially a corporate fad for a number of years. However, in current times, mainstream national governments, such as the United States and United Kingdom, have started adopting the discourse and fabricating new economic policies to support these visions. For example, the UK Central Government spoke of a "Green New Deal" where the nation's economic direction would be based on a postcarbon economy. In the United States, presidential candidate Barack Obama ran partially on a "green jobs" platform, which sought to reskill workers whose jobs were rendered obsolete after the economic crisis of 2008. China, the heir apparent to become the world's economic superpower, put its industrial machine into green technology. Most recently, as part of a green economy initiative—but veiled as a "good global citizen" initiative—Switzerland, a country that uses nuclear power to obtain 37 percent of its energy, announced a plan to reduce its CO_2 output to below 50 percent of 1990 levels, all while decommissioning its nuclear power system.

Back at Rio +20, there remained room for skepticism for some. In fact, as the conference sponsored by the United Nations was being held at the site of the 2016 Summer Olympics, some 50,000 people took to the streets of Rio proper to protest the green economy as it was being framed by the United Nations. Who could be against a green economy? After all, doesn't the green economy help polar bears, benefit ecologically sensitive areas, and create wealth and jobs? Maybe. But, for the United Nations (and others), it did. In 2011, for example, the UNEP published a report entitled *Towards a Green Economy: Pathways to Sustainable Development and Poverty Eradication*, which argued that the green economy results in "improved human well-being and social equity, while significantly reducing ecological risks and environmental scarcity" (2011: 16). What, then, could the protestors be so upset about? For one, they were concerned about the institutional mechanisms associated with the "free" market that would supposedly deliver these goals. For them, the market had neither brought economic security nor social justice. One need only to look at the composition of the protestor groups to see this: labor unions, Indigenous rights organizations, women's groups, and, of course, some environmental organizations. For them, the work on the green economy, taking place on the future Olympic grounds, was adopting the words of sustainability but invoking the same delivery mechanisms that had led to previous rounds of environmental destruction, economic downturn, and uneven distribution of wealth.

URBAN REGENERATION AND RENEWABLE ENERGY

Policies about renewable energy development and urban regeneration in the United States offer another example of the instrumental use of the rhetoric of sustainability. In 2008, the United States Environmental Protection Agency established the "RE-powering America Lands" initiative. This initiative sought to convert tens of thousands of acres of America's most contaminated lands to sites of green energy production. For many, these are "sustainable" solutions in that the United States' growing electricity demand will be met by green sources, thus producing fewer greenhouse gases. It will help the economy by providing much-needed jobs to rural and urban America. It will take the stress off of undeveloped land (greenfield sites) and thus help maintain natural carbon sinks, and it will help clean up sites in communities that need development. The rhetoric, the *words*, of this policy discourse suggests that this is a sustainable outcome. Who could argue against creating jobs, hazardous site clean-ups, and fewer carbon emissions? But do the words belie the concept of sustainability? The answer is, "It depends." It certainly provides "sustainable" benefits for some, yet for others the benefits are less clear. Consider those living around a contaminated site (or brownfield) in a city programmed for a green energy development. Their level of economic security is lower because they live proximate to such a site (Bullard, 2000). They have borne a higher level of risk over time because of their proximity to such sites. Moreover, the clean-up standard will be lower because the land use is industrial, not recreational or housing. Further, chances are that the jobs produced won't be from their neighborhood. Finally, because of the way grid infrastructure works, the electrons produced by the green system on the converted brownfield site will not benefit those living near it. So, the winners do not compensate the losers, a key concept called *pareto optimality* in market-oriented economic thinking.

PLANNING FOR PARKS AND RECREATION

Inequity becomes more evident when using an example from public parks and green space. Green space and public parks have been found to be both desirable and an improvement to the quality of life for those who use them. Yet, as Agyeman (2013) has noted, the park design in 1980s London with green spaces for "all" to enjoy are not equally accessible to everyone, and thus privilege a certain social class and racial group. Why? There are several reasons. First, housing in close proximity to parks is typically more desirable than housing without access to green spaces. Parks provide recreation, better air quality, and a place for families to interact outside the home. Yet, increased demand for housing near parks translates into higher home prices. Without requirements or provisions for affordable housing, many middle-class and working-class people are priced out of these housing markets and must settle for housing further away from the green space. And when they do have access to these spaces, they often find the spaces are designed for the middle-class, white, nuclear family. How so? Think of park benches and picnic tables. How many people do they seat? Four, comfortably? Six, but uncomfortably? This presents a problem for some families, such as immigrant families, which tend be larger. These families also tend to congregate with their extended families. For them, a family of four on a weekend outing is an exception, not a rule.

What message does this send to social groups who do not fit the design? Imagine a sign reading "No more than six people at this site." Might that affect their interest in using green space? In their place, would you have argued against park development or "improvement"?

SUSTAINABILITY AND THE PLANNER'S DILEMMA

Thus far we have argued that sustainability is a socially constructed concept. We have used renewable energy and parks as examples. But how do planners, the people who allocate resources for sustainability projects, think about how they ply their trade? For Scott Campbell (1996), it is a triangle of conflicts that arise from different understandings and meanings that are attributed to the notion of sustainability. Campbell enters the enduring debate on whether emphasis should be on the economy, the ecology, or social justice—and how to reconcile these seemingly opposing concepts. He calls this the "planners dilemma." In discussing this dilemma, he identifies three approaches to planning that are fundamentally different, but connected, to different conflicts in urban planning: property conflict, resource conflict, and equity-versus-nature conflict.

Property conflict is about the space allocated for innovation, distribution, production, and consumption. Following this logic, urban space, often private property, is a rare and contested good that needs to be used in order to promote and stimulate economic growth, create or save jobs, and guarantee profits. Here, cities transform or regenerate in order to adapt to new economic challenges and circumstances. For example, large-scale industries were once key to economic prosperity, but nowadays many cities focus on the creative class with its distributed demands for urban space. Property conflict arises when planners consider how to allocate urban space to different activities.

Let's create an image to give these conflicts a concrete form. In recent years, many cities around the world have undergone profound transformations due to significant technological changes in logistics and transportation. Inner-city harbors are no longer needed for freight; containers are more practical, cheaper, and mobile. So, what's to be done with all these inner-city harbor areas? From an economic perspective, these areas were always a significant engine of the urban economy, so why change it? Water used to be a "hard" location factor, meaning that water was a basic requirement for economic activity such as a mill or a microprocessor manufacturer. Today, urban economies think of water differently. Water can now be seen as a "soft" location factor, one that is attractive and desirable but not a basic requirement. Following this logic, harbor areas are transformed into office spaces for new service industries. Old industrial buildings are retrofitted into modern lofts, the desired form of living for the new creative class. Fancy restaurants invite views over the waterfront. Well-designed public spaces are converted into elegant promenades and plazas that invite them for a walk after dinner. They do not offer respite for those who lack a place to live. This is exactly what the property conflict is about: for whom and what purpose do we design our cities—profit or people (Chomsky, 2011)? Are attractive areas in the city primarily aimed at accommodating the wealthy (c.f. Lees, Slater, and Wyly, 2013)? Or, are planners obliged to plan for everybody since everybody has a "right to the city" (Harvey, 2012; Brenner, Marcuse, and Mayer, 2012)?

This problematizes Campbell's second concern: resource conflict. Resource conflict sees cities as sites where natural resources are consumed and transformed. Cities consume much of the global energy resources and significantly contribute to global warming. Following this, urban space needs to be protected from further exploitation—that is, human use. Buildings, roads, plazas: they all contribute to the sealing of soil, preventing rain water from draining or plants from growing. In our example of inner-city waterfront regeneration, the vacant harbor area is an excellent opportunity to transform this area back into "nature." With technological progress come new opportunities. While new areas outside of the cities are transformed into container terminals, the inner-city areas are now no longer used. So why not "renaturalize" inner-city harbor areas? Instead of office buildings, there could be larger park areas. Instead of cemented promenades flanked by expensive restaurants, there could be areas reserved for more natural flood prevention with new biotops, such as in Hamburg. Sure, there is certainly quite a romanticized idea of nature behind this strategy. But instead of dedicating space to economic activities, production, and consumption, this approach aims at reclaiming nature and reintroducing biodiversity into the city.

Campbell's third conflict refers to the question of social equity and justice and ecological objectives. Here, the focus is on the distribution of ecological amenities, as described above, and the question of whether they will be equally accessible for all. The central question is, does the preference of ecological goals over economic growth hit poorer people harder because it limits their access to job markets even further? Does the implementation of sustainable buildings automatically lead to higher rents and thus exclude lower-income groups from the amenities of low-energy standards or green neighborhoods? The transformation of an inner-city harbor area into a natural park that contributes to environmental protection might indeed imply that job opportunities in surrounding neighborhoods are spatially dislocated, because lower-income groups must now travel or commute to reach their work places. From this perspective, the ecological transformation would have contributed to social injustice.

These are important questions that have dominated urban planning for some time. And to be honest, this typology has its blind spots. In the center of Campbell's (1996) perspective is the idea that urban planning is the rational act to manage or trade these different foci—the environment, the economy, and the social. Successful urban planning is about finding solutions to these conflicts. And according to Campbell (1996), the best planning project is the one situated at the center of the triangle comprised of property conflict, resource conflict, and equity-versus-nature conflict. Urban regeneration, from this perspective, needs to reconcile these aspects by stimulating economic interests to the same degree as referring to environmental protection or social equity. This book is about exploring these conflicts—not in ideal ways, but in their messiness of urban-planning practice.

So, does sustainability exist in practice? The answer is no . . . yes . . . well, *maybe*. It depends on who you ask. Our approach is not only about imagining what a more sustainable future might look like, as the examples above suggest, but also about realizing the range of knowledge and analytical tools one will need if they hope to deliver it. As we will see in the coming pages, despite the consensus regarding the term "sustainability," it remains a contested concept.

The Contribution of this Book

In this book we explore the many concepts, norms, processes, programs, and practices of sustainable urban development. Our goal is not only to expose these to you but that they will become part of your analytical toolkit. While we will lead you through the conceptual scholarly research, the practitioner literature, and even look at sustainable urban development programs and practices, our objective is to not constrain your thinking to some arbitrary endpoint of what "sustainable" is. Instead we seek to offer both conceptual and practical material as a starting point for you to develop your own ideas about sustainable urban development and to examine these ideas in new and creative ways. This book comes from our own frustration with the limits of thinking about and acting in the name of "sustainability." As part of the next generation of thinkers and policy-makers, you should realize that "thinking sustainably" *should* be difficult. It should require careful examination of well-established tradeoffs, and actively seeking to render visible "new" ones. It should be about making tough decisions and struggling over what we can accept and what we cannot. In other words, thinking sustainably is itself a process of constant political struggle and should be consciously regarded as so. This does not mean equitable decisions cannot be made. Rather, we must strive to think beyond norms, to recognize the histories of policy formations and their impacts on conceptual and policy outcomes.

We believe that cities can and will play an important role in setting the foundation for sustainable development. Cities are sites of power, inno-vation, and transmission; they can be seen as forerunners and trendsetters that are instrumental in transforming themselves, as well as other places and regions throughout the world.

Our Invitation: A User Guide for the Book

To promote critical and creative thinking, we have presented the material in this book in an innovative format that allows you to assemble your own personal reading path. If you wish to dive into the adventures of the field trips immediately, you may come back later to the conceptual chapters. You need not embark on the field trips in the order that we have presented them. Our hope is that you will move through the chapters in a way that you might an actual field trip, wandering, exploring, and letting curiosity be your guide as you reflect on the material presented.

We would like to point out that our field trips are *not* case studies. Rather, they are told through a first-person narrative from the perspective of our well-informed and experienced contributors, and are designed to lead you through a district or several districts. What separates these field trips from conventional case studies is that they are not written to build theory or to illustrate a conceptual point. They are there for you to explore from a variety of perspectives. We offer some conceptual frameworks for you in the first chapters, but we would consider it a lost opportunity if you limit your examination of the field trips to them. In fact, we challenge you to imagine what postsustainable urbanism might look like. Whether you are a student of urban planning, geography, sociology, or a related discipline, we want you to see these field trips as complex puzzles with moving pieces, or as a pallet of colors, canvas, and other materials—much like the artwork that accompanies each field trip—that you can disassemble, reassemble, or adjust by mixing "colors" in new ways. We invite you to develop your own field trips of new models and practices, or to identify other sustainable urban development fallacies. The book's final chapter should help you to better understand how political, economic, and other factors in sustainable urbanism appear to be framed in particular settings and perspectives.

Our key idea is to take up field trips as an old and established instrument of teaching and to implement them into a new textbook format. Field trips can serve as an important and powerful approach to observe, analyze, and better understand spaces; and they form an integral part of teaching and learning in a wide range of disciplines, including geography, history, archeology, social and cultural sciences, as well as the natural sciences and related disciplines. As mentioned, it is important to keep in mind that field trips and case studies are not the same. A case study is a form of research that analyzes a specific (geographical) case, taking into account the specificity of place (including historicity, path dependency, local resources, etc.), wider theoretical debates, and overarching structures and trends. Case study research starts with research questions and combines empirical and theoretical approaches. The aim of a case study is to give a concluding explanation on the basis of field research and analysis.

Our field trip approach is different. Field trips are based on the idea of *visiting* places in order to gain experience and new insights. Most of the field trips invite readers to explore specific sites, neighborhoods, or projects linked to the overarching topic of sustainable urbanism. Contributors were asked to point out political and social aspects in their field trips and to explicitly address the different, sometimes competing, meanings and practices of social sustainability to be observed. The field trips tell the story of the projects and focus on particular problems, controversies, and major challenges for present and future developments. The degree to which the authors' positionalities are reflected varies among the field trips.

Usually, a field trip is not framed within a particular theoretical perspective; rather, its primary aim concerns exploration, not analysis. In this book, we would like to engage with different forms of sustainable urban development as part of a "traveling experience" in the sense that the field trip experiences are presented to the readers as place-based *stories of sustainability*. As mentioned, these sustainability stories are related by contributors with international expertise in their field, but—far different from the manifold research articles and books they have written and published—they were asked to tell their own subjective story of their cases, drawing on their subjective perceptions and theoretical insights, and without explicit reference to a theoretical framework. Just like going on an actual field trip, readers are invited to discover and experience the presented stories, some of which appear to be unfinished—and thus to be regarded as "raw material"—and still open to further interpretation and reflections that can build on different angles and perspectives to read (or rather *see*) these stories.

The potential of our field trips relies on the following benefits:

1. *Openness.* The field trips are presented as open stories in order to stimulate further reflection. The aim of the field trips are to raise questions, not give answers. The field trips thus end without conclusions, as it is up to readers to reflect on them and make sense of them. Obviously, the same field trip may be read and understood in various ways by different readers.

2. *Interpretation.* The absence of a theoretical framework provides methodological freedom to readers to reinterpret the presented stories. Stimulated by the storyline, readers can develop further questions and interpretations based on their own experiences, judgment, and creativity. While the place-specific details of the field trips may fade into the background, the readers' thoughts and interpretations are likely to touch on broader questions of environmental injustice, social exclusion, neoliberalism, and commodification of the environment.

3. *Relatedness.* We take students/readers on these field trips because we want them to discover places and environments. Right from the start, they tend to interpret and cope with the new impressions by relating them to their previous experiences. They relate the *new* to the *well-known*, the *unfamiliar* to the *familiar*. In this sense, our field trips have

the potential to help readers identify similarities and differences and, in doing so, make sense of their new and old experiences. Thus the reflection of their own experiences is rationalized and sharpened by the otherness of the material provided in the field trips. Further, the field trips offer the possibility to comparatively relate them to each other.

4. *Learning from the field.* The field trips help readers understand and challenge the theoretical claims, the empirical evidence, and the meaning of social sustainability in particular and sustainable urban development in general. As part of an iterative process, the field trips complement the overarching theoretical concept presented in the first part of the book. In addition, we invite readers to assess and collect complementary information about the sites visited in the field trips and to develop a more in-depth perspective. In order to facilitate this process, we have suggested further readings at the end of each field trip chapter. We also plan to set up an Internet platform where further material can be found.

In a nutshell, our book invites readers to engage with the raw materials provided in the field trips, to mobilize their knowledge, and to transfer their interdisciplinary and cross-cultural experiences in order to reflect on, discuss, and better understand different forms of sustainable urbanism. We hope you will enjoy taking an active part in this adventure, and identify new kinds of solutions to the problems that plague urban development, in general, and sustainable urban development, in particular.

References

Agyeman, J. (2013). *Introducing just sustainabilities: Policy, planning, and practice.* London: Zed Books.

Brenner, N., Marcuse, P., and Mayer, N., eds. (2012). *Cities for people, not for profit: Critical urban theory and the right to the city.* London, New York: Routledge.

Brenner, N., ed. (2014). *Implosions/explosions: Towards a study of planetary urbanization.* Berlin: Jovis.

Bullard, R. D. (2000). *Dumping in Dixie: Race, class, and environmental quality.* 3rd ed. Boulder, CO: Westview Press.

Campbell, S. (1996). Green cities, growing cities, just cities? Urban planning and the contradictions of sustainable development. *Journal of the American Planning Association*, 62(3), pp. 296–312.

Chomsky, N. (2011). *Profit over people: Neoliberalism and global order*. Cambridge, MA: MIT Press.

The Economist. (2011). *Welcome to the Anthropocene*. Available at: www.economist.com/leaders/2011/05/26/welcome-to-the-anthropocene [Accessed 3 Sept. 2016]

Harvey, D. (2012). *Rebel cities: From the right to the city to the urban revolution*. London, New York: Verso.

IPPC (Intergovernmental Panel on Climate Change), ed. (2014). *Climate change 2014. Mitigation of climate change*. Cambridge: Cambridge University Press.

Lees, L., Slater, T., and Wyly, E. (2013). *Gentrification*. London & New York: Routledge.

Rorty, R. (1991). *Objectivity, relativism, and truth*. (Philosophical Papers, Vol. 1). Cambridge: Cambridge University Press.

UNDES (United Nations Department of Economic and Social Affairs). (2014). *World urbanization prospects: The 2014 revision*. 1st ed. [pdf]. Available at: esa.un.org/unpd/wup/publications/files/wup2014-highlights.pdf [Accessed 3 Sept. 2016]

UNEP (United Nations Environment Programme). (2011). *Towards a green economy: Pathways to sustainable development and poverty eradication*. 1st ed. [pdf] St-Martin-Bellevue: 100 WATT. Available at: sustainabledevelopment.un.org/content/documents/126GER_synthesis_en.pdf [Accessed 3 Sept. 2016]

Chapter 1

Constructing Sustainable Development

Robert Krueger, Tim Freytag, and Samuel Mössner

Introduction

For some, sustainability is an unprecedented and conscious effort to create a profound transformation of the Earth's social and ecological systems. This transition did not happen as many thought it might, by "nature" talking back to us—limits to growth, resource scarcity, ecological overshoot, or whatever. Rather, it has been socially constructed through a sociopolitical process that seeks to creatively address the challenges of living in an increasingly complex nature–society relationship. Sustainability, then, is about the human adaption to the changing physical, material, and social life conditions. Further, the concept while often used in a normative sense—what ought to be—is not transhistorical, but changes over time and is adapted to specific human wants and needs in the context of ever-changing human–environment relationships.

When we use the concept of sustainability, we do so against a backdrop of these constant and fluid transformations: shifting ideologies that complement, replace, and sometimes jockey for influence. Hence, it is not possible to search for a commonly shared or fixed definition of sustainability.

In this chapter we focus on sustainable development as a social construct by examining key scientific, sociocultural moments and the actors working within them. We start with a long look back at sustainable development's antecedents. We then move forward to show the influence of ideas as they are reproduced in new shapes through the years.

Sustainability:
From Its Antecedents to the Twenty-First Century

This section positions the sustainability debate in its deeply rooted and long historical context. Our goal here is to tease out the roots of the norms that inform today's sustainability debates by focusing on key historical and intellectual moments that provide a context to sustainability's conceptual, institutional, and practical foundations.

EARLY COMMENTATORS AND DISCOURSES

Sustainability has played an important role in human activities since the knuckle-dragging era when Neanderthals formed groups and began hunting. As humans developed, agricultural techniques and sustainability took on additional meaning regarding adequate food and sustained production for the group. Humans organized their societies around food production, but power played a major role too. For example, in Germany, early use of the sustainability concept emerged from both resource scarcity and concerns about class. In *Sylvicultura oeconomica, oder haußwirthliche Nachricht und naturmäßige Anweisung zur wilden Baum-Zucht*, published in 1713, Hans Carl von Carlowitz sought to bring together the concepts *continuity*, *stability*, and *maintenance* as the basis for cultivating productive forests. Carlowitz was concerned about the extensive consumption of wood and depletion of forests at a faster pace than they could be reproduced. These notions also underwrote social divisions and definitions of class. In addition to the value they provided as fuel and raw material, forests were also important resources for emerging states, nobles, and aristocrats. For them, forests secured not only an income but also symbolized societal prestige and exclusivity, from which they derived power. The example shows that among other stakeholders, there were royals, land owners, and peasants, each with a role in food provision—consumption and production. Our key point here is that the concept of sustainability cannot be divorced from its societal context and sociocultural relations of power.

As the eighteenth century continued, the concept of long-term, efficient management of natural resources achieved a greater level of societal importance. This development was accompanied not only by growth in the human population but also by industrialization, which drew people away from the fields and into the cities. In England, for example, population, carrying capacity, and resource substitution were concepts forwarded by scholars who were concerned with increasing population, changing settlement patterns, and industrial scale production strained resources proximate to urban centers. Philosophers and other scholars raised concerns about the scarcity of (material) resources. We are all familiar with names like Malthus, Ricardo, and the French physiocrats who concentrated their studies on the capacity of land, food, and other resources to support human communities. Their views of nature, concepts of the problem, and its various solutions were different, but this coterie of scholars was interested in a common question: how does the *human* economy coexist with *nature's* economy?

One reference point of scholarly work at the time is the work of British Aristocrat and Pastor Thomas Robert Malthus (1766–1834). Malthus, while highly controversial, elucidated well the disputatious and controversial nature of sustainability. Malthus is best known for his "Essay on the Principle of Population" (1798), in which he employs "natural laws" that assert (1) food is basic for the existence of human beings, and (2) passion between man and woman leads to natural reproduction. These axioms created and supported the incontrovertible interdependence between food and human reproduction. As a corollary, rising reproductive rates lead to an ever-increasing need for food, which require a finite resource—land. Malthus was the first scholar to explicitly question the relationship between resources and scarcity. To ameliorate the problem, Malthus proposed state control of the food/population nexus. In particular, he proposed that poorer populations needed an area of particular concern as he believed they were less able to "restrain their sexual urges" (Robertson, 2012: 4). Malthus's work captures issues relevant in today's debates. For example, his work reveals class and race biases and the concept of technological determinism, which we will address below.

Before moving on, let us position Malthus and his work historically. Class concerns were central to Malthus's views. Higher education, at least theoretically, played a factor in reproduction. Malthus deduced that Englishmen with more education would be prevented from marrying if their income after marriage would not enable them to keep their position within the social hierarchy. Moreover, he deduced, this was a consideration less-educated and poorer people would certainly lack. The issue of education and class could also be found in race, as at this time people with darker skin were deemed less human than the white European aristocracy. While Malthus's views play into the role of the rational actor that is highly contested, but still widely present today, his notion of technological determinism is quite the opposite of today's view. Indeed, Malthus (1798) was quite skeptical that any technical improvement or engineering could delay or prevent the impasse between land capacity and human reproduction. Malthus's work captures key antecedents—though not all of them—of today's debates around sustainability.

In Malthus's time, the disciplines of economics or political science had not yet been developed. This gave philosophers a free range to synthesize ideas through deduction—the method of choice at the time—as Malthus and others (e.g., Smith, Kant, and Machiavelli) did to speculate, without crossing disciplinary debates or boundaries, the virtues of industrial expansion for liberty or peacemaking through commerce. In the mid–nineteenth century, the disciplinary features of economics started to coalesce. Indeed, they harnessed scientific advances from physics and biology and sought to uncover the same kinds of generalizable rule governing society that were found in the universe and among the evolution of organisms. You might be asking yourself at this point, "why is this relevant?" The answer is: because the very ideas that came from Malthus and his contemporaries informed the basic assumptions that would become economic theory, in general, and equilibrium theory, in particular. There is no space to develop these ideas further here, but we can see the historical connections between philosophical deduction about technology and human behavior codified in neoclassical economic theory, which has been the basis of our normative assumptions about how economies function and about the people who exist within them. Let us illustrate this point by reinterpreting an often overlooked and more contemporary example.

In the early 1950s, with the full onset of the Cold War, a great deal of uncertainty arose around the scarcity of natural resources. A key question for the United States and the West was would there be enough raw materials to defeat the Soviets? Defeat here wasn't in military terms per se but in winning the economic war by providing industry with the materials it needed to create the goods and services that were growing in demand in postwar Western Europe. The US commodity prices rose dramatically during the first year of the Korean War (1950–1953), which implied increasing scarcity (think "peak oil"). To examine the problem, the US Congress created a special commission, The Paley Commission, named after its chairman William Paley, the president of the Columbia Broadcasting System (CBS) in the United States. This commission examined commodity needs based on population projections until the year 1975. The basic findings of the study were that US demands would grow significantly and that, based on price, supply of some resources was adequate to support the economy. Other raw materials, however, were in short supply. The report thus suggested that supplies could be sustained if acquired from other sources, but at an increasing cost. The Commission recommended that the government identify and procure new supplies, as well as search for substitutes. Two elements of this report informed future discussions about sustainable development. First, the Paley Commission recognized the difference between absolute scarcity and relative scarcity. The former arises from the lack of *control* over existing resources. The second was the doctrine of technological substitution, which means that technologies could change to require fewer or different resources to support the same function. Both of these points would later figure in the version of "sustainable development" famously proposed in the United Nations report *Our Common Future*, or the so-called Brundtland Report (WCED, 1987), which can be traced back to Malthus.

First, in response to its insight about relative scarcity, the Paley Commission looked to identify actions that the government could take to secure the resources necessary to sustain the Western economies and its military. For decades, governments, including the United States, had been funding explorers to identify and map the location of key natural resources: oil in the Middle East, copper in Chile, gold in South Africa, to give some well-known examples (Smith, 2003). Also well-known is the "relationship building" undertaken in the 1950s, 1960s, and 1970s by the United States, its allies, and their agents. The International Bank for Development and Reconstruction (The World Bank) used technocratic decision tools grounded in economics, such as the planning, programming, and budgeting system or PPBS and cost–benefit analysis to (hopefully) improve their investment decisions. Another key theory these approaches were based on was W. W. Rostow's notion of economic development and modernization.[1] An academic economist and advisor to President John F. Kennedy, Rostow had developed stages of economic growth that non-Western countries would have to pass through in order to be "modern" or "developed" (think Malthus's virtues of the wealthy versus the poor). These steps provided Western governments with a framework to model policy inventions, aid packages, and consulting to countries seeking to "modernize." As a result, the Western countries nurtured a new regime in Iran; new regimes, economic and otherwise, in Chile; and a convivial relationship with a regime that legislated blacks and other nonwhites as subhuman (South Africa). This support was built on the foundation of the basic producer–consumer economics of "modernization" you might have learned in grammar school. Often overlooked with this doctrine are the uneven and unjust implications for those places that served as producers.

The second important insight of the Paley Commission, the doctrine of technological substitution, proved to have even more powerful and longstanding implications. Indeed, the notion that technology will provide solutions to our environmental and economic problems remains a core belief for many. Technological substitution was popularized by Paley's Commission and codified a decade later by academic economists Harold Barnett and Chandler Morse in their 1963 book *Scarcity and Growth*. Barnett and Morse echoed the Commission's findings that under conditions of increasing scarcity, rising raw material prices would trigger innovation and a process of technological substitution. These concerns revived the neoclassical economists' notion from the previous century: that material scarcity and economic development could possibly be *decoupled*. Of course, the notion of "sustainable development" as we now conceive it results from myriad conditions, but the arguments of the Paley Commission and Barnett and Morse would have a lasting effect on the political, economic, and discursive underpinnings of the sustainable development discourse. In contrast to the arguments put forth in the Paley report, which characterized economic development as a deliberate effort requiring risky and unethical international policies, the sustainable development concept argued that development is a sociopolitical process that works on its own in some deterministic way.

Now, if one thinks back to Malthus, he would have been unaware of both these notions. First, absolute scarcity versus relative scarcity would have been a problem for him because he lived on an island. Further, when his essay on population growth came out, the British Empire had been set back by the loss of the American Colonies, and its eastern expansion had not yet begun in earnest. Therefore, without political stability outside of the United Kingdom, relative scarcity could not exist. The notion of "technological substitution" is a concept also unavailable to Malthus. In the world he lived in, agricultural intensity was a factor of space, not of technology and space. This means that for Malthus a hectare of land could support X number of livestock or produce Y tons of crops. Today, through agro-related technology, we can grow crops where fifty years ago it would have been impossible. We can increase crop yields through chemical fertilizer and genetic and other interventions that would have baffled Malthus.

With this backdrop in place, we now turn to the slow evolution to reshape "scarcity and growth" into a discourse of environment and sustainable development.

From "Scarcity and Growth" to Environmental Values

During the 1970s and 1980s, a series of events and intellectual moments began to shift beliefs regarding what is sustainable. In contrast to previous decades, the dominant view focused on the physical capacities of the environment to sustain human life through the provision of resources. After World War II, technical innovation and sophisticated resource management strategies extended the environment's productive capacity. Prosperity increased in Western Europe and North America, as did production and consumption. While the spoils of increasing wealth were distributed through Western societies, so were the environmental impacts of production. In the United States, rivers caught fire, the act of breathing suffocated people, fish kills were common, and the consequences on human health of all of these incidents were increasingly well documented. In Western Germany, it was nuclear energy being promoted as "clean" energy, animal experimentation by the cosmetic industry, and acid rain that set off the first generation of environmental protests.

The environmental histories of these times are well documented elsewhere, so there is no reason to go into them deeply here. Suffice to say that this period witnessed dramatic interest in the environment as an amenity and the deleterious effects of large-scale industrial production on human health through environmental pathways. As a result, the US federal government, for example, acted to pass a bevy of environmental laws in the 1960s and early 1970s to protect human health and the environment. The key point to take here is that, much like in previous decades, the federal government was the primary site of responsibility for executing and delivering environmental policy. Questions of scarcity and growth still took precedence, and resource scarcity arguments, which were seen to have economic implications, often trumped environmental ones.

Beginning in the 1970s, all of this began to change. Scholars enlarged their scope of interest and, together with forward-thinking policymakers, worked behind the scenes for a decade to shift the scarcity and growth paradigm.

SIMPLY SUSTAINABLE DEVELOPMENT?

In the 1980s, after two decades of the environmental movement and the broad recognition that our material relationship to nature was bad for humans and the Earth systems they depend on, the concept of "sustainable development" emerged as a would-be set of organizing principles for future economic growth. A growing environmental movement that resulted from industrial disasters and risks in the United States fueled these debates. In academia, the Romanian economist-mathematician Nicholas Georgescu-Roegen (1993) published his radical ideas that linked economic systems to the second law of thermodynamics. International coalitions, like the Club of Rome, published the famous system dynamics model in 1972 and laid its argument for limiting growth in the context of ecological capacities. The Club of Rome and the works of Donella Meadows and colleagues (1972) raised awareness, and criticism, of this way of examining what was sustainable and what looked sustainable, but was in fact a delay in the negative consequences of overconsumption, or "ecological overshoot." A few years later, Herman Daly, father of ecological economics, published his work calling for a steady-state economy, which required a mildly fluctuating population growth and energy input.

The concept of "sustainable development" entered public discourse in the early 1980s when the International Union for the Conservation of Nature and Natural Resources (IUCN) and World Wildlife Fund (WWF) published their *World Conservation Strategy* (1980). The IUCN report was concerned about the increasingly rapid, environmentally destructive, and systemically damaging approach to taking natural resources. The report cites a long list of hazards and disasters that include soil erosion, loss of agricultural lands, industrial pollution, deforestation, ecosystem degradation, species extinction, and more. The report also calls for a new global ethic grounded in the "interrelatedness" of global development. The ethic makes it the duty of all nations, calling into question the hegemony of Rostow and others, to offer coordinated global strategies that outline strategic development and conservation measures. At the core of this approach is positioning development and conservation as equal and mutually reinforcing goals. Further, it offers recognition that development is a sociopolitical process that works on its own through an internal logic.

Published years later by the United Nations World Commission on Environment and Development (WCED) (1987), *Our Common Future* picked up many of the themes of the IUCN report. *Our Common Future*, also known as The Brundtland Report,[2] is celebrated as a mighty step forward in thinking on economic development, the environment, and the human condition. Like its predecessors, the report was grounded in concepts of "limits"—that is, economic and technological activities can be improved, but we are still limited by the "biosphere to absorb the effects of human activities" (WCED, 1987: 8). Distinguishing itself, where the IUCN report linked conservation as the remedy to environmental degradation, the Brundtland Report repositioned environmental quality and social equity as a fundamental goal of development. For example, "[g]rowth must be revived in developing countries because that is where the links between economic growth, the alleviation of poverty, and environmental conditions operate most directly. Yet, developing countries are part of an interdependent world economy; their prospects also depend on the levels and patterns of growth in industrialized nations" (WCED, 1987: 51). Given this interdependent relationship, it is not surprising that Brundtland was explicit about the role of social and economic conditions in shaping sustainable and unsustainable behavior. "Sustainable development is a process of change in which the exploitation of resources, the direction of investment, the orientation of technological development, and institutional change are all in harmony and enhance both current and future potential to meet human needs and aspirations" (WCED, 1987: 46).

Brundtland and its authors sought to support the aspirations of *Our Common Future* by creating a clear and concise definition of sustainable development. For them, sustainable development simply is "development that meets that needs of the present without compromising the ability of future generations to meet their own needs" (WCED, 1987: 46). It is by this standard, this norm, from which a development program's success ought to be measured.

To support this broad goal, the Brundtland Commission offered a system of governance that extended from the global to the local scale. Key features of the proposal were to have an ecology-first approach to governance. In other words, policymakers would develop regulations and policy to set the stage for economic activity that was first and foremost ecologically appropriate. Brundtland also called for a system of regulations to be developed to address existing problems of environmental protection and resource management. These were to be defined by a rigorous risk assessment using sophisticated indicators and other methods of assessment. Finally, these actions would be based on the participation of stakeholder groups and marshaled evidence so that deliberations could be inclusive and actions appropriate. The Earth Summit in Rio was the event that was to bring these and other issues together. Here, policymakers from around the world, the largest gathering of high-level officials ever, deliberated on these issues. A series of subsequent events and projects were put in place to support the goals of Agenda 21. A key project, discussed below, was Local Agenda 21.

Five years later, in June 1992, the United Nations Conference on Environment and Development was held in Rio de Janeiro. This was a crucial step in making sustainability concerns a priority on the agenda of international politics. The Rio Earth Summit took place just a few years after the fall of the Iron Curtain, the end of the Cold War, and the breakdown of the Soviet Union. At that particular moment in time, the bipolar political divide of the globe was to be replaced by a new era in which the protection and preservation of the planet would be a key concern of the Earth's citizens—at least, this was the hope of many participants in the Earth Summit, journalists assisting in the event, and people following the conference in the media. Never before had such a great number of politicians (172 governments including 108 heads of state or government, and roughly 2,400 NGO representatives) participated in an environmental event, which was accompanied by a parallel NGO forum attended by 17,000 people.[3] The conference was widely perceived as a turning point toward global sustainability as a guiding principle in our world. In this spirit, a large majority of the nation-states signed Agenda 21, a contractual program of this particular and dominant understanding of sustainability at the local level. Although some of the guiding ideas were already addressed at the United Nations Conference on the Human Environment in 1972 in Stockholm—notably with the instauration of the United Nations Environmental Program—the 1992 Earth Summit was widely perceived as the starting point of a new era and the institutionalization of the new understanding of sustainability that continues to dominate and direct political action.

Please recall the tensions we presented in the opening section on scarcity and technological optimism through substitution. In some ways, the Brundtland Report reshaped the key features of the "sustainable development" debate. Scarcity, while still an issue of concern, was largely replaced with "natural capital." In other words, the cost of a commodity, such as gold or copper, otherwise known as "rare earths," should include the cost for depletion or destruction of ecosystem services. This idea has also become part of some countries' building codes, saying that new developments destroying "natural" areas must compensate for this in different places. Extending this principle further, today's developers, municipalities, investors, and travelers can buy into compensations that have been produced at other places, enhancing the mobility of natural capital. The concept of "natural capital" was supposed to supplant scarcity as the ultimate value because the concept of scarcity itself had no relationship to the environment where ore or other resources are hosted. Climate change is a great example of this. We don't talk about scarcity of clean, or carbon-free air. But we do think about the atmosphere's carrying capacity of carbon and the effect of this on our lives and livelihoods. Defining what the environment is and who is affected by its transformation entered the political sphere as a site of contestation.

The shift from resource scarcity to ecosystem integrity, we argue, is underwritten by the assumption that economic systems can innovate to (1) reduce resource intensity (using less raw material in a product); (2) substitute one resource for another; (3) find new sources (e.g., recycling); and (4) reuse old products (e.g., repairing), among others. Hence, the Brundtland concept of sustainable development is fundamentally based on growth and technological substitution. Like the concepts of absolute scarcity and relative scarcity mentioned above in the context of the Paley Commission, the concept of limits to growth is said to be mediated by the absolute limits of the Earth, but perhaps is relative in practice because of the unfettered belief in technological innovation.

These points are best illustrated through an example. As we said above, the "scarcity and growth" debate emerged in a certain political-economic context. The sustainable development debate did so as well, and it's important to recognize these underlying factors because it provides a lens for examining sustainable development as not only a set of goals but also a set of practices embedded in a particular context.

ECOLOGICAL MODERNIZATION AND SUSTAINABLE DEVELOPMENT

Cold war *détente* (1947–1991) coupled with efforts to contain the geopolitical expansion of Soviet-style communism helped shape the scarcity and growth paradigm of sustainable development. In the 1980s, this struggle, though very real as a suite of foreign affairs, opened up a new front in domestic quarters. In particular, after the fall of the Iron Curtain, as the 1980s progressed and turned into the 1990s, the role of the state came increasingly into question. What was perceived as centralized control of economies, and therefore development, via nation-states began to give way to state restructuring and an increasing role of private enterprise to regulate itself and "the market" to be the adjudicator of economic, social, and environmental relations, not the nation-state.

Why is this important to the sustainable development debate? It is critical to explore these changes in the context of the emerging sustainable development paradigm because, like the generation before, it influenced how sustainable development would be rolled out. Further, it was the theory of "ecological modernization" that molded sustainable development into something more than a plan: a realized policy discourse.

In the 1980s, ecological modernization theory was being discussed by a relatively small group of scholars in the social sciences, primarily from Germany and Northern Europe. Ecological modernization was a theory, or an understanding, that environmental problems could and should be addressed through the transformation of production via the development and implementation of new technologies and processes that were less resource intensive than their predecessors. It was economic actors, entrepreneurs, and the private sector that were to be the drivers of this transformation, not the state. Ecological modernization is a macroeconomic structural change that identifies sectors capable of combining higher levels of growth with lower levels of material input. For followers of this approach, industrialization and technological substitution and innovation offered a way out of ecological crisis. Ecological modernization is more than a theory. In the 1990s, it became a key part of the European Union's Environment Programme. Key aspects of the approach as codified in policy focus on the precautionary principle, integrated regulation (carrot and stick), and voluntary mechanisms. Indeed, countries like Germany, The Netherlands, and Japan are said to be paradigmatic examples of this approach in practice.

The rhetorical similarities between ecological modernization and sustainable development should be pretty clear. There is a clear interest demonstrated by both groups that the environmental integrity of the Earth should be maintained and can be done so through continued—but less resource intensive—growth. While not explicit, the intergenerational equity piece is addressed by ecological modernization by using fewer resources in the present so more will be available in the future. Both visions rely heavily on technological innovation to reduce environmental impacts. While sustainable development goals are in countless official documents worldwide, it is the vision of ecological modernization, of "greening the economy," that drives the practice. Ecological modernization is the operant of macrolevel sustainability. It is here that we can see the tension of sustainable development's three pillars: economic prosperity, ecological integrity, and social equity.

Ecological modernization as a theory of social change and a set of policy prescriptions emerged from established and newer thinking on "how the economy works." What Paley Commission debates could not have anticipated is the shrinking role of the government, as one actor among many in a *governance* structure, rather than the traditional architect and organizer of economic and social activity. This change is clear in ecological modernization. An outcome of this is worth punctuating here, how these ideas shape the operationalization of sustainable development. First, the issue of ecological integrity has largely been reduced to a series of technological fixes. Technology can mediate, replicate, and augment the natural processes. Further, the "signal" for addressing these issues comes not from a state regulation, but from social movements (maybe) or consumer demand. It's the market that determines which environmental systems are integrated into the economy. When, for example, was the last time you heard of the importance of biodiversity outside the potential benefits that "big pharma" can derive from it? Thus, abstract forces define what the environment is and how it is integrated (or is not) into the larger social system of economic activity. As mentioned, it has implications for aspects of the ecosystem that are deemed necessary, but it also has implications for social equity. How? Different people engage with and are affected by their environments. Whether it's gender relations and water distribution in Ghana, elderly people suffering in heat waves in Chicago, or non-whites and the economically disadvantaged bearing a greater burden of environmental risks in the world's cities, different groups of people are affected by their environment in myriad ways. Sustainable development as a framework calls for the integration of these issues. It is not, however, capable of changing the broader set of social relations that help to define who is suffering from inequity and who is not.

Step-by-step green technology was integrated into the mainstream economy. What was previously widely perceived as a fundamental opposition of ecological and economic interests has been reconciled in the logics of a green growth economy. Pushing forward ecological concerns no longer meant to question economic growth per se and to ask for alternative economic visions, but leading economic actors subsequently discovered and made use of ecological concerns as a resource for economic growth in the context of ongoing competing and emerging moral economies.

Similar to this shift in the economy, we can see changes in the political arena. In politics, the integration of ecological concerns and the idea of an emerging green economy was taken up by decision makers and has gained a position very close to unquestionable mainstream awareness. In other words, economic and political actors appropriated ecological concerns and the notion of sustainability as a resource. However, the social dimension of sustainability was not given much consideration in the process, although it is difficult to imagine how to implement sustainability in the world without engaging larger parts of society.

More than twenty-five years after the Earth Summit in 1992, we have to acknowledge that much of the enthusiastic hope to start a new era could not so easily be put into practice. Taking up what was meant to be an alternative approach and implementing this into *Realpolitik* was not possible without making compromises. From a critical stance, it might be stated that the price to pay for moving sustainable development into the center of mainstream politics consisted of betraying the counterhegemonic momentum inherent in the sustainability concept. All in all, we have experienced that sustainable development has become widely accepted to an extent that you can hardly find anybody who would argue openly against the concept. However, the gap between general awareness and acceptance of the concept and the achievement we have made thus far is striking. Key indicators suggest that not much progress has been made since 1992. This is particularly dramatic in the field of international climate politics against global warming and the subsequent rise of the sea level and the increase in meteorological hazards. It seems that in spite of numerous initiatives, the target of a global reduction of CO_2 emissions is further away today than it was at the Earth Summit in 1992, or when the Kyoto protocol was signed in 1997. The subsequent United Nations Climate Change Conferences and the research findings transmitted by the Intergovernmental Panel on Climate Change (IPCC) give little hope that the existing problems can be solved. Obviously, an increasing awareness of the need for sustainable development does not automatically result in action. At global, national, regional, local, and individual scales, we can observe one and the same phenomena: a considerable gap between wide-ranging sustainability talk and actual sustainability action. A key challenge in making sustainable development happen thus consists of finding a way not only to increase awareness but also to foster measures that will help put sustainability into practice.

Our discussion now turns to the local scale and Local Agenda 21. A discussion of sustainable development at an urban scale is important for a variety of reasons. First, it gives us an opportunity to further ground the ideas mentioned above. Though there are scalar differences, these narratives are complementary and can help the reader understand the underlying point: that sustainable development is a set of normative principles that exist within a broader cultural context. In addition to providing a further opportunity to ground the ideas, the Local Agenda 21 and sustainable urban development experience is fraught with conceptual richness and political controversy. To take up this debate, we return to the 1990s to recount key historical developments in sustainable urban development.

Rio, Local Agenda 21, and Sustainable Urban Development

Recall that in 1987 the WCED produced *Our Common Future* (aka The Brundtland Report). This milestone document helped identify a set of policy goals that would be explored and implemented, particularly in the case of cities and towns. It was not until the Earth Summit in Rio de Janeiro that these issues were taken up in earnest. Here, delegates from around the world discussed Agenda 21. A core aspect of the Agenda 21 governance approach was the concept of subsidiarity. Subsidiarity holds that decisions should be made where the most relevant decision makers are, and those who are closest to the people. To address this, Agenda 21 architects proposed Local Agenda 21 (LA 21). Chapter 28 codified LA 21 in that it recognized that local governments play a key role in bringing about sustainable development across scales. LA 21 principles emphasized that local authorities need to make considerable changes to their policy-making approaches so they can incorporate the perspectives and views of a range of interests. Chapter 28 of Agenda 21 states:

> Each local authority should enter into a dialogue with its citizens, local organizations and private enterprises and adopt "LA 21." Through consultation and consensus building, local authorities would learn from citizens and from local, civic, community, business and industrial organizations and acquire the information needed for formulating the best strategies. The

process of consultation would increase household awareness of sustainable development issues. Local authority programmes, policies, laws and regulations to achieve LA 21 objectives would be assessed and modified, based on local programmes adopted. (UNCED, 1992)

Key to LA 21 is a broad-based, multi-stakeholder planning process focused on balancing economy, social equity, and the environment. It was believed that the success of LA 21 would also turn on the ability of a local authority to redirect its policies, laws, and regulations to align with principles that emerged from the planning efforts. By 1996, according to LA 21 architects, cities should have engaged the public in a consultation process and achieved consensus regarding a local sustainability program.

ICLEI, the international environmental nonprofit association, spearheaded the effort to assist communities in developing their LA 21 activities. Indeed, ICLEI hatched the LA 21 idea a year before the 1992 Rio Summit. The goal of ICLEI's LA 21 Campaign is to "to build a worldwide movement of local governments and associations dedicated to achieving sustainable development through participatory, multi-stakeholder sustainable development planning and the implementation of resulting LA 21 action plans" (ICLEI, 2006). The process is quite simple. By 1996, 1,119 communities in Europe had initiated LA 21 programs. To accomplish this goal, in 1994, ICLEI organized the European Sustainable Cities and Towns Campaign, which led to the Aalborg Charter. Two years later, steps for implementing the Aalborg Charter were drafted and ratified under the Lisbon Action Plan. Since Lisbon, ICLEI has worked with hundreds of communities on their LA 21 plans and organized thousands of communities.

According to ICLEI (2006), over 2,000 European communities have now signed onto the Aalborg Charter. In addition to their organizing efforts, ICLEI also provides technical assistance, research and evaluation, and assistance in piloting new participatory approaches. The purpose here is not to trumpet the efforts of ICLEI, but to suggest that the organization has a very high level of influence over LA 21 in Europe (where 5,000 of the 6,400 LA 21 initiatives exist worldwide). The influence, both formal (through Aalborg) and informal (through its consulting), suggests that the idea of multi-stakeholder planning exercises where the three legs of the sustainable development stool—economy, social equity, and environment—was agreed upon by many European cities, at least rhetorically, as worthy and politically palatable goals. Moreover, the intention was to use the information from these processes to develop policies that captured the community's vision for itself. Finally, municipalities would develop policies to create norms in development that support these goals.

A survey published in 2002 by ICLEI showed that some 6,400 communities from 113 countries worldwide had become involved in LA 21 activities over the previous decade (ICLEI, 2006). The popularity of LA 21 as a local and regional development strategy was again affirmed when 400 European Communities, representing 100 million Europeans from thirty-six countries, signed the Aalborg Charter in 1994. The Aalborg Charter, which was facilitated by ICLEI as part of their European Sustainable Cities and Towns Campaign, committed its signatories to develop local sustainability action plans in parallel with LA 21.

Another critical area to examine is how LA 21 agendas are supported by the functions of the state. Despite calls for fundamental change, it is not surprising that the adoption of LA 21 was not a total paradigm shift in Europe (or in the United States, as described below). It emerged in the context of existing state functions and regulatory mechanisms. Typically, these occur along two axes, market-oriented regulation and state-based command and control. In Europe, state-based regulation, while waning, remains a dominant force that influences development patterns and land use. This is to say that local authorities (as well as regional and national ones too) have the capacity to clearly direct outcomes of urban development through performance standards and other forms of command and control regulation. The Dutch, for example, set minimum density standards at thirty-three units per hectare in an effort to promote compact cities with smaller ecological footprints. There is a sense among some that in The Netherlands, as in other places, such as Germany and Denmark, the rural fringe of cities is not transitional and up for grabs for development. Thus, market forces in these countries *can* be closely regulated so they more appropriately align with the dictates of the LA 21 process.

In contrast to European cities and towns, who adopted the LA 21 process in large numbers, North American cities did not do so. Roughly twenty US cities, for example, are LA 21 cities. However, this is not to say that US cities did not adopt sustainable development principles. Like other sustainable development policies, US governments at the local, regional, and national scales eschewed the global standard and came up with their own approach. Also similar were the mechanisms adopted by US cities: they were incentive based, voluntary, and largely development driven (i.e., driven by the market and not by the state), instead of being process driven.

This American variant of local sustainability is often referred to as "smart growth." With its roots in the state of Maryland, it spread rapidly across the United States. Over 500 US cities and towns have adopted principles of smart growth. Indeed, smart growth now extends beyond US borders, as policy entrepreneurs have exported them to Europe and Asia. To understand the rapid spread of smart growth policies and practices, we must return to the discussion of political economic context.

Sustainable development has been referred to as a stool metaphor, as opposed to a ladder. This is to say that a stool has three legs, and to this point we have discussed only two—economy and environment. The social leg, neglected thus far, we turn to now.

Toward a Post-Sustainable Society?

As we have seen, natural and social scientists, and particularly geographers, have for forty years examined sustainable development from an understanding grounded in ecological modernization. For example, economic geographers continue to focus on technological innovation and substitution by examining businesses like green manufacturing and environmental services, as well as supply chains and other economic networks. Scholars thus rely on the traditional development paradigms described above, which is to say they rely on traditional growth paradigms (or business as usual). For Schulz and Bailey (2014), this focus also dominates most of the recent scholarly work on the economic impacts of climate policy and energy transitions. While focusing on the (spatial) dynamics of emerging industries (e.g., related to renewable energies), underlying innovation processes, regional economic trajectories, or international trade, scholars overlook the implications of these development trends for alternative growth models and sufficiency imperatives. In the final section we will briefly introduce one of these alternative development scenarios.

POSTGROWTH?

Can we sustain our seemingly open-ended appeal to economic growth, even as more and more people are recognizing that this model creates more problems than it addresses? The push for continuous growth undermines economic security, communities, the environment, a sense of place and continuity, and even mental health. Increasingly, policymakers at a variety of spatial scales are mobilizing new indexes, such as the Happy Planet Index, the Human Development Index, or the Index of Sustainable Economic Welfare.

Alongside these new ways of measuring sustainability and prosperity is an alternative approach to development that eschews growth in its current form. This concept, termed "postgrowth," should be understood as a departure from dominant growth paradigms in the sense of Serge Latouche's *décroissance* (2009), that is, a rejection of the maxim that private and societal prosperity can only be ensured via a continuous growth of materially and monetarily measurable economic performance. Tim Jackson's book *Prosperity without Growth* (2009) captures the orientation of a transition toward sustainable lifestyles and economic systems envisioned by the postgrowth concept. Both Jackson and Latouche place strong emphasis on distributive justice in growth and wealth, both at the level of international development policies and within individual national economies.

Drawing on the work of Georgescu-Roegen, especially his steady-state economics theory, Latouche (2009) has refocused the discussion of environmental sustainability, suggesting that the objective of economic growth has endangered the goal of environmental sustainability and banished the principle of justice. His principle of *décroissance,* which rejects growth-oriented forms of production and consumption patterns, has been influential in the Italian, Spanish, and French sustainability movements. In this way, Latouche (2009) warns us against the trap of ecological modernization, rejecting its belief that a transition to a sustainable economy can be possible within present market principles. Latouche (2009) and the postgrowth approach point to a possible way forward, exposing new analytical terrain and the limits of previous works. Bearing in mind the history of sustainable development, its promises and pitfalls, we can begin again to look for new alternatives to what sometimes seems an intractable global challenge.

Notes

1. Remember that *modernization*, at the time, was a process where less or least developed countries move from what used to be called "underdevelopment" to more developed systems by modeling wealthy Western countries.

2. We will use the Brundtland Report and *Our Common Future* interchangeably throughout the text.

3. UN Environment and Development (1992). See www.un.org/geninfo/bp/ enviro.html

For Further Reading

Beatley, T. (2000). *Green urbanism: Learning from European cities*. Washington, DC: Island Press.

D'Alisa, G., Demaria, F., and Kallis, G. (2014). *Degrowth: A Vocabulary for a New Era*. London: Routledge.

Gibbs, D. (2005). *Local economic development and the environment*. London: Routledge.

Robertson, T. (2012). *The Malthusian moment: Global population growth and the birth of American environmentalism*. New Brunswick, NJ: Rutgers University Press.

References

Barnett, H. J., and Morse, C. (1963). *Scarcity and growth: The economics of natural resource availability*. Baltimore: Johns Hopkins University Press.

von Carlowitz, H. C. (1713). *Sylvicultura oeconomica, oder Haußwirthliche Nachricht und Naturmäßige Anweisung zur Wilden Baum-Zucht*. Leipzig: Braun.

Georgescu-Roegen, N. (1993). The Entropy Law and the Economic Problem. In: H. E. Daly and K. N. Townsend, eds., *Valuing the Earth: Economics, Ecology, Ethics*, 1st ed. Cambridge, MA: MIT Press, pp. 75–88.

ICLEI (International Council for Local Environmental Initiatives). (2006). *Second local agenda 21 survey*. New York: United Nations Commission on Sustainable Development.

IUCN (International Union for Conservation of Nature) and WWF (World Wildlife Fund). (1980). *World Conservation Strategy: Living Resource Conservation for Sustainable Development*. Gland: IUCN.

Jackson, T. (2009). *Prosperity without growth? The transition to a sustainable economy*. 1st ed. [pdf] London: Sustainable Development Commission. Available at: www.sd-commission.org.uk/data/files/publications/prosperity_without_growth_report.pdf [Accessed 3 Sept. 2016]

Latouche, S. (2009). *Farewell to growth*. Cambridge: Polity Press.

Malthus, T. R. (1798). *An essay on the principle of population; or, A view of its past and present effects on human happiness; with an inquiry into our prospects respecting the future removal or mitigation of the evils which it occasions*. Reprint 1872. London: Reeves and Turner.

Meadows, D. H., Meadows, D. L., Randers, J., and Behrens, W. W. (1972). *The limits to growth: A report for the Club of Rome's project on the predicament of mankind.* New York: Universe Books.

Robertson, T. (2012). *The Malthusian moment: Global population growth and the birth of American environmentalism.* New Brunswick, NJ: Rutgers University Press.

Schulz, C., and Bailey, I. (2014). The Green Economy and Post-Growth Regimes: Opportunities and Challenges for Economic Geography. *Geografiska Annaler: Series B, Human Geography,* 96(3), pp. 277–291.

Smith, N. (2003). *American empire: Roosevelt's geographer and the prelude to globalization.* (California Studies in Critical Human Geography, Vol. 9). Berkeley: University of California Press.

UNCED (United Nations Conference on Environment and Development). (1992). *Report of the United Nations Conference on the Environment and Development.* Rio de Janeiro & New York: United Nations.

WCED (World Commission on Environment and Development). (1987). *Report of the World Commission on Environment and Development: Our common future.* 1st ed. [pdf] New York: United Nations. Available at: www.un-documents. net/our-common-future.pdf [Accessed 3 Sept. 2016]

Chapter 2

The Rise of Sustainable Urban Development

ROBERT KRUEGER, TIM FREYTAG, AND SAMUEL MÖSSNER

> Since its early definition in the Brundtland Commission report of
> 1987, the concept (but not much the practice) of "sustainability"
> has really taken off. A cursory glance at both popular and academic
> publications will quickly suggest a whole array of "sustainabili-
> ties" . . . I have not been able to find a single source that is against
> "sustainability." Greenpeace is in favor. George Bush, Jr., and Sr., are,
> the World Bank and its chairman . . . are, the Pope is, my son Arno
> is, the rubber tappers in the Brazilian Amazon are, Bill Gates is, the
> labor unions are. All are presumably concerned about the long-term
> socioenvironmental survival of (parts of) humanity; most just keep
> doing business as usual.
>
> —Swyngedouw, 2007: 20

Introduction:
The Rise of Sustainable Urban Development

Our discussion now turns to the dynamics of economic development policy, in general, and sustainable urban development policy,
in particular. Examining sustainable development at an urban scale is
important for several reasons: (1) it provides grounding for the ideas we
explored in the previous chapter; (2) it reveals the inherent complexity of
sustainable urban development; and (3) it can help the reader to better
understand the underlying perspectives, conflicts, and processes that come

along with urban sustainability. What we offer here can be used to frame the field trips that follow. However, we think of these as starting points, rather than endpoints, for this exploration. Thus we hope the reader will employ these perspectives critically and creatively—to see them not as constraining, but as inspirational.

Some scholars might take issue with limiting our analysis to the urban scale. They argue that the urban scale is quite difficult to circumscribe since urbanization processes occur across the globe at all spatial scales. "Planetary urbanization" (Brenner and Schmid, 2015; Merrifield, 2013) and "methodological cityism" (Angelo and Wachsmuth, 2015) are two conceptual perspectives that pursue this scale of urbanism. We appreciate this and some of the other upheavals going on in urban theory literature. However, it's one thing to conceptualize "the urban" to understand broader capitalist social relations, and it's another to be able to make sense of different urban sustainability plans and projects at the local, urban scale. Sustainable urban development is fraught with conceptual richness and political controversy, and this is our entry point for engaging you in and challenging you to think differently about sustainable urbanism.

Despite disagreements about whether everything is urbanized, even the moon, many urban theorists agree that cities are the main site of development, sustainable or otherwise. In 2009, a property market bubble burst in the United States, ending a period of unprecedented global urban growth, both in terms of GDP production and population. This is also the time that, for reasons we explain below, sustainable urban development became more deeply rooted in the vernacular of architects, developers, city boosters, and others.

In this chapter we present conceptualizations of how we can understand sustainable urban development and the conflicts and the political challenges that surround it. Our Ariadne's thread through the labyrinth of these conceptualizations is our premise that sustainable urban development is not a harmonious concept but comprises the tensions and contradictions of larger society, in general, and in city development, in particular. Accordingly, sustainable urban development can be seen from different realities, or social constructs, which legitimate different processes and outcomes. For example, how can something as earnestly utopian as Local Agenda 21 get transformed into an economic engine of growth? We explore this issue in the section below. To return to our metaphor from the previous chapter, for some, a possible consequence of the tensions placed on the structure of the three-legged stool is becoming less than comfortable. To help with this, we suggest a few key readings at the end of the chapter. Meanwhile, we intend in this chapter to offer some conceptual resources to use as you participate in the field trips to come, as well as to inspire you to look more deeply into these accounts and others.

Economic Engines: Urban Sustainability, Local Agenda 21, and Greening the City

In large part, the sustainable development discourse has shaped the way many cities have been remade. It's hard to find a city that doesn't have sustainability as part of its "brand." In the 2000s, the mode of urban development—remaking long-derelict urban cores into vibrant urban utopias and sites of consumption—was synonymous with sustainable urban development (see below). Sustainable urban development plans go by monikers such as compact urban development, transit-oriented development, smart growth, and smart cities. These developments rely on existing infrastructures, remediating and regenerating brownfields; they were often built on (or planned as) public transit lines.

Coincidentally or not, these landscapes appealed to the imagery of an urban utopia to the emerging "creative class." Scholars have argued that the creative class was an important ingredient to urban development because "creatives" are the new raw materials for the entrepreneurial, new economy city (Krueger and Buckingham, 2012). The sustainable city, or its rhetoric at least, was thus viewed not only as a good goal but as a driver in shaping a city for the new economy; city boosters, urban development consultants, and even some scholars perceived that creatives attracted the kind of labor needed to support the supposedly less resource intensive information and service economy, which were the engines of the postindustrial city, or the ecomodern city. Those adopting this development approach also believed that such practices made them more competitive in the global labor market. A development-driven "sustainable city as economic engine" rhetoric supplanted the more utopian rhetoric of Local Agenda 21. Like ecological modernization tried to accomplish with sustainable development on the macroscale, urban areas "greened" but were not grounded in environmental or social concerns, but economic ones. Sustainable urban development's time had come, but not as it was imagined by its architects in the early 1990s.

No matter which moniker one chooses—sustainable urban development, LA 21, smart growth, compact urban development—sustainable development has been adopted as a set of policy goals in many cities. This does not mean that the process of urbanization has become more "sustainable" in recent times. Sure, we have more mass transit nodes, more green buildings, more viable ecosystems in our cities than before. This is all good. And what's interesting is that while ecological modernization has influenced macroeconomic change, it has influenced urbanization too. The value of being green is viewed by many cities as a foregone conclusion. Freiburg, Germany, proudly calls itself the greenest city in Europe, as does Växjö, Sweden. Despite the accolades and media attention these cities have had, they have not realized what it means to be a sustainable city. The actions of these cities have brought economy and environment closer together in ways aligned with the norms established by Brundtland. Many commentators have noted that for many cities the single most important element in a city's sustainability effort revolves around environmental concerns (Portney, 2003). As we pointed out above, these environmental aspects coupled nicely with economic development visions, which made them palatable for city policymakers and boosters. Fully integrating, or having environment-led development remains an elusive goal, but in the last round of urban regeneration, these two goals articulated by Brundtland and operationalized at the local level have more closely aligned visions when, a generation earlier, they were seen to be at odds with one another.

In this section, we present the broader urban political economic context in which sustainable urban development exists. Indeed, sustainable urban development has found spatial expression in the context of broader urban economic drivers. It may seem ironic that the "sustainable city" sits so comfortably within the tableau of the "neoliberal city." The appearance is both an illusion and a construction of reality. As Agyeman (2013) reminds us, it is an illusion because, as a set of *principles*, sustainable urban development fails to deliver on its commitment to social equity and economic security. It is also a *construction of reality* in that sustainable urban development has found its spatial expression in the context of urban neoliberalism. City boosters tout their stock of high-performance, energy-efficient buildings, green roofs, compact and dense developments, adaptive reuse of existing infrastructures, and transit-oriented development. To develop these points further, we turn our discussion now to a selection of urban theory. Our purpose here is to provide a set of perspectives that allows one to further examine this tenuously imbricated connection between the sustainable city and the neoliberal city.

The Art of the Urban:
The Social Construction of Urban Theory and Urban Space

At the beginning of this book we described our approach as social constructivist. A social constructivist ontology of reality takes the belief that
the world around us is based less on objective, "hard" facts than on ideas,
perceptions, and beliefs that people hold about reality. The implication of
this ontology is an epistemology that requires us to understand how people
create reality. In this case, we are looking at how urban actors—residents,
planners, developers, politicians, and others—create reality. Another key
aspect of social constructivism is that reality is fluid and requires interpretation as it changes over time.

Urban scholars and analysts are as diverse as the spaces that they
examine. Therefore, there is no generally agreed upon general urban theory,
though some who follow a positivist ontology would suggest that there is.
Like the architects and inhabitants of cities, urban scholars have different
experiences, perceptions, and beliefs that influence their understanding of
the urban condition. Our constructivist view of the "urban" or the "city"
(urban space) informs us that urban space is not a fixed objective entity.
It is conceived as a set of social constructions that are highly contingent
on a series of events, experiences, practices, and power geometries that
shape relations among diverse urban inhabitants. Following Lefebvre
(1991), urban space thus reflects a set of social practices that is enacted
by individuals and social groups as they move through time and space.
Urban space is thus an *oeuvre* of its citizens—a work of art constantly
being made and remade under different social relations, practices, and
power geometries (Lefebvre, 1991).

We use the next section of this chapter to explore perspectives of
how scholars explain the processes that citizens use to create urban space.
One key thing to remember here is that theories, like social practice, are
accountable to the tenets of social constructivism (Barnes, 1996). In our
view, no single theory can explain the politics of the production of urban
space. This can be problematic, especially when one is engaged in urban
politics and trying to make an argument to, say, a politician who has a
two-year window to "make something happen." Your five-year argument
about gentrification may fall on deaf ears, especially if the politician believes
that the market is the most efficient and fair mechanism for distributing
wealth. These are all things you need to consider as you participate in

the field trips presented in the upcoming chapters. This situation might seem intractable. It is certainly a challenge, a difficult one, at that—just ask anyone who has tried to break through the detritus covering boosterist politics of urban economic development. We will not leave you without a way forward. In the final section, we present a perspective on how better decisions might be made and new theories might emerge.

Planning as a Top-Down Technical Activity

By the end of the nineteenth century, many cities began designing land use plans in a more technically sophisticated way. Among the most famous are the plans by John Nash (early eighteenth century), Georges Eugène Haussmann in Paris, France (mid–nineteenth century), Cesare Beruto in Milan, Italy (between 1884 and 1889), James Friedrich Ludolf Hobrecht in Berlin, Germany (1862), and certainly Ildefons Cerdà i Sunyer, in Barcelona, Spain (1859). Even if these big plans vary in their perspectives, political orientation, and expected outcomes, they represent a new phase of planning as a professionalized, if not technocratic, activity from which the public was largely excluded.

In the late nineteenth century, some planning circles took a more utopian angle, such as the United Kingdom's Ebenezer Howard and his "Garden City" (see also Frank Lloyd Wright of the US) and Le Corbusier, of France. Howard founded the Garden City Association, which morphed into the Town and Country Planning Association (TCPA) in the United Kingdom. Britain's postwar government enlisted the prestigious TCPA to help it design a national planning law. In 1947, the Town and Country Planning Act passed parliament. The TCPA of 1947 shifted the power of development to local authorities, which it also established, away from private property owners. Even if one owned a large swath of land, it had to be anointed by the local authority to become part of the spatial plan for the district. In contrast, if one's land fell within a development area planned by the local authority, the authority had to purchase the land from the landowner. Further, the Law required private citizens to get planning permission for smaller improvements to individual homes. The TCPA of 1947 model spread outside the United Kingdom to Europe, too. For example, the British during their post–World War II occupation of West Germany integrated aspects of the historic planning law into the postwar German context. It also influenced planning in the United States. In the

1960s, the US congress considered a national planning law developed by Richard Babcock (1918–1993), a Chicago lawyer and planning scholar. Ultimately, the plan failed to pass the US Congress, in what is known as the Quiet Revolution that occurred in several American states, including Florida, Vermont, Oregon, and Hawaii, after the federal government failed to enact a national planning vision.

Urban planning was becoming increasingly professionalized. The University of Liverpool established the first planning department in the United Kingdom in 1909. In 1923, Harvard founded the first city and regional planning department in the United States, followed by MIT in 1932, and then Columbia University, the University of Washington, and the University of California, Berkeley. After World War II, planning became an academic field of study, and planning programs proliferated around the United States.

The paradigm that emerged after World War II was called "rational planning." During this period, planning required technical studies, such as labor market, tax base, and consumer buying power analyses. Local planning had been broken down to a set of discrete tasks that would later be analyzed collectively. Planners had to collect quantitative data and be able to analyze them. They had to understand these data in order to set local development goals and to create appropriate strategies and assessment criteria. They also had to be able to adjudicate where to use resources. They thus had to understand development financing, feasibility, and cost–benefit analysis.

Another aspect of this period driving rational planning was the notion that all the big social questions had been answered and that planning could be a science, like regional science or spatial science; the best options could be discovered through technical planning. Further, there was the notion that all of the great questions surrounding urban economic activities had been resolved. As Dahl and Lindblom (1953) argued:

> In economic organization and reform, the "great issues" are no longer the great issues, if they ever were. It has become increasingly difficult for thoughtful men to find meaningful alternatives posed in the traditional choices between socialism and capitalism, planning and the free market, regulation and laissez-faire, for they find their actual choices neither so simple or so grand. Not so simple, because economic organization poses knotty problems that can only be solved by painstaking

attention to technical details—how else, for example, can inflation be controlled? Not so grand, because, at least in the Western world, most people neither can nor wish to experiment with the whole pattern of socio-economic organization to attain goals more easily won. (1953: 3)

In the mid 1960s, then, few urban planners and activists saw the value of everyday knowledge for urban planning. Consider the iconic American planner, Edmund Bacon, who exemplified this perspective and often drew criticism, even in the 1960s, because his notion of design was top-down. He argued that great cities are great not because of one person, but because of the way they fit together. This period in planning is defined by the belief that it was "the technocratic elite" who would guide our planning systems (and political and economic ones, too) (Fischer, 2003). A dominant view in the planning and economic realms, technocratic decision making did see challenges, and ultimately calls for more democratic and participatory forms of planning decision making. The tension here became defined by the rational scientific approaches to planning (think British "New Towns," or urban renewal, or Jane Jacobs versus Robert Moses) against the public's irrational reaction to "good design." The response from the 1960s through the 1980s was to throw an increasing amount of scientific data—standardized scientific data—at the public to counter "irrational" arguments.

Today, it seems foolhardy to try to implement new projects without any participation. Indeed, in many countries, participation has been institutionalized within their legal planning codes. LA 21 built off this culture of participatory planning and the normative principles of democratic decision making. LA 21 is based on the belief that good governance occurs when participants are equal in the process, creating place-specific constellations of governance at different scales—the local, urban, and supraurban levels. Ironically, the beliefs that planning can be in fact democratic come from the ideology of neoliberalism. In contrast to the 1960s when, in the United States at least, the power of the federal government remained generally unquestioned, in the 1980s that began to shift as the tools of economics, such as cost–benefit analysis, became dominant in planning, in particular, and policymaking, in general. For example, in the Reagan-era 1980s growth management regimes, which were once dominated command-and-control-style regulation, were supplanted by rigorous cost–benefit analysis requirements (Breyer, 1982). Especially at the national scale, government's appetite for centralized mandates began to crumble significantly during this period. Government agencies were increasingly required to use cost–benefit analysis more stringently to justify new regulations. Moreover, the ideology of spreading social costs (e.g., schools funding or the environmental costs of development) to the market increasingly gained traction. In planning, this translated into the notion of Adequate Public Facilities Ordinances (APFOs). APFOs shifted the focus from explicitly stated environmental priorities and required local planning boards to consider whether the pace of local development outpaced the ability of the local authority (based on planned capital expenditures) to provide adequate public infrastructure (e.g., roads, sewerage, schools). If the authority could not keep pace with its obligations, then a development could not move forward unless the developer was willing to fund the improvements (Knapp and Nelson, 1992). As DeGrove (1992) states:

> Growth management . . . is deeply committed to a responsible fit between development and infrastructure needed to support the impacts of development, including such things as roads, schools, water, sewer, drainage, solid waste, and parks and recreation. Thus, growth management is closely linked to, and necessary for, the achievement of "quality of life."

This form of planning expanded beyond environmental concerns to issues of infrastructure cost management and quality of life. Flight from the cities to the suburbs strained infrastructure in newly developing suburbs while shifting the tax base away from the inner city, especially in relation to school funding (Glaeser and Berry, 2006). Fiscal restraint imposed by cost–benefit analysis in the 1980s paved the way for a broader strategy of limiting the power of the government, especially in those areas where it was believed the government restricted the ability of the market to allocate resources. The Republican revolution of 1994 and the so-called "Contract with America" exemplify this shift.

In this section we have briefly discussed the evolution of elite-driven, technical rationalist planning to more participatory approaches. More importantly, we have discussed the culture in which these shifts have taken place, characterized by an erosion of the power of the state in planning and economic decisions. In the 1960s, planning was strongly dedicated to elite-fueled and state-driven technical approaches to design and implementation. In the 1980s this state-centric approach eroded, giving in to new forms of techno-planning using economic tools, such as cost–benefit analysis. Academics and forward-thinking practitioners developed participatory approaches, but the general approach was that of "decide-announce-defend," or DAD. This meant that the decision-making responsibility remained with the elite technical planners, but instead of implementing their designs without public input, they would decide on a course of action, announce it, and defend their decision. This very much reflected the general policy of government decision making at the time, especially around environmental regulatory decisions.

The production of urban space shifted during this time. Revisiting our definition of the production of space: urban space is a set of social constructions that are highly contingent on a series of events, experiences, practices, and power geometries that shape relations between diverse urban inhabitants. It reflects a set of social practices enacted by individuals and social groups as they move through time and space. These changes also affected spatial relations since the locus of power was no longer held by states, especially in the United States, but was devolved to local governments or markets. At the local scale, or scale of the city, local government became one actor among many involved in the politics of urban development. Moreover, expertise shifted from being within the local state to a broader set of actors, such as consultants, private planners, and developers. In the next section we will examine some of the conceptual frameworks that emerged to capture the change nexus of sociospatial relations that would produce new forms of "sustainable space."

"Fixing" the Regimes:
Pro-Growth Coalitions and Sustainable Urban Development

In this section we pick up the theme of governance in sustainable urban development in the broader context of market triumphalism in urban governance. Doing so requires us to examine conceptual frameworks specifically designed to examine urban politics and spatial change. In particular, we are interested in exploring how the seemingly paradoxical goals of the market and sustainable development coexist with one another. Do the aspirational goals of sustainable urban development compete with the market, or are they complementary to each other? We argue that they are co-producing new forms of urban policies and spatial relations that are decidedly post-Fordist because they are based on different ideologies and political perspectives and conflicting forms of coalition building. These new urban politics are reframing policy and reshaping spatial development.

The "new urban politics" seeks a significant reduction in the local provision welfare policies, basic service provision (e.g., waste management), and pursue the rolling back of local government authority and rolling out market-based approaches to urban development (Cox, 1993; Peck, 2004). For Hall (2013: 154), there has been a scramble to reap the rewards of an increasingly competitive—and lucrative—free market. Facing increasing fiscal constraints cities have reoriented their inclination being inward looking—fixing potholes, picking up rubbish, and ensuring the school buses run on time—and placed emphasis on new forms of "place marketing" of the revitalization (Porter and Shaw, 2013). This new urban politics thus seeks the complete commodification of urban resources and the unconditional subjugation of previous responsibilities for ensuring healthy communities. Some are that these services will be more efficiently provided if they are placed within the paradigm of economic growth.

The purpose of the new urban politics thesis was, as Boyle puts it, to provide a framework "to make sense of epochal transformations in the governance of the contemporary capitalist city" (2011: 2674). While the globalization of capital flows has constrained cities to adopt progressive policies environmental issues have become important drivers to urban politics. With its emphasis on the ecological consciousness of "protecting and enhancing the natural environment" (While, Jonas, and Gibbs, 2004: 549) that also involves businesses and capital, social values and a demand for social justice, political transparency, and social heterogeneity, sustainability seemingly contrasts with the goals and framework of the "new urban policy" (Raco, 2005). Some authors have labeled these conditions paradoxical (Krueger and Gibbs, 2007) or even "schizophrenic" (Krueger and Agyeman, 2005); others have stated that sustainable development in this logic is "simply impossible" (Swyngedouw, 2007). Raco points out that sustainable urban policies and the demand for entrepreneurial and growth-first approaches were only "ostensibly very different interpretations of contemporary development" (Raco, 2005: 324) and instead reflect a "hybridity of development discourses" (Raco, 2005: 343).

Let's explore this further with an example. Austin, Texas, has been one of the United States' fastest growing cities for several decades. Development was led by high tech companies, such as Dell, IBM, and Oracle. But Austin is also weird (as locals remind us); it's different from much of the rest of Texas. Indeed, it has acquired a reputation as a progressive, tolerant, and creative city, topping many of the indices that rank these features. Both Austin's business community and its environmental community have embraced this identity. As Tretter (2013) points out: the enlightened business class saw it in their long-term interest to embrace aspects of environmentalism in order to make Austin the technopolis of the Southwest.

To examine this phenomenon, Trettor (2013) adapted Molotch's growth coalition theory, which argued that green coalitions and growth coalitions have a necessarily antagonistic relationship, in the context of creative cities and sustainable cities. In their view of growth coalition theory, Logan and Molotch (1987) argued that city governments have been required to increase growth for tax and other purposes. Since taxes are key here, cities need to increase the value of land on the tax rolls. Often this was done through suburbanization. But as many cities reach "build out," a new cycle of development had to occur. However, in the 1990s and 2000s, many cities took stock of their local resources, including old factories and blighted inner-city land parcels and neighborhoods. Deindustrialization made many of these quarters lose their property value. As cities began the process of place-making in the 1990s and 2000s, these derelict inner-city spaces became valorized as they were thought to attract new economy workers, or the creative class (Florida, 2005). Developers could see the value of inner-city redevelopment for the first time in over a generation, and environmentalists praised the intensification of development on brownfield sites rather than the greenfield sites that existed in would-be suburbs. Thus a compromise between these two antagonistic groups was forged. Other authors have described this epochal shift in urban politics as leading to a rethinking of the "whole terrain" of urban politics (Hall 2013: 154). The new urban politics that had been developed in order to respond to the new challenges are described by Cox (1993) as "new urban politics." These politics are the "conceptual umbrella" (Ancien, 2011: 2477) of what is later described by While, Jonas, and Gibbs (2004) as the "sustainability fix."

In Europe, issues of sustainability started to hit the urban scale with the emergence of early environmental grassroots in the 1970s (Béal, 2012; Miller, 2000). During "roll-back environmentalism" (Béal, 2012), the mainstreaming of sustainability in urban politics has weakened the goals and ideologies that appeared during the 1970s. Consequently, during the phase of "roll-out environmentalism" the goals and principles of sustainability—in the meantime manifested in the literature and dominating political programs (see Leipzig Charter of the EU in 2007)—were challenging the goals and principles of the "new urban politics" (Béal, 2012: 410). Urban elites, policymakers, and politicians were in search for new ways of reconciling these opposing strategies within a new sustainable urban development agenda. This is the moment of searching for a "selective incorporation of ecological goals in the greening of urban governance" (While, Jonas, and Gibbs, 2004: 551).

In the 1980s, David Harvey conceptualized the "spatial fix," a practice in which firms would relocate from one place to another to lower their labor and/or environmental costs. In other words, they would build new branch plants and production facilities in places where labor costs were cheaper or environmental regulations less stringent (e.g., BMW building factories in the southern United States, or Mexican maquiladoras reestablishing on the US–Mexico border). In the context of urban development, While, Jonas, and Gibbs (2004) conceptualized a new kind of fix, the "sustainability fix," which they define as the "selective incorporation of environmental goals, determined by the balance of pressures for and against environmental policy within and across the city" (552). In the context of new urban green-growth politics, While, Jonas, and Gibbs argue that sustainable urban development propels the change the economy needs. Similar to spatial fixes, the sustainability fix reconciles the "tension between spatial flow and spatial fixity that then impels the changing geography of capitalism" (Barnes, 2006: 38). "Sustainability fixes" to urban growth and development have been manifold across time and space and have affected the oeuvre of urban space. For example, according to While, Jonas, and Gibbs (2004), Manchester and Leeds focused on waterfront developments, inner-city revitalizations, and flagship projects. These strategies are easily recognizable in other cities, too, such as Barcelona (Gomes de Matos, 2013) and Hamburg (Dörfler, 2011). Liverpool, after falling behind expected profits from its cultural marketing, added a "low carbon economy" objective with particular focus on the city's wind and tidal sector to its strategic plan merging the paradigm of growth with green aspects (North, 2010). Under the label "EcoDensity," Vancouver continued existing policies under a new label, "making Vancouver healthy, clean and green" (Rosol, 2013: 2238). By "linking the discourse of densification to sustainability" and "promoting development that serves the environment, economy and community," the city exerted hegemonic power over antagonistic opinions (Rosol, 2013: 2239). Temenos and McCann (2012: 1389) show how Whistler, a small town near Vancouver, has mobilized sustainability to its development agenda, and Long researched how Austin, Texas, has emerged as a "sustainable city" as it recognized "the ability of [its] green reputation to attract talent, capital and industry" (Long, 2014: 8). Drawing on Tianjin eco-city in China, Pow and Neo analyze the "eco-flagship prestige projects" (2014: 133) "as an entrepreneurial project" (2014: 138).

Sustainability fixes are implemented in many cities around the world. Urban regeneration projects play a key role in this process. There are (at least) three points that all these examples have in common. First, they demonstrate how environmental and sustainability aspects are superimposed by economic interests. It's a three-legged stool of sustainability, with the strongest leg being the economy, a weaker ecology leg, and a social leg that seems to be broken off—the stool is obviously unstable. Second, and with regard to the broken social leg, these cases show how principles of justice and equity are not included in these sustainability fixes. This brings Jonas and While to conclude that "an important task for future research of a more critical orientation will be to identify whether or not the contradictions of urban entrepreneurialism are opening up possibilities for an urban-scaled politics constructed around a stronger and more socially just 'sustainability fix'" (2007: 152). Third, most of these studies focus on the urban and cities as analytical frameworks. While some of them argue with the mobility of policies (McCann, 2011) and explicitly refer to a relational perspective on sustainability fixes, only a few take into account the interscalar connectivity and relationality of sustainability fixes. Temenos and McCann point out that "local sustainability fixes are [. . .] always also 'extra-local' in their construction and legitimation" (2012: 1390–1391) and, by doing so, claim for a stricter spatial perspective of the sustainability fix approach.

Participation from the Bottom-Up: Politicizing Sustainable (Urban) Development

Besides a focus on the built environment (the spatial configuration), technological innovations (instruments and tools), and impact on climate change (output), sustainable development had also been discussed in terms of new and innovative planning practices (process). A significant element of Local Agenda 21, as outlined previously, was the idea to involve all kinds of social actors in order to achieve a more sustainable form of development. Because it involved governments, businesses, trade unions, academics, educators, and local citizens, decisions were thought to be better. All these actors were thought to play an active role contributing to develop ideas of how to implement the principles defined by the Earth summit. Thus, participatory planning approaches, already discussed since the 1960s, came to a new renaissance in this field. The main ideas behind the concept of participation are representation, knowledge, and the professionalization of planning.

Over the last two decades, urban sustainability research has developed in two strong, yet opposing, directions. Besides the form of technical-scientific research that strives to develop sophisticated principles and guidelines that offer "solutions for citizens and their governments" (Roseland, 2012) and facilitate the implementation of "best practices," there is an alternative perspective emerging that critically approaches best practices and technical-scientific framings of sustainability questions by uncovering power relations, contradictions, and conflicts (Freytag, Gössling, and Mössner, 2014) that are linked to "actually existing sustainabilities" (While, Jonas, and Gibbs, 2004; Krueger and Agyeman, 2005; Krueger and Gibbs, 2007). At the very center of the latter, a relatively new debate discusses the lack of democracy that occurred in the context of a consensual understanding of the need for sustainable development. At first glance, this seems paradoxical: wasn't it precisely the planning of sustainable (urban) developments that employed innovative planning tools and strategies such as participatory approaches or forms of bottom-up, direct local democracy? Why are new authors concerned with the decline of democracy to an "egalitarian project" (Crouch, 2008: 13), particularly in urban green contexts? Different from a few decades ago, when sustainable development was still subject to engaged social movements and intense protests (most famously against the construction of nuclear weapons plants; see Miller, 2000), sustainability policies today in a great many cities appear to be broadly consensual, yet simultaneously "suspend the proper political dimension" (Swyngedouw, 2013: 2). Indeed, as Swyngedouw (2013) has noted, it turns out to be difficult to find anyone opposed to the idea of sustainability. It seems as if sustainability has won the battle of predominating, hegemonic ideas in Western societies and beyond. Depending on the theoretical perspective, sustainable development occurs as either a new hegemony (Jessop, Peck, and Tickell, 1999; Lauria, 1997) that is no longer subject to debate (at least until a new counterhegemonic bloc arises.) or, as other authors (e.g., French political theorist Jacques Rancière) have asserted, the consensus of sustainable development is the result of mechanisms of exclusion (1995; 2001). Both perspectives raise critical questions and express severe concerns regarding the qualities of local democracy as well as environmental and sociospatial justice (Harvey, 2009), as summarized under the critique of postpolitics (Gill, Johnstone, and Williams, 2012; Swyngedouw 2007, 2013).

Freiburg, Germany:
The Postpolitical Sustainable City?

A good example that illustrates these arguments is the sustainable development of Freiburg im Breisgau, Germany. Since the mid-1990s, Freiburg has been hailed as one of the leading examples of sustainable urban development in Europe. According to some authors, it is among Europe's leading "eco-cities" and, indeed, the city markets itself as "Freiburg Green City." Freiburg has won several awards for its sustainable development; at the Rio 20+ conference it was recognized by Sustainia 100, and in 2010 the city won the German Sustainability Award. At the center of all this homage are the city's innovative cycling network, public transit, solar energy initiatives, strict energy standards for new constructions, as well as the high level of social acceptance for sustainable policies among citizens. Most famous is the eco-quartier Vauban, constructed in the mid-1990s as a model for sustainable (urban) development. All buildings in the city meet the strict Freiburg energy standards, and many of them are passive energy buildings. A few houses are "plus energy" buildings that produce more energy than they consume, transforming these residential buildings into small power plants. The neighborhood is well connected by the public tram, and even alternative forms of housing are accepted in the neighborhood, highlighting the high level of political tolerance toward other forms of living and thinking. A supermarket selling exclusively organic products guarantees local supply, and a weekly market sells regional products. It seems as if the theoretical ideas of Serge Latouche (2009) have been successfully put into practice in Vauban, Freiburg. In an interview with the *Guardian* about his last and new book *Good Cities, Better Lives: How Europe Discovered the Lost Art of Urbanism* (2013), the late Sir Peter Hall described Freiburg's political efforts toward sustainable development in this way: "they have created good jobs, built superb housing in fine natural settings and generated rich urban lives. But not only that: simultaneously these cities have become models of sustainable urban life, minimizing energy needs, recycling waste, and reducing emissions" (Rogers, 2014). When awarded most sustainable city in Germany, Freiburg's lord-mayor

Dieter Salomon mentioned the active citizenry that "pushes him every day" toward a more sustainable urban development.

What is remarkable here is that, as the mayor contests, the sustainable politics result from the citizenry, not the political class. It appears that sustainable development in Freiburg has been accepted by all citizens, and has become common sense for everyday practices. And in fact, in Freiburg and elsewhere, sustainable (urban) development emerges as what Gill, Johnstone, and Williams (2012) call "meta-consensual politics." It seems as if all citizens have uncritically accepted the predominating norms and routines for a better life in the city. There is a predominating consensus that sustainable development, in whatever form, is normatively positive and thus not subject to political quarrels.

However, while Freiburg's sustainable development continues with great success, inequality is worsening, affordable housing is in increasingly scarce supply, and the poor continue to be displaced to make way for new development. This raises the question: sustainability for whom? Vauban is among the most expensive neighborhoods in the city. The "plus energy" buildings produce a 5 to 6 percent return of investment to a solar farm owned by large investors outside of Freiburg (Freytag, Gössling, and Mössner, 2014). As with any capitalist development, sustainable (urban) development has also created huge social and spatial disparities in the city. Why is it, then, that there is consensus among citizens about this form of development and that no debate takes place about the form, content, and possible consequences of a (technically) sustainable development that lacks reference to social inclusion and justice?

Following the theoretical perspective of a critique of postpolitical conditions, no general and overarching consensus is possible in society, as people are radically different from one another. Consensus therefore does not simply "exist," but is politically produced and heavily fortified against opposing ideas, perspectives, and alternatives. Consensus, then, is highly instrumentalized and aimed at specific interests and outcomes for those groups at the center of the consensus. Thus a sophisticated apparatus exists for maintaining consensus. Rather than contrasting opinions being expressed in public space, most decisions are made behind closed doors, away from the public, yet these decisions become accepted afterward as kind of natural laws. This form of post-parliamentarianism (Crouch, 2008) goes in line with new forms of "politainment" (Jörke, 2005: 482), where making politics is transformed into an entertaining act. We are all well aware that televised political debates before presidential elections are staged by marketing professionals and media experts. Political decision making has become quasi-privatized and removed from the public realm: it is politics outside of the political, as French political philosopher Jacques Rancière (2001) has described it. There is a pacifying consensus in society over the principles and direction of policies to which protest and any form of political debate has been subordinated, "reduced to the administration and management of processes whose parameters are defined by consensual socio-scientific knowledges" (Swyngedouw, 2009: 602). Antagonist interests and perspectives are subordinated to the dogmatic search for societal consensus leading to the unification and standardization of society.

The exclusionary power of consensual politics, which suppresses any alternative form of political resistance, results from what Marchart (2010) calls the "political difference," that is, the difference between—in the words of Rancière (2001)—*police* and *the political*. Following Jacques Rancière, "police" is defined as specific procedures that constitute power and create or stabilize the consensus (Marchart, 2010: 179) about what is visible and audible in society (Rancière, Tornell, and Vamvakidis 2010). The consensus denies these parts of the society, which are metaphorically not given a "language to be heard." From this perspective, sustainable development in Freiburg appears as consensus-oriented *police order*, aimed at hegemonies (Chambers, 2011: 306) that disallow different meanings, contrary opinions, and societal dissensus. In Freiburg and Vauban, people with higher incomes clearly benefit from the consensus of sustainable development and secure their societal status and position. People with lower incomes are excluded to cheaper areas or fringes of the city.

Reasserting Justice and Equity in Sustainable Development?

Indeed, sustainable urban development, in particular, and sustainable development, in general, has privileged environmental over social sustainability. From a macrolevel sustainable development policy, we see REDD (Removing Emissions through forest Degradation and Destruction) and REDD+ as examples. At the urban scale, we see issues of gentrification and environmental injustice flourish, even when adjacent to sustainable development projects. Environmental justice and sustainable development advocate and scholar Julian Agyeman notes that "a truly sustainable society is one where wider questions of social needs and welfare, and economic opportunity, are *integrally* connected to environmental concerns" (2013: 5). Agyeman (2013) and colleagues coined the phrase "just sustainability" as a moniker for those activities that attached all three legs to the sustainability stool. It might seem repetitive to some who already understand social equity and justice as an integral part of the sustainable development agenda. It's not. Rather, it is an explicit effort to remind scholars and practitioners alike that what often looks like "proper" sustainable urban development is only a creative use of the environmental and economic legs. Arguably, it presents the state-of-the-art in critical sustainability theory. By bringing together the sustainability literature and the environmental justice literature, these authors sought to create a vocabulary for political opportunity and mobilization both in the grassroots and local government.

To date, this work has focused largely on the organization aspects of a vision of movement leaders rather than the "extensive" politics of economic development. Indeed, there remains a critical need to examine how sustainability might be "mapped" onto the current geography of neoliberal capitalism and, more importantly, where the opportunities for broader political engagement with sustainability might present themselves. Further, this conceptualization should be a sobering reminder that some groups of people are disempowered and have no voice, or whose voices are marginalized, in the policy process. Thus, by rendering the concept of justice explicit we have a more difficult time placing justice and equity in a subservient position. We lack space here to develop the concept of just sustainability further. What we will do is provide four examples of scientific research that complement and add to the just sustainability thesis.

Urban greening has been one area central to the sustainable urban development discourse. Green space has increased and/or improved in many cities in the name of "sustainable development." Green space has been preserved from development because of its aesthetic, recreational, and ecological service values. In addition to these green infrastructures, bike lanes, bike share programs, shared car schemes, additional miles of trams and public transport, and smarter public transport have been developed. Planners have developed "green infrastructure toolkits" to help mobilize and disseminate how cities might turn unmanaged or derelict space into sources of economic value and cost savings through relying on ecological services. Finally, inner-city redevelopment and brownfield rehabilitation have contributed to convivial relationships between green and the city.

Adopting green practices in cities makes sense in terms of transaction costs and other development costs they contribute to the economic value of nature and a city's competitiveness. Urban spaces, regional and local alike, are using their greening strategies—branding them and marketing them—to attract new economy workers, and thus those highly-sought high-tech jobs that bring more advantageous multiplier effects.[1] We can see this well documented in the policy mobility literature.

There are negative consequences of sustainable urban development, too. Gentrification is an important problem. When areas are regenerated and branded "sustainable," property values tend to rise because their market value increases. When these properties that have been redeveloped were formerly rental units or near neighborhoods where incomes are below the average median income, many of the current residents get priced out of the housing market. This process of gentrification happens both when the market is left to regulate, as often happens in the United States, or through state-led gentrification, such as in London's East End. Further, the people who are forced out of what was already marginal housing must move to other marginal housing and further from their jobs, making these already disadvantaged groups involuntarily suffer additional disadvantages (longer commutes, higher fuel costs, time away from family, lower quality housing, etc.).

Sustainable urbanism as a set of policies and practices has become more adversarial. People are being displaced, while no real gains are being made with regard to ecological improvements, such as reduced CO_2. The benefits of a sustainable lifestyle are limited to certain people, and society is no more just or stable. Yet, sustainable urbanism has a strong consensual element to it (Krueger and Buckingham, 2012). Indeed, those who often have the most to lose do not speak up because, as Erik Syngedouw's quote at the beginning of this chapter suggests, who can possibly be against more sustainable societies, in general, and sustainable cities, in particular? Sustainable urbanism works because it often fits neatly into the ideology of "how things work." It can be an economic engine of growth; it can be a vehicle for attracting a desirable labor force; and it can support a city's "brand" of being innovative or creative. As Swyngedouw points out:

> The fantasy of "sustainability" imagines the possibility of an originally fundamentally harmonious Nature, one that is now out-of-synch but which, properly managed, we can and have to return to by means of a series of technological, managerial, and organizational fixes . . . Disagreement is allowed, but only with respect to the choice of technologies, mix of organiza-

tional fixes, the details of managerial adjustments, and the urgency of time and implementation. (2007: 23)

The people in the professions who are given responsibility to plan for sustainable cities frame the issue of sustainable urbanism around the acres of wetlands preserved, number of electrons consumed, the amount of trash diverted from the waste stream, "holistic" forms of decision making,[2] and reducing complex environmental, economic, and social issues to technical choices that bear the mantle of "sustainability."

These actions suggest a certain level of pluralistic decision making, where all stakeholders are assumed to hold an equal position and work together dispassionately to set the terms of sustainable development. This approach is informed by the concept of "deliberative democracy." Following Dryzek (1994), deliberative democracy assumes that (1) deliberation involves equal individuals with stated preferences, and (2) the forms of argument and persuasion are limited to rational approaches. Nonrational forms of expression, which are determined by power relations, are marginalized. For example, arguing for additional affordable housing in a "sustainable urban development" can be quickly nixed because costs of these structures require a certain price point that would be compromised. According to Slovenian philosopher Slavoj Žižek (1999), this creates a postpolitical condition in which decisions are made dispassionately and based on so-called facts. As Žižek puts it:

> In post-politics, the conflict of [global ideological] visions embodied in different parties which compete for power is replaced by the collaboration of enlightened technocrats (economists, public opinion specialists) and liberal multi-culturalists, via the process of negotiation of interests, a compromise is reached in the guise of a more or less universal consensus. Post-politics thus emphasizes the need to leave old ideological visions behind and confront new issues, armed with necessary expert knowledge and free deliberation that takes people's concrete needs and demands into account. (1999: 198)

The ultimate sign of a postpolitical sustainable urbanism is the growth of a managerial approach to government (and governance), where government is reconceived as a managerial function, not a crucible for the deliberation of ideas, policies, and practices.

Several times in the book we have invited you to be active participants in engaging and critiquing current forms of sustainable urbanism. We have called upon you to develop creative ideas and solutions around the field trips that come in the next section. Following Bernstein (1988: 6), we agree that "[w]e can best appreciate the vitality and diversity of . . . tradition[s] when we approach it as an ongoing engaged conversation consisting of distinctive—sometimes competing voices." We now ask you to get out into the field to pursue your own adventures in sustainable urbanism.

Notes

1. A multiplier effect is the number of times a dollar (or pound, or Euro, or Yen) is circulated in a place. Historically, higher levels of income in some sectors increase multipliers, which can be converted to new jobs and taxes.

2. For example, former Massachusetts governor Mitt Romney combined the Departments of Transportation, Housing, Energy, and Environment under a single super-secretariat. The stated goal of this organizational structure was to bring together people responsible for key areas who, if working together, could make better decisions about resource allocation and environmental sustainability.

For Further Reading

Agyeman, J., Bullard, R. D., and Evans, B., eds. (2003). *Just sustainabilities: Development in an Unequal World.* Cambridge, MA: MIT Press.

Gibbs, D. (2005). *Local economic development and the environment.* London: Routledge.

Krueger, R., and Gibbs, D., eds. (2007). *The sustainable development paradox: Urban political economy in the United States and Europe.* New York: Guilford Press.

References

Agyeman, J. (2013). *Introducing just sustainabilities: Policy, planning, and practice.* London: Zed Books.

Ancien, D. (2011). Global city theory and the new urban politics twenty years on: The case for a geohistorical materialist approach to the (new) urban politics of global cities. *Urban Studies,* 48(12), pp. 2473–2493.

Angelo, H., and Wachsmuth, D. (2015). Urbanizing urban political ecology: A critique of methodological cityism. *International Journal of Urban and Regional Research*, 39(1), pp. 16–27.

Barnes, T. J. (1996). *Logics of dislocation: Models, metaphors, and meanings of economic space*. New York: Guilford Press.

Barnes, T. J. (2006). Between deduction and dialectics: David Harvey on knowledge. In: N. Castree and D. Gregory, eds., *David Harvey: A Critical Reader*, 1st ed. Oxford: Malden, pp. 26–46.

Béal, V. (2012). Urban governance, sustainability and environmental movements: Post-democracy in French and British cities. *European Urban and Regional Studies*, 19(4), pp. 404–419.

Bernstein, R. J. (1988). Pragmatism, pluralism, and the healing of wounds. *Proceedings and Addresses of the American Philosophical Association*, 63(3), pp. 5–18.

Boyle, M. (2011). Commentary. The new urban politics thesis: Ruminations on MacLeod and Jones' six analytical pathways. *Urban Studies*, 48(12), pp. 2673–2685.

Brenner, N., and Schmid, C. (2015). Towards a new epistemology of the urban? *City*, 19(2–3), pp. 151–182.

Breyer, S. G. (1982). *Regulation and its reform*. Cambridge, MA: Harvard University Press.

Chambers, S. A. (2011). Jacques Rancière and the problem of pure politics. *European Journal of Political Theory*, 10(3), pp. 303–326.

Cox, K. R. (1993). The local and the global in the new urban politics: A critical view. *Environment and Planning D: Society and Space*, 11(4), pp. 433–448.

Crouch, C. (2008). *Postdemokratie*. Frankfurt: Suhrkamp.

Dahl, R. A., and Lindblom, C. E. (1953). *Politics, economics and welfare: Planning and politico-economic systems, resolved into basic processes*. New York: Harper & Brothers.

DeGrove, J. M. (1992). *The new frontier for land policy: Planning & growth management in the States*. Cambridge, MA: Lincoln Institute of Land Policy.

Dörfler, T. (2011). Antinomien des (Neuen) Urbanismus. Henri Lefebvre, die HafenCity Hamburg und die Produktion des posturbanen Raumes: Eine Forschungsskizze. *Raumforschung und Raumordnung*, 69(2), pp. 91–104.

Dryzek, J. S. (1994). *Discursive democracy: Politics, policy, and political science*. Cambridge: Cambridge University Press.

Fischer, F. (2003). *Reframing public policy: Discursive politics and deliberative practices*. Oxford: Oxford University Press.

Florida, R. (2005). *Cities and the creative class*. London & New York: Routledge.

Freytag, T., Gössling, S., and Mössner, S. (2014). Living the green city: Freiburg's Solarsiedlung between narratives and practices of sustainable urban development. *Local Environment: The International Journal of Justice and Sustainability*, 19(6), pp. 644–659.

Gill, N., Johnstone, P., and Williams, A. (2012). Towards a geography of tolerance: Post-politics and political forms of toleration. *Political Geography*, 31(8), pp. 509–518.

Glaeser, E. L., and Berry, C. R. (2006). Why are smart places getting smarter? *Rappaport Institute/Taubman Center Policy Briefs*, 3(2), pp. 1–4.

Gomes de Matos, C. (2013). Das Modell Barcelona—Partizipation, Protest und Post-politik. *Sub\urban. zeitschrift für kritische stadtforschung*, 1(2), pp. 121–140.

Hall, P. (2013). *Good cities, better lives: How Europe discovered the lost art of urbanism.* London: Routledge.

Harvey, D. (2009). *Cosmopolitanism and the geographies of freedom.* New York: Columbia University Press.

Jessop, B., Peck, J., and Tickell, A. (1999). Retooling the machine: Economic crisis, state restructuring, and urban politics. In: A. Jonas and D. Wilson, eds., *The Urban Growth Machine: Critical Perspectives Two Decades Later*, 1st ed. Albany: State University of New York Press, pp. 141–159.

Jonas, A.E.G., and While, A. (2007). Greening the entrepreneurial city. In: R. Krueger and D. Gibbs, eds., *The Sustainable Development Paradox*, 1st ed. London, New York: Guilford Press, pp. 123–159.

Jörke, D. (2005). Auf dem Weg zur Postdemokratie. *Leviathan—Berliner Zeitschrift für Sozialwissenschaften*, 33(4), pp. 482–491.

Knapp, G., and Nelson, A. C. (1992). *The regulated landscape: Lessons on state land use planning from Oregon.* Cambridge, MA: Lincoln Institute of Land Policy.

Krueger, R., and Agyeman, J. (2005). Sustainability schizophrenia or "actually existing sustainabilities?" Toward a broader understanding of the politics and promise of local sustainability in the US. *Geoforum*, 36(4), pp. 410–417.

Krueger, R., and Buckingham, S. (2012). Towards a "consensual" urban politics? Creative planning, urban sustainability and regional development. *International Journal of Urban and Regional Research*, 36(3), pp. 486–503.

Krueger, R., and Gibbs, D., eds. (2007). *The sustainable development paradox: Urban political economy in the United States and Europe.* New York: Guilford Press.

Latouche, S. (2009). *Farewell to growth.* Cambridge, UK: Polity Press.

Lauria, M., ed. (1997). *Reconstructing urban regime theory: Regulating urban politics in a global economy.* Thousand Oaks, CA: Sage Publications.

Lefebvre, H. (1991). *The production of space.* Oxford: Blackwell.

Logan, J. R., and Molotch, H. L. (1987). *Urban fortunes: The political economy of place.* Berkeley: University of California Press.

Long, J. (2014). Constructing the narrative of the sustainability fix: Sustainability, social justice and representation in Austin, TX. *Urban Studies*, 53(1), pp. 149–172.

Marchart, O. (2010). *Die politische Differenz. Zum Denken des Politischen bei Nancy, Lefort, Badiou, Laclau und Agamben.* Frankfurt: Suhrkamp.

McCann, E. (2011). Urban policy mobilities and global circuits of knowledge: Toward a research agenda. *Annals of the Association of American Geographers*, 101(1), pp. 107–130.

Merrifield, A. (2013). The urban question under planetary urbanization. *International Journal of Urban and Regional Research*, 37(3), pp. 909–922.

Miller, B. A. (2000). *Geography and social movements: Comparing antinuclear activism in the Boston area*. Minneapolis: University of Minnesota Press.

North, P. (2010). Unsustainable urbanism? Cities, climate change and resource depletion: A Liverpool case study. *Geography Compass*, 4(9), pp. 1377–1391.

Peck, J. (2004). Geography and public policy: Constructions of neoliberalism. *Progress in Human Geography*, 28(3), pp. 392–405.

Porter, L., and Shaw, K., eds. (2013). *Whose urban renaissance? An international comparison of urban regeneration strategies*. London: Routledge.

Portney, K. E. (2003). *Taking sustainable cities seriously: Economic development, the environment, and quality of life in American cities*. Cambridge, MA: MIT Press.

Pow, C. P., and Neo, H. (2014). Modeling green urbanism in China. *Area*, 47(2), pp. 132–140.

Raco, M. (2005). Sustainable development, rolled-out neoliberalism and sustainable communities. *Antipode*, 37(2), pp. 324–347.

Rancière, J. (1995). *On the shores of politics*. London: Verso.

Rancière, J. (2001). Ten theses on politics. *Theory and Event*, 5(3), pp. 17–34.

Rancière, R., Tornell, A., and Vamvakidis, A. (2010). Currency mismatch, Systemic risk and growth in emerging Europe. *Economic Policy*, 25(64), pp. 597–658.

Rogers, B. (2014). UK planning expert: There is something wrong with Britain. *The Guardian*. Available at: www.theguardian.com/artanddesign/2014/jan/17/uk-planning-expert-peter-hall-britain-wrong [3 Sept. 2016]

Roseland, M. (2012). *Toward sustainable communities*. Gabriola Island, B. C: New Society Publishers.

Rosol, M. (2013). Vancouver's "EcoDensity" planning initiative: A struggle over hegemony? *Urban Studies*, 50(11), pp. 2238–2255.

Swyngedouw, E. (2007). Impossible "sustainability" and the postpolitical condition. In: R. Krueger and D. Gibbs, eds., *The Sustainable Development Paradox: Urban Political Economy in the United States and Europe*, 1st ed. New York: Guilford Press, pp. 13–40.

Swyngedouw, E. (2009). The antinomies of the postpolitical city: In search of a democratic politics of environmental production. *International Journal of Urban and Regional Research*, 33(3), pp. 601–620.

Swyngedouw, E. (2013). The non-political politics of climate change. *ACME: An International E-Journal for Critical Geographies*, 12(1), pp. 1–8.

Temenos, C., and McCann, E. (2012). The local politics of policy mobility: Learning, persuasion, and the production of a municipal sustainability Fix. *Environment and Planning-Part A*, 44(6), pp. 1389–1406.

Tretter, E. M. (2013). Contesting sustainability: "SMART growth" and the redevelopment of Austin's eastside. *International Journal of Urban and Regional Research*, 36(1), pp. 297–310.

While, A., Jonas, A. E. G., and Gibbs, D. (2004). The environment and the entrepreneurial city: Searching for the urban "sustainability fix" in Manchester and Leeds. *International Journal of Urban and Regional Research*, 28(3), pp. 549–569.

Žižek, S. (1999). *The ticklish subject: The absent centre of political ontology*. London: Verso.

Chapter 3

A Tale of Two Cities

Christchurch, New Zealand, and Sustainable Urban Disaster Recovery

Tim Baird and C. Michael Hall

Introduction

Christchurch is the second largest city in New Zealand and is situated on the east coast of the South Island. Once believed by scientists and the public to be situated in a low-risk seismic zone, the city was struck by a series of devastating earthquakes (known as the Canterbury earthquake sequence) that started on September 4, 2010 (hereafter referred to as the "September earthquake"), with a 7.1 magnitude earthquake situated forty kilometers west of the city. The earthquake caused widespread structural damage to buildings, but no fatalities were reported. Less than six months later, on February 22, 2011, the city was struck by an even more devastating earthquake (the "February earthquake"); the close proximity to the central city, shallow depth and high peak ground acceleration combined to produce a violent earthquake that claimed 185 lives, destroyed a large proportion of Christchurch's Central Business District, and caused substantial damage in the suburbs, especially in the low-lying and lower socioeconomic Eastern suburbs, as well as to urban infrastructure. Powerful aftershocks on June 13, 2011, and December 23, 2011, also took a toll on already damaged

49

areas. Needless to say, this sequence of events has altered the physical and psychological fabric of the city and its inhabitants, including that of your two tour guides.

Before these events, Christchurch was called "The Garden City"—a term historically associated with the city since the International Exhibition of 1906–1907. This phrase was adopted by the Christchurch Beautifying Association, which sought to market the city in terms of its English landscape heritage. This is important, as it has long been reinforced in the minds of visitors and inhabitants that the city is "green," although of course whether this has meant that it was or is sustainable remains open to question. The parks and gardens of the city are/were (since the earthquake we find that we shift uneasily and hesitantly between tenses while thinking of specific locations, trying to remember whether or not they are still there) not the only defining features, however; the city was also noted for having many public buildings designed in the Gothic Revival style of architecture, as well as some classic Edwardian streetscapes. This gave parts of the city substantial heritage value as well as a degree of architectural integrity. The Edwardian buildings also provided relatively cheap inner-city rents and locations for the shops of what some would call the creative classes. In other words, it is where authors would often have coffee and buy books and music.

The last part of the scene setting is about how we are governed in a post-earthquake world. In response to the devastation of the earthquake events, the New Zealand National Party–led central government appointed Christchurch Member of Parliament Gerry Brownlee as the Earthquake Recovery Minister; this role saw Minister Brownlee granted special powers under the *Canterbury Earthquake Recovery [CER] Act* (New Zealand Parliamentary Counsel Office, 2011). One of the first acts under this legislation was the creation of the Canterbury Earthquake Recovery Authority [CERA] in March 2011, with the mandate of being "a government department with the purpose of leading, facilitating, coordinating and partnering with communities to respond to, and recover from, the impacts of the Canterbury earthquakes" (Christchurch Central Development Unit, 2013a). The CER Act also included the amendment, Section 38, under which the Minister was given power to order "the demolition of all or part of a building, or structure" (New Zealand Parliamentary Counsel Office, 2011: 26). This affected individuals and other bodies who were therefore powerless to act against such unprecedented measures.

In order to hasten what Minister Brownlee termed the "rebuild" phase of the recovery, the Christchurch Central Development Unit [CCDU] was created. This unit was tasked with delivering a blueprint known as the Central City Recovery Plan [CCRP] in a hundred days (Christchurch Central Development Unit, 2013a). The CCDU identified the following goals for the Recovery Plan:

- Identify anchor projects based on those in the Christchurch City Council's draft.

- Locate those anchor projects and consider how they would integrate with each other as part of the new central city.

- Provide guidelines for areas surrounding anchor projects including precincts (Christchurch Central Development Unit, 2013a).

Minister Brownlee further endorsed the CCRP with the following statement:

> Success in central Christchurch depends on everyone working under a shared vision. At first, the Canterbury Earthquake Recovery Authority, particularly the Christchurch Central Development Unit, will provide leadership. But cities are ultimately created by the people who decide to be part of them—who choose to invest their talent, capital and heritage. (Christchurch Central Development Unit, 2013a)

The CCRP is to be anchored by five key projects modeled on the desire for a city that is "green," "prosperous," and "accessible to all" (Christchurch Central Development Unit, 2013a). These projects include the development of a new convention center, the building of new multi-purpose stadium, the setting aside of parts of the central city for a "Justice and Emergency Services Precinct," the formation of an "Innovation Precinct," and the creation of a precinct dedicated to the performing arts (Christchurch Central Development Unit, 2013a). The plan requires the compulsory acquisition and amalgamation of some properties. However, not all local people shared Minister Brownlee's passion for this plan. According to the Minister, "international examples show that it is important to have a broad and flexible plan to guide development, and to listen to the voices of the community. The people of greater Christchurch have said they want a distinctive, vibrant, green and accessible city" (Christchurch Central Development Unit, 2013a). In contrast, the City Owners Rebuild Entity [CORE], who represent a group of central city property owners, have been vocal in their criticism, stating that it is "disingenuous [and] is cultivating a level of distrust and suspicion. Owners feel aggrieved by the process and do not feel there is any degree of negotiation given, that there can only ever be one outcome with the threat of compulsory acquisition. This is not a willing seller willing buyer scenario" (quoted in *National Business Review*, 2013).

The scene setting is important. How do we take you on a field trip in which—in many cases—there is nothing to see? Unless you count empty and demolished space as something to gaze on, that is. In our case, we can close our eyes and imagine what was there. It has gone. What remains are the links to websites to show you what was, and a continued sense of displacement and wondering what will come next within the different contested visions of what comprises a green and sustainable city. In this way, participants on the field trip are just like the locals whose understanding of what is going on around them in the city is mediated as much by reference to information gleaned from the Web as it is from actually looking at the spaces around them—if not more. This will remain for a while as, in such a time of deconstruction and reconstruction, representation and misrepresentation, things are changing even quicker than usual from one day of wandering through the city to another until perhaps some new sense of place is established. The role of governance, and the behind-the-scenes negotiations of capital, insurance, and real estate will shape the supposedly green city of Christchurch and express themselves in the intensely visible new streetscapes of Christchurch.

Field Trip

The field trip that you are about to go on through post-earthquake Christchurch illustrates the realities that exist on the ground. This is a tale of two cities—one that is seemingly stagnating under the imposition of central government plans, and one where residents are responding to the earthquake aftermath in an organic and creative direction—often embracing the past, or what's left of it, instead of dreaming of a "distinctive" and "vibrant" future. It is a walking tour especially as, at this stage at least, we do not always know which roads are open and, in true local fashion, we will start at a pub. Plus, as two people who study tourism, we cannot help at times but be typical tour guides going from sight/site to sight/site, letting you know what was there and why. But, at this stage at least, we do not need to put our red flag into the air so that you can follow us.

THE CARLTON HOTEL

The Carlton Hotel (Figure 3.1) is situated on the high-profile corner of Bealey Avenue and Papanui Road just outside the main Christchurch central business district (CBD). There have been two previous incarnations of the hotel on the site. The first hotel was built in 1865 and demolished in 1902 (Christchurch City Libraries, 2013). The replacement for the original hotel was designed in the Italian Palazzo style, "so that the city could show a cheery face to visitors to the 1906–07 International Exhibition" (Christchurch City Libraries, 2013).

In 1981, the hotel was deemed a Category 2 building on the register of the New Zealand Historic Places Trust (New Zealand Historic Places Trust, 2013a). The September earthquake badly damaged the facade of the

Figure 3.1. Demolition of the Carlton Hotel on April 19th, 2011. Photo by Tim Baird.

building (see Figure 3.1), but the hotel remained open. It was the February earthquake that sealed the fate of the hotel, as part of the Papanui Road façade collapsed, and the building was finally demolished in front of a large crowd of onlookers on the evening of April 19, 2011.

The third incarnation of the Carlton Hotel (Figure 3.2) has since been built on the site. Local heritage supporters have been vocal in their opposition to the design of the new building, which they claimed was a "departure from its predecessor's historic look" (Wright, 2012). Echoing the sentiment of many property developers, building owner James Murdoch stated in his defense that "People keep bringing up 'it's not built the way it was,' but the one [hotel] prior to this one wasn't built 'the way it was.' The original pub was an old weatherboard place . . . [and] many earthquake rebuilds would be built in the era. The era at the moment is 2012" (Wright, 2012).

Figure 3.2. Rebuild of the Carlton Hotel as viewed on September 2nd, 2013. Photo by Tim Baird.

Christ Church Cathedral

Christ Church Cathedral is arguably the most iconic of all the buildings in the central city that have been badly damaged by the earthquake sequence. Opened in 1881, the building is situated in the focal point of the city, Cathedral Square. It had previously been damaged in earthquakes in 1881, 1888, and 1901, when the top of the spire was replaced by hardwood covered in copper as a result of damage, although this was forgotten about until September 2010.

After emerging relatively unscathed with no major structural damage from the September earthquake, the Christ Church Cathedral was severely damaged in the February earthquake. The bell tower collapsed, and there was also damage to the front entrance area of the building. The building was deconsecrated on November 9, 2011.

Since the February earthquake, the fate of the building has generated heated debate among heritage advocates and the Anglican diocese. "Christchurch has a reputation for unholy rows over heritage buildings, but the debate over Christ Church Cathedral has polarised the city like no other civic battle in recent memory" (Cropp, 2012). Church officials have expressed their desire to demolish the building and build a modern replacement; public opinion, however, has been divided between groups who would prefer it either left as a ruin, rebuilt with a mix of old and new elements, or razed to the ground and replaced by a new modern cathedral that reflects a "new" city. Given the core social function of Cathedral Square as the meeting place of the city, many people are just fed up with the endless wrangling over a space that has long been regarded more as public and secular than religious.

The Transitional ("Cardboard") Cathedral

From the loss of the Christchurch Cathedral emerges possibly one of the most unusual responses to the earthquake recovery yet. Designed by renowned Japanese architect Shigeru Ban, the Transitional Cathedral (or more commonly known among locals as the "Cardboard Cathedral") was commissioned by the Anglican Church as a temporary replacement for the Christ Church Cathedral. Built on the site of the former St. John's Church and opened in August 2013, the Transitional Cathedral has been the subject of much debate among locals who argue that it represents an inappropriate use of insurance money that should have been used to rebuild the Christ Church Cathedral (Cropp, 2012).

The Arts Centre

The Arts Centre of Christchurch (Figure 3.3) is one of the most significant clusters of heritage buildings in New Zealand. First opened in 1877, it was the original site of the University of Canterbury until the mid-1950s, when the campus began relocating to the suburb of Ilam. Damage from the earthquakes resulted in the closure of twenty-two of the twenty-three buildings in the precinct, and this has led to the creation of one of the largest heritage restoration programs currently being undertaken in the world (The Arts Centre of Christchurch, 2013a). The following statement communicates the vision that The Arts Centre of Christchurch has for their restoration program:

Figure 3.3. Damage to the historic clock tower at the Arts Centre of Christchurch as viewed on September 7th, 2010. Photo by Tim Baird.

In restoring the Arts Centre, our focus is on ensuring the longevity and survival of its unique architectural and historical importance for future generations of New Zealanders. In doing so, the restoration programme has been developed in accordance with the requirements of the Resource Management Act and the Historic Places Act, as well as many of the principles of the International Council for Monuments and Sites New Zealand Charter. (2013b)

This vision behind this restoration project stands in stark contrast to the loss of other Christchurch's heritage buildings undertaken though the special powers of the CER Act (2011). Like Cathedral Square, the Arts Centre has a major cultural and social function. These are now absent from the city's life. In the aftermath of a disaster, this poses the question of how can social sustainability be enacted when many of the spaces in which connections are made have been lost, are excluded, or soon will be used to build another office building in which real estate value can be maximized. The maintenance of exchange value in a post-disaster city does not mean the support of public social exchange, but is instead predicated on the artificial restriction of space to maintain or enhance real estate value, because that is how the sustainability of the city is defined by central government.

CHRISTCHURCH CASINO

Situated on Victoria Street, the Christchurch Casino opened in 1994. Although the building suffered some damage in the February earthquake, the building's owners deemed the structure could be quickly fixed. Such is the cultural significance of the casino that Earthquake Recovery Minister Gerry Brownlee even offered to grant the Christchurch Casino a license to operate in a temporary location under the special earthquake legislation (Gorman, 2011). The main problem for Sky City Group, owners of the Christchurch Casino, was not simply the fact that the building was initially in the inner-city Red Zone (an area from which the public was excluded as demolition and other earthquake related work occurred), but that it was deemed to be in the fall zone for a nearby badly damaged building. The post-earthquake refurbishment of the Christchurch Casino included the development of a new Russian-themed bar called Mashina, which opened in October 2013.

CHRISTCHURCH TOWN HALL

The Christchurch Town Hall (Figure 3.4) opened in 1972. Listed as a Category 1 heritage building (New Zealand Historic Places Trust, 2013b), the building is internationally recognized for its acoustic design. The status of this building within the canon of New Zealand architecture is also significant, with architects Warren and Mahoney (2013) summing up the effect of the Christchurch Town Hall on subsequent civic urban design in the following statement:

> If ever there was a landmark building in the development of New Zealand civic architecture, it is the Christchurch Town Hall. What made it particularly unique was that it was the first totally new town hall in New Zealand for nearly 50 years. To this day, it is still the benchmark by which all other civic buildings are measured.

The structure of the building emerged relatively unscathed from the September 2010 earthquake, but it was seriously damaged in the February

Figure 3.4. The Christchurch Town Hall as viewed on June 8th, 2013. Photo by Tim Baird.

earthquake, and the facility has remained closed since then. Geotechnical reports have stated that there had been a significant lateral spread of the land underneath the building, and that parts of the building have since slumped toward the Avon River. Nevertheless, the city council has agreed to fund the restoration of the building, although the national government had stated a preference for a new performing arts precinct. Many people would have also liked to have seen greater provision of funds for social housing for lower socioeconomic groups given the rapid increase in the cost of rental properties in Christchurch as a result of the loss of many houses to the earthquake and zoning as well as the influx of migrants to assist in the rebuild.

CROWNE PLAZA HOTEL

The Crowne Plaza (formerly Park Royal) Hotel opened in 1988. Situated on the edge of the historic Victoria Square, the Crowne Plaza Hotel (Figure 3.5) was one of the premier hotels in the city center, and was noted as having "the city at its doorstep" (Finest Hotels, 2010). It was also situated close to the former convention center, and linked by an air bridge to the

Figure 3.5. Demolition of the Crowne Plaza Hotel as viewed on April 13th, 2012. Photo by Tim Baird.

Christchurch Town Hall. After suffering only minor damage from the September earthquake, the Crowne Plaza Hotel was condemned after the February earthquake caused severe damage and was subsequently demolished.

The owners decided not to rebuild the hotel, which left a rather prominent gap not only in the luxury hotel market in Christchurch, but also in the architectural fabric of the city center. Since demolition work on the hotel was completed, the site has been occupied by a temporary initiative created by Gapfiller (2012) known as the Pallet Pavilion (Figure 3.6). Built from "over 3000 wooden blue CHEP pallets, [it] is a showcase for the possibilities of innovative transitional architecture in a city that is ready to embrace new ideas" (Gapfiller, 2012). The structure was designed to provide a venue for weekend markets as well as music and theater performances. A far cry from the former monolith that once occupied the same site, the Pallet Pavilion stands as a symbol of the organic community-level grassroots idealism that emerged in the city in response to the earthquakes. However, this is perhaps symbolic in more ways than one, as

Figure 3.6. The Pallet Pavillion which has been constructed as a Gapfiller initiative on the former Crowne Plaza Hotel site as viewed on August 20th, 2013. Photo by Tim Baird.

what happens to such community space as the rebuild occurs? Are such spaces maintained, are they shifted elsewhere, or are they just built over?

RE:START MALL

The retail sector of the Christchurch CBD was severely affected by its closure after the February earthquake. The loss of many businesses from this area has been noted by CCDU as having had "a substantial cost to the economy, with preliminary estimates suggesting that the lack of a central city [in Christchurch] is costing the New Zealand economy between $200 and $400 million per year" (let alone the cost to local people, of course) (2013a). In an attempt to encourage locals back to the central city, the Christchurch Property and Business Owners Group came up with an ambitious plan to develop the Re:START container mall (Figure 3.7) in Cashel Street. The design of the "mall" is made up of "60 shipping containers—stacked and placed in various configurations, pierced with windows and folding doors and painted in a bright and cheerful palette—[which] have been fitted out as high-end shops and cafes" (Strongman, 2012).

Figure 3.7. The Re:START Container Mall as viewed on August 20th, 2013. Photo by Tim Baird.

The designers of Re:START had to overcome the challenge of building a retail precinct in what was, at the time of construction, still a disaster zone that remained cordoned off to members of the public. However, a great deal of thought went into attempting to address these issues:

> I'm particularly struck by the sociability of the public spaces. The edges of the colourful container buildings are as important as what is inside them. People sit, chat, drink coffee, listen to music and the spaces are intimate, sheltered, on a human scale—they find a receptive public. People clearly feel safe there and they relax. There are many lessons to be learned from Re:START about the construction of public space in a new city. (Strongman, 2012)

There is no definite date set for the end of the Re:START Mall; it was originally thought by Christchurch Property and Business Owners Group that the development would be in place until the end of 2013 (Re:START, 2012), but as property developers contest the land rights in this area, it appears that the mall will operate longer than was originally anticipated, especially as it remains one of the few drawcards for people to come and visit the CBD.

NEW REGENT STREET

New Regent Street (Figure 3.8) is situated in the northeast quadrant of the Christchurch CBD. Built over a three-year period in the Spanish Mission architectural style, the street was officially opened on April 1, 1932 (mere months after the deadly 1931 Napier Earthquake). The timing of the opening of this development was in order to offer the people of Christchurch "a beautiful ray of colour and hope in the midst of the depression" (Gates and Lee, 2013).

Damage from the February earthquake forced the closure of all businesses in the street, and the future of the buildings remained in question until a plan was announced to restore the street. "This street was built as a brave new development with a new style of architecture right in the middle of one of the hardest times in New Zealand history, the depression, and now Christchurch is facing one of the hardest times in its history since then, and New Regent St is once again a symbol of new life coming back to the city" (Gates and Lee, 2013). The street offi-

Figure 3.8. New Regent Street as viewed on August 20th, 2013. Photo by Tim Baird.

cially reopened in April 2013, with seven shops open for business (Gates and Lee, 2013). As one of the few clusters of heritage buildings left in the central city after the earthquakes, New Regent St. is being marketed toward both tourists and locals under the tagline "Indulge Yourself," with the view toward providing a boutique shopping and heritage destination. In the new Christchurch, will it be the fate of the remaining heritage to go upmarket as landlords seek to increase rents to recover lost returns and/or the cost of post-earthquake refurbishment? Is there therefore a hidden dimension of the rebuild for the social sustainability of the city that will serve to exclude people from the city as a result of the real estate need to generate returns on investment?

High Street and the Lichfield/Poplar Lanes Development

The former boutique shopping and entertainment areas of High Street (Figure 3.9) and the surrounding Lichfield/Poplar Lanes (Figure 3.10) development were among the areas hardest hit by the February earthquake. After many of the heritage buildings in the area were significantly weakened by the September earthquake, their unreinforced masonry facades collapsed into the street in the February event. This led to most of the heritage buildings in the area being demolished under Section 38 of the

Figure 3.9. High Street as viewed on August 20th, 2013. Photo by Tim Baird.

Figure 3.10. Poplar Lane as viewed on October 7th, 2010 after being damaged in the September 4, 2010 Canterbury earthquake. Photo by Tim Baird.

CER Act (2011). The High Street and Lichfield/Poplar Lanes development had been designed to entice people back into the center of the city to live and was part of a proposed multicultural and multiple socioeconomic group new urbanism strategy that focused on the creation of a "livable city" (Hall, 2008). These plans have not been heard of since the rebuild got underway. The area is now slated to become part of the Innovation Precinct (Christchurch Central Development Unit, 2013a).

PROPOSED STADIUM SITE

Due to earthquake damage to the existing AMI Stadium, part of the Central City Recovery Plan has involved the development of a proposed new stadium within the Eastern Frame of the CCDU Blueprint (Figure 3.11) as a joint venture between the Christchurch City Council, CERA, the Ministry of Business Innovation and Employment, the private sector, NGOs, and the philanthropic sector (Christchurch Central Development Unit, 2013b). This has proven to be arguably the most controversial of the five anchor projects proposed by the CCDU (McCrone, 2013). Opponents to the development have cited the NZ$506 million price tag for the covered 35,000 capacity stadium as unrealistic (Greenhill, 2013), while the failure of the recently completed Forsyth Barr Stadium in Dunedin to

Figure 3.11. The proposed site for the controversial stadium development as viewed on September 11th, 2013. Photo by Tim Baird.

generate a return for the city has also raised questions regarding financial viability (Hall and Wilson, 2016). This is especially the case because the temporary 17,000 seat stadium, built in one hundred days following the February earthquake, is not at capacity for most of the sporting events it hosts. The positioning of the proposed stadium development has also caused debate among heritage advocates, with the historic Ng Gallery Building under threat of demolition, as it borders the Madras Street side of the site (Berry, 2012).

TE PAPA ŌTĀKARO /AVON RIVER PRECINCT

Designed in part as an attempt to recapture the meaning behind Christchurch's "Garden City" brand, the Central City Recovery Plan also includes the concept of the Te Papa Ōtākaro/Avon River Precinct, which is based on the "winding path of the Ōtākaro/Avon River [and] will define Christchurch's new river precinct" (Christchurch Central Development Unit, 2013c). The first part of the development, known as "Watermark" (Figure 3.12), opened in August 2013. The concept has been marketed to the people of Christchurch as being based on the "over 100,000 community suggestions via the 'Share an Idea' campaign; [the park] aims to deliver on aspirations for a 'Green City' and align with the design principles of

Figure 3.12. The initial stage of the Te Papa Ōtākaro/Avon River Precinct as viewed on September 11th, 2013. Photo by Tim Baird.

Te Papa Ōtākaro" (Christchurch Central Development Unit, 2013d). In terms of urban planning, it is hoped that "the visual contrast between the curving river and the linear grid of the streets is a key element of the city's distinctive urban form" (Christchurch Central Development Unit, 2013d). Unfortunately, other ideas shared by the people of Christchurch with respect to being a green and sustainable city, such as a light rail system, greater use of renewable energy and environmentally friendly construction methods in building design, and increased focus on public transport and cycleways, have not been incorporated in the new city plan, which appears green on the basis of the grassed areas in which the CBD will sit. In a city where the idea of public consultation has been proven to be somewhat of a misnomer after campaigns such as "Share an Idea," and in which normal democratic rights remain suspended, the notion of sustainable urban development is grounded in maintaining real estate values.

As someone who walked along the river every day until his house was lost to earthquakes and government zoning (Michael), I can report that the Watermark is little more than an upgrade on the existing path that was already there and the replacement of the grassed verge with bark and natives (although the introduced deciduous trees remain). What then has really changed except the facade?

References

Berry, M. (2012). Owners unhappy with plans to take building. *The Press*. Available at: www.stuff.co.nz/the-press/news/christchurch-earthquake-2011/city-blue-print/7396130/Owners-unhappy-with-plans-to-take-building [Accessed 3 Sept. 2016]

Christchurch Central Development Unit. (2013a). *Christchurch central recovery plan*. 1st ed. [pdf] Christchurch: Canterbury Earthquake Recovery Authority. Available at: ccdu.govt.nz/sites/ccdu.govt.nz/files/documents/christ-church-central-recovery-plan-single-page-version.pdf [Accessed 3 Sept. 2016]

Christchurch Central Development Unit. (2013b). *The stadium*. Available at: ccdu.govt.nz/projects-and-precincts/stadium [Accessed 3 Sept. 2016]

Christchurch Central Development Unit. (2013c). *Te Papa Ōtākaro/Avon River precinct*. Available at: ccdu.govt.nz/projects-and-precincts/te-papa-otaka-ro-avon-river-precinct [Accessed 3 Sept. 2016]

Christchurch Central Development Unit. (2013d). *Watermark*. Available at: ccdu.govt.nz/projects-and-precincts/te-papa-otakaro-avon-river-precinct/watermark [Accessed 3 Sept. 2016]

Christchurch City Libraries. (2013). *The Carlton Hotel*. Available at: my.christ-churchcitylibraries.com/the-carlton-hotel/ [Accessed 3 Sept. 2016]

Cropp, A. (2012). *The unholy row over Christ Church Cathedral*. Available at: amanda cropp.co.nz/wp-content/uploads/2012/05/chch-cathedral.pdf [Accessed 3 Sept. 2016]

Gapfiller. (2012). *The Pallet pavilion*. Available at: www.gapfiller.org.nz/summer-pallet-pavilion/ [Accessed 3 Sept. 2016]

Gates, C., and Lee, F. (2013). Rain dampens new Regent St. reopening. *The Press*. Available at: www.stuff.co.nz/the-press/news/city-centre/8574400/Rain-dampens-New-Regent-St-reopening [Accessed 3 Sept. 2016]

Gorman, P. (2011). Temporary Christchurch casino site not an option. *The Press*. Available at: www.stuff.co.nz/the-press/news/christchurch-earth quake-2011/4847215/Temporary-ChCh-Casino-site-not-an-option [Accessed 3 Sept. 2016]

Greenhill, M. (2013). Roofed stadium to cost $506 million. *The Press*. Available at: www.stuff.co.nz/the-press/business/the-rebuild/8856802/Roofed-stadium-to-cost-506m [Accessed 3 Sept. 2016]

Hall, C. M. (2008). Servicescapes, designscapes, branding and the creation of place-identity: South of Litchfield, Christchurch. *Journal of Travel and Tourism Marketing*, 25(3–4), pp. 233–250.

Hall, C. M., and Wilson, S. (2016). Mega-events as neoliberal projects: "Realistic if we want Dunedin to prosper," or "the biggest civic disgrace . . . in living memory"? In: J. Mosedale, ed., *Neoliberalism and the Political Economy of Tourism*, 1st ed. Farnham, UK: Ashgate, pp. 37–54.

McCrone, J. (2013). The $100 million dollar question. The debate is heating up: Do we need this? *The Press*. Available at: www.stuff.co.nz/the-press/business/the-rebuild/8689845/The-100-million-question [Accessed 3 Sept. 2016]

National Business Review (2013). Property owners launch stinging attack on CERA. Available at www.nbr.co.nz/article/property-owners-launch-stinging-attack-cera-ch-138530 [Accessed 3 Sept. 2016]

New Zealand Historic Places Trust. (2013a). *Lost heritage Christchurch City I-P*. Available at: www.historic.org.nz/theregister/heritagelost/lostheritage-cantyearthquakes/lostheritagecanterburyearthquakeschristchurchi-p.aspx [Accessed 3 Sept. 2016]

New Zealand Historic Places Trust. (2013b). *Welcome to High Street stories: The life and times of Christchurch's High Street precinct*. Available at: www.high-streetstories.co.nz/ [Accessed 3 Sept. 2016]

New Zealand Parliamentary Counsel Office. (2011). *Canterbury Earthquake Recovery Act 2011*. Available at: www.legislation.govt.nz/act/public/2011/0012/latest/DLM3653522.html [Accessed 3 Sept. 2016]

Re:START. (2012). *About Christchurch city: Re:START*. Available at: www.restart.org.nz/about-christchurch-central-restart.php [Accessed 3 Sept. 2016]

Strongman, L. (2012). *Re:START Mall, Christchurch*. Available at: www.australian-designreview.com/architecture/23596-restart-mall-christchurch [Accessed 3 Sept. 2016]

The Arts Centre of Christchurch. (2013a). *About us*. Available at: www.artscentre.org.nz/about-us.html [Accessed 3 Sept. 2016]

The Arts Centre of Christchurch. (2013b). *Rebuild and restore*. Available at: www.artscentre.org.nz/rebuild---restore.html [Accessed 3 Sept. 2016]

The Arts Centre of Christchurch. (2013c). *Annual report 2012*. Available at: www.artscentre.org.nz/assets/ac-annual-report-1213.pdf [Accessed 3 Sept. 2016]

Warren and Mahoney [architects] (2013). *Christchurch Town Hall*. Available at: www.warrenandmahoney.com/en/portfolio/christchurch-town-hall/ [Accessed 3 Sept. 2016]

Wood, A. (2013). Development plans for Christchurch casino. *The Press*. Available at: www.stuff.co.nz/the-press/business/8910711/Development-plans-for-Chch-Casino [Accessed 3 Sept. 2016]

Wright, M. (2012). Carlton Hotel rebuild begins. *The Press*. Available at: www.stuff.co.nz/the-press/business/7998794/Carlton-Hotel-rebuild-begins [Accessed 3 Sept. 2016]

Chapter 4

Reworking Newtown Creek

WINIFRED CURRAN AND TRINA HAMILTON

It's an incredible story. Between seventeen and thirty million gallons of oil seep into Newtown Creek, the body of water that separates Brooklyn from Queens, and under the surrounding neighborhood of Greenpoint. Revealed briefly by an underground explosion in 1950, the oil plume goes largely unnoticed because of the volume of other pollutants in the water until 1978, when the Coast Guard, on routine helicopter patrol, reports a massive oil sheen on Newtown Creek. Even after this discovery, nothing happens. In 1990, an agreement is signed between the State of New York and Mobil to begin clean-up. Nothing happens. In 2002, the environmental organization Riverkeeper, charged with protection of the Hudson River, takes a detour on their boat patrol into Newtown Creek and rediscovers this massive oil spill. They begin negotiations with what is now ExxonMobil. Nothing happens . . . until 2004, when Riverkeeper, frustrated by ExxonMobil's intransigence, files suit. In 2007, New York State Attorney General Andrew Cuomo (now governor) joins the River-keeper suit. Things start to happen. In 2010, the State and ExxonMobil settle the lawsuit, with ExxonMobil promising a more vigorous clean-up as well as settlement funds for the state and community, and the US Environmental Protection Agency (EPA) declared Newtown Creek an official Superfund site.

How does a massive oil spill in New York City, nearly twice the size of the Exxon Valdez spill, go largely unnoticed and unremediated for over sixty years? And, more important, what do you do with the polluted water and land that resulted from the spill when you do start to address the massive environmental injustice? And how does the Newtown Creek spill coexist with the rampant gentrification happening in the surroundings neighborhoods of Greenpoint and Williamsburg? These are the questions that motivated our interest in Newtown Creek.

The invisibility of the environmental contamination in Greenpoint mirrors the invisibility of the area's industrial sector within New York as global city. While Greenpoint and neighboring Williamsburg have gentrified, there is still a vibrant industrial sector that is a legacy of the area's industrial history that gets too little attention. Indeed, it is ignorance of the industrial activity in the area that sparked interest in the area for one of us (Winifred). In 2001, I was researching a strike by the International Longshoremen at what was then the Domino Sugar plant (now rezoned and slated for luxury residential development), and as I conducted interviews, what amazed me was that people in the immediate vicinity (many living in industrial buildings converted to residential use, both legally and illegally) not only weren't aware of the strike, but didn't even realize that it was still a working plant. As a Brooklyn native, I was fascinated by the coexistence of this major manufacturing facility with the hipsters that have come to define this section of Brooklyn. How can these things coexist? Well over a decade later, this question still defines my research.

It's very difficult to know that a major oil spill occurred in Greenpoint even when one is in Greenpoint. For us as researchers, the oil spill was knowable only through the maps we had consulted, and even these have been contested, with different entities using different maps with different estimations as to the extent of the spill (see Figure 4.1 for a few examples). Long-term residents had a clue; there was the "black mayonnaise" (Prudhomme, 2011) that stained laundry drying on the line, the oil seeping up through vegetable gardens after a good rain (personal interview with long-term resident, June 2009), the toxic fumes that gave people headaches, but no one really knew exactly what it was or where it had come from. Even after the discovery of the spill in 1978, Newtown Creek got very little attention from the City or anyone else. More recent in-movers, attracted by Greenpoint's proximity to Manhattan, had no idea of the neighborhood's toxic legacy. As one of our informants told us, "I had no idea about the Newtown Creek and what had gone on with this oil spill. I mean, it's just incredible that I had no idea about it, being in the field [of public health], prior to living here, but even living here, I mean it took me a good couple of months to even learn about this" (personal interview, June 2009). It was this lack of public attention that intrigued Trina about the case. After spending several years researching media-savvy public campaigns against large American corporations, including several against ExxonMobil over issues from climate change to oil spills and community compensation around the globe, Trina began to ask how such a massive spill had gone so long without being subject to the spotlight of a national or international campaign.

The pervasiveness of the pollution in Greenpoint and Newtown Creek makes it surprising that few knew of it. As one legislative aid explained to us, "You can't dig a hole in the ground up there and not find something. It was a manufacturing district for over 150 years; there's something everywhere" (personal interview, June 2009). A lawyer involved

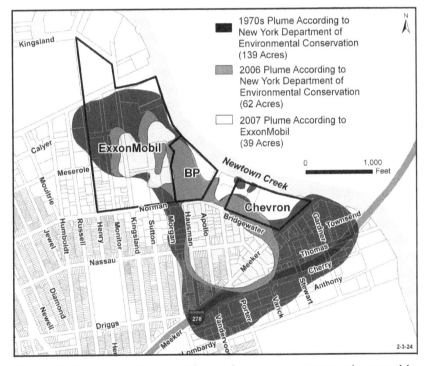

Figure 4.1. Greenpoint oil plume. This rendering is an estimate only, created by Eric Montz for the research project based on publicly available maps; acreage refers to estimated area as shown on the map, not official estimates.

in one of the suits related to the spill commented, "we don't really know the extent of the contamination, we don't know all the possible effects of the contamination, and there may be other unrelated contaminants," such as a recently discovered vapor plume related to dry-cleaning chemicals (phone interview, December 2008).

The mystery surrounding the existence and extent of oil and other pollutants in Newtown Creek and under the ground in Greenpoint is at least in part because of the historic difficulty of getting down to the water and seeing what was going on there. For decades, the best, and really only, way to see Newtown Creek was in a boat. Industry lined the Creek and much of the rest of the Brooklyn and Queens waterfront, denying waterfront access. There was no green space along the Creek allowing residents access to the water. In this way, the invisibility of the Creek, and indeed the invisibility of Greenpoint as a working-class immigrant enclave in term of public policy attention, allowed for the development of the "constellation of toxicity" (personal interview, June 2009) that exists in Greenpoint today. As one activist involved in the fight for clean-up explained:

> If this had happened anywhere else . . . I think you would have had a different response from the polluter and from the State. The fact that it happened in an urban area, industrialized area, working class, dirty, "dirty river" already anyway, the fact that the river was kind of walled off from the community so that even now with all the interest in it, it's hard to get down to it, you know, all these things contributed to this sort of apathy, I think, at the State level and the Feds for that matter, too. Local agencies and people just saw a hundred years of industrialization on the Creek and figured that was the status quo. (personal interview, June 2009)

Field Trip

The Newtown Creek Nature Walk aims to rectify this, exposing the industrial past and present of the Creek and the intimate connection between the water and New York's emergence as a global metropolis. In the way it brings together nature, industry, and culture, the Newtown Creek Nature Walk is part of the process of creating what Matthew Gandy (2006) calls new urban ecological imaginaries, which of course, have very real policy implications (Millington, 2013). We invite you to explore the nature walk and to consider how it changes your perception of nature and the city.

Even for those of us who know the neighborhood well, this does seem the most unlikely place for a nature walk. To get to the nature walk from the rest of the neighborhood, you must cross under the overpass of the Pulaski Bridge (a favorite hangout for pigeons), which connects to Queens, walk past an oil storage facility, and pass a major Time Warner Cable outpost before you see the stainless-steel pipe fence that marks the entrance to the nature walk. You then walk up the forty-foot ramp to the first major feature of the nature walk, a concrete walkway with curved walls called the vessel. This is meant to mimic the great ships like the USS *Monitor* that were once built along this waterfront. Like a ship, the walls of the walkway have portholes. Peek through the portholes (Figure 4.2), and you can see the workings of the feature that defines this nature walk as much as, if not more than, the Creek itself: the Newtown Creek Wastewater Treatment Plant, the largest of the city's fourteen treatment plants (New York City Department of Environmental Protection, 2012).

Figure 4.2. View of Newtown Creek Wastewater Treatment Plant from the Nature Walk. Photo by Winifred Curran (2012).

THE WASTEWATER TREATMENT PLANT: WHERE THE NATURE WALK BEGINS

While it may seem ironic that this long-awaited nature walk borders a wastewater treatment plant, without the plant there would be no nature walk. The nature walk is a concession to the community, which had long been demanding more green space in this open space–starved neighborhood, as part of the update and expansion of the treatment plant. But wait. Better views are yet to come.

At the end of the vessel, you can catch your first peek of the Creek. But turn around, and an even better view surprises you, that of the Empire State Building (Figure 4.3). There's no better place to get a view of the Manhattan skyline than from the Brooklyn waterfront. This is one of the factors fueling the real estate boom and gentrification of the area.

Figure 4.3. View of Empire State Building from Nature Walk. Photo by Winifred Curran (2012).

From here, the path opens up and you get to what starts to actually look like a nature walk. There are a series of seven stone circles, each etched with native place names used by the Lenape people who originally inhabited the area. This reference to the Native American residents of the area reminds us that the Creek has virtually always been defined by human activity.

NEWTOWN CREEK

And there it is, Newtown Creek, one of the most polluted bodies of water in the country (Figure 4.4, pg. 78). On a sunny day, it can be a sparkling blue. On cloudy days, it can be as gray as the asphalt produced along its shores. But always, you will see an oily sheen that has come to define the Creek (Figure 4.5, pg. 78). For decades before the nature walk, few could get this close to the water. You might think that, given the pollution, no one would want to. But Joe Lentol, the long-time state assemblyman for this area, told us, "If you know this neighborhood, there's a great desire to be close to the water . . . I'd like to swim in the Creek. I used to swim in it as a kid. Probably got a mouth full of oil" (personal interview, July 2009).

Get close to the water here. There is a series of wide granite steps, etched with geologic eras and life forms, leading down to the water and no guardrail. This feels very inviting, but all around you signs warn of the dangers lurking in this water. "CAUTION: Wet Weather Discharge Point. This outfall may discharge rainwater mixed with untreated sewage during or following rainfall and can contain bacteria that can cause illness"; "This waterway is heavily used by ships and it's [sic] sediment may be contaminated with chemicals"; "Wash hands & clothing if contact with water or sediment occurs"; "Do not swim in these waters. Do not eat fish caught in these waters" (emphasis in original).

From this vantage point, you can really see Newtown Creek as a working waterway. On any given day, you will see barges sailing up the Creek to the East River. Docked on the banks of the Creek are barges loaded with the city's detritus: crushed cars, old tires, mounds of waste (Figure 4.6, pg. 79). It's not especially scenic, except in a ruin porn kind of way. It may not be pretty, but it is important. There are still 119 businesses along the Creek, employing 4,822 people (estimate including Queens and Brooklyn side, Brownfield Opportunity Area, 2012).

Turn from the view of the Creek as it is, to one of the Creek as it was. There is a large granite table (1,400 pounds, to be precise) upon which is etched a map that at first appears unrecognizable (Figure 4.7, pg. 79).

Figure 4.4. Newtown Creek Nature Walk. Photo by Winifred Curran (2012).

Figure 4.5. Oil sheen on Newtown Creek. Photo by Winifred Curran (2012).

Figure 4.6. Barges on Newtown Creek. Photo by Winifred Curran (2012).

Figure 4.7. Historic map of Newtown Creek watershed. Photo by Winifred Curran (2012).

Then you recognize the basic outline of Brooklyn and realize that this is a map of the original watershed of the Newtown Creek, before European inhabitants arrived. The map is on a slight gradient, "so falling raindrops can replicate the journey of the Creek's own, original waters" (New York City Department of Environmental Protection, 2012).

Whale Creek and the Culmination of the Walk

Follow the path around the curve to Whale Creek. From this angle, we have a great view of the wastewater treatment plant digester eggs, just on the other side of Whale Creek. These egg-shaped Gehry-esque behemoths (Figure 4.8) are such an architectural and engineering marvel that the Department of Environmental Protection runs monthly tours of them for the public. Each of the eight digester eggs holds three million gallons of sludge.

The remainder of the path is where you'll find the most nature on this nature walk. Native plants line the path, but even here the design of the path makes the human impact visible (Figures 4.9 and 4.10). The plaque describing each tree or shrub lists not only the species name, but

Figure 4.8. Newtown Creek Wastewater Treatment Plant digester eggs. Photo by Winifred Curran (2012).

Figure 4.9. Newtown Creek Nature Walk at Whale Creek. Photo by Winifred Curran (2012).

SEASIDE GOLDENROD
(Solidago sempervirens)
Autumn blooming tall clusters of aromatic flowers attract bees and butterflies. Powdered leaves were applied to wounds and saddle sores on horses. Thomas Edison experimented with its stem milk to produce latex. Plant milk produces an instant sealant for wounds.

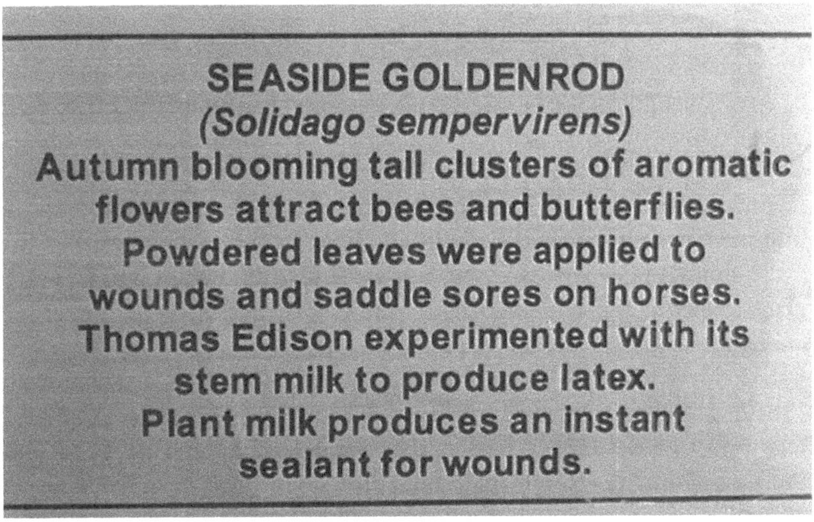

Figure 4.10. Example of sign explaining uses for native plants. Photo by Winifred Curran (2012).

also what medicinal or economic value it had historically. Weeping willow, for example, was spun to make rope. It could also be made into a tea to reduce fever and is a source of salicylic acid, which was developed into aspirin. Thomas Edison experimented with the stem milk of seaside goldenrod to produce latex. Early spring sprouts of horsetail were eaten raw or cooked as greens. It's a locavore paradise.

Picnic tables located on this stretch of the path remind us of what happened to the native species planted here; they were displaced to make way for the industrial development that is commemorated on the maps, etched into metal plates attached to the tops of the stone tables. These maps depict the businesses that used to line this section of the Creek, compiled from Sanborn maps 1887–1951. The maps give a glue as to the diversity and centrality of the industrial economy to this area: cooperage (barrel manufacture), chemical manufacturing, oil works and refining, ironworks, ship welder, wooden box company, plaster board manufacturer, lumber companies, asphalt production, granite works, coal and brick yard, bronze foundry, and steam laundry.

Next to the historical business map is a current map—that of the wastewater treatment plant. Herein lies the challenge for many industrial neighborhoods like Greenpoint. In many cases, when industry left, noxious uses followed. The same zoning designation that allowed for the heavy industry that built New York City also allows for things like waste transfer stations, incinerators, power plants, and wastewater treatment plants. This stigmatizes neighborhoods and unfairly burdens specific populations, in the case of Greenpoint, the largely Polish immigrant working class. There are nineteen waste-transfer stations lining the Creek and twenty-three combined sewer outflows that disgorge into the water (Stern, 2012). The environmental justice issues in Greenpoint are not simply historic, a legacy of the industrial past, but rather a continuing issue in this ever-expanding city.

Though often mocked (one Yelp reviewer commented, "Great secret place to swim! . . . The water itself is mildly refreshing and interestingly enough has a molasses like viscosity & taste. Wow 2 for 1!"[1]), the nature walk is loved. As one informant told us of people in the neighborhood, "They want to be connected to nature, even if it is a little dirty . . . people just want to have the walls knocked down a little bit and have access to the waterfront" (personal interview, June 2009; Curran and Hamilton, 2012). Of course, this is not an ideal nature walk. One of the triumphs of the nature walk is that it doesn't idealize nature, but rather shows it to us as a social construction. This is not the green space that residents of Greenpoint have long been demanding. No one wants to live in a polluted wasteland. And yet, these people have done so, and for generations. So what are we going to do about it?

PULASKI BRIDGE AND BOX STREET

Evidence of the changes and contradictions of modern-day Greenpoint abound as we trace our way from the nature walk back to the main thoroughfare of the neighborhood. Crossing back under the Pulaski Bridge, on Box Street, we come upon an anomaly—an old-fashioned checkered cab, parked outside what at first glance looks like any other industrial warehouse in the area (Figure 4.11, pg. 84). But on closer inspection, we see that this is not a warehouse, but a four-star hotel, the Box House, with its own fleet of checkered cabs to ferry visitors wary of the mean streets of Greenpoint. As of this writing, rooms start at $289 a night. As with much of the development in Greenpoint and Williamsburg, the hotel is in a converted factory, in this case a door factory. Industrial chic is essential to the way the Box House sells itself. This kind of architecture and space has been one of the driving forces for the gentrification of the area. This gentrification can lead to the displacement of other industrial businesses (Curran, 2004). It's much more profitable to rent out rooms for $300 a night than to actually make things.

Just down the block, at 48 Box Street, we find a "boutique neo townhouse style condominium"[2] with prices ranging from $669,000 for a one-bedroom to $995,000 for a three-bedroom (Figure 4.12, pg. 84).

And this is the conundrum of cleaning up Newtown Creek. Will clean-up simply attract more uses like the Box House hotel and 48 Box Street? Does clean-up necessarily mean the displacement of long-term residents who can't afford the increases in rent that come with these luxury uses?

A different perspective emerges as we turn the corner of Box Street onto Manhattan Avenue, the main thoroughfare in Greenpoint. Here, we can stop for a coffee at the Ashbox, a cute café that might seem the very embodiment of the hipster takeover of Greenpoint. And yet, as we sit for a break during this particular field trip, we hear the young, seemingly hipsterish group next to us speaking not of bars or shows or condos, but of various remediation plans for the Creek, including micro-remediation

Figure 4.11. Box House hotel. Photo by Winifred Curran (2012).

Figure 4.12. 48 Box St condominiums. Photo by Winifred Curran (2012).

in the form of mushroom cultivation and alliances with industries along the Creek. Indeed, this particular project, an attempt to clean the water by seeding hay with oyster mushroom spawn to create mycobooms, was funded by Metro Fuel Oil (Newtown Creek Alliance, 2012).

THE GREENPOINT MANUFACTURING DESIGN CENTER

We like to meet at the Ashbox because it is right across the street from one of the major environmental and industrial institutions in Greenpoint, the Greenpoint Manufacturing and Design Center (GMDC). Situated in a classic loft building right at the mouth of the Newtown Creek (Figure 4.13), GMDC is an icon of the industrial retention movement in New York. GMDC is a nonprofit industrial developer that provides affordable space for small-scale manufacturers and is so successful that there tends to be a waiting list for space in any of the four buildings they manage. The institution has been a forceful advocate for the viability of manufacturing in New York City, and has also been an important player in the clean-up efforts for Newtown Creek.

Figure 4.13. Greenpoint Manufacturing and Design Center. Photo by Winifred Curran (2012).

Just outside GMDC on the waterfront is the first official kayak launch on Newtown Creek. As with some of the other improvements along the Creek, there has been some controversy about the launch. How to balance the needs of recreational boaters and sustained barge traffic? Will the kayaks end up displacing the industrial traffic on the Creek?

There is a pocket park at the kayak launch from which to ponder these questions. As with the nature walk, there is the balancing of the scenic with the industrial. Signs at the park celebrate the industrial history of Newtown Creek. A map points out historically and architecturally significant sites in the neighborhood. There are many "former" industrial sites on the list: the former Union Porcelain Works, the former Greenpoint Flint Glassworks, the former Havemeyer Sugar Refining Company. And is that what is to become of industrial use in Greenpoint? Is the decline of industry in a global city like New York, where real estate is so valuable, inevitable? The fairly steady stream of barge traffic that will pass as you sit asking yourself these questions provides a valuable counterpoint to that sense of inevitability. The GMDC and adjacent pocket park mark the physical confluence of competing visions and disparate regulatory trajectories for Greenpoint's waterfront. And so we end our tour with two future renderings of the Greenpoint waterfront, one a community plan for ecological and industrial regeneration along Newtown Creek itself, and the other a developer's vision for a high-rise community along the East River waterfront at the mouth of Newtown Creek (Figures 4.14 and 4.15).

GMDC partnered with the Newtown Creek Alliance and Riverkeeper to form a Brownfield Opportunity Area (BOA) funded by a grant from New York State in 2008. The goal of the BOA plan (and subsequent, ongoing community planning processes), as described to us by various partners in the project, is to develop the Creek into "a functioning waterway, which means ecologically functioning" (phone interview, June 2009), as well as economically viable, as part of "a twenty-first-century industrial corridor" (personal interview, February 2012).

Indeed, the final BOA report released in 2012 represents Newtown Creek as "a valuable urban asset: an area of working industry at the center of a thriving urban mega-region" (Brownfield Opportunity Area, 2012: i). It notes that "[j]obs in urban manufacturing have traditionally provided higher wages and better benefits than the lower-paying retail and service sectors, and have helped to build stable and equitable communities." Moreover, "Newtown Creek is New York City's largest Significant Maritime and Industrial Area (SMIA)," as defined by Vision 2020, New York

City's Comprehensive Waterfront Plan. "Despite declines in the industrial and manufacturing sectors due to regional shifts related to containerized shipping and globalization, the Newtown Creek shoreline remains characterized by heavy industry, several still water-dependent. Its employment is the highest among the six New York City SMIAs" (Brownfield Opportunity Area, 2012: i). In other words, the shores of Newtown Creek are not sitting toxic and idle, awaiting high-rise developer saviors. As the BOA describes it, "very little land within the BOA lies fallow" (Brownfield Opportunity Area, 2012: i).

It's no wonder, then, that the BOA's future renderings for Newtown Creek include hard hats, barges, and factories—active industry!—alongside restored wetlands and wildlife. The report describes a future *"industrial ecosystem where waste and production are connected"* (emphasis in original), joining "industrial users and processes in an Industrial Symbiosis, or 'Cradle-to-Cradle' cycle, where the waste or by-product of one process becomes an input for another. Products created in Newtown Creek can supply consumption streams in the rest of the City with new consumer and industrial products. Natural and industrial waste treatments can process the unclaimed by-products to spur the production processes of other symbiotic enterprises within the area and the City at large" (Brownfield Opportunity Area, 2012: viii).

The BOA's industrial outlook is in stark contrast to many portrayals of industrial decline in New York City and other metropolises. The BOA report explains: "The outlook for the next decade may be more positive than overall sector-level data suggest. Rather than the manufacturing sector being comprised of larger manufacturers, such as the apparel industry, there appears to be a trend, evident in the BOA, for smaller firms with long term growth potential, assuming available space at an acceptable cost" (Brownfield Opportunity Area, 2012: 90).

GREENPOINT LANDING

Just on the other side of GMDC, however, where an 800,000-gallon wastewater sludge tank used to sit, is the site of a new development called Greenpoint Landing. The plan calls for ten towers, thirty to forty stories each, and 5,500 apartments (Curbed, 2013), of which 1,400 will be affordable (Warerkar, 2018). Residential use is allowed on this site as a result of the 2005 rezoning. At a May 2013 community meeting, "Melanie Meyers, a representative for the Greenpoint Landing development, caused an uproar when she explained, 'We're creating a neighborhood on the waterfront.' [T]he response from the audience was clear: Greenpoint already has a neighborhood, thank you very much" (Greenpointers, 2013).

The neighborhood envisioned by the Greenpoint Landing developers along the East River is far different from the one proposed by the BOA along Newtown Creek. The focus of the development is on the waterfront as high-end residential with Manhattan views (Figures 4.14 and 4.15), with no reference or orientation toward the remaining industry to the East. The images shown here do not do justice to the massive scale of the development and the profound break this project represents from the area's history.

At the May 2012 Greenpoint Landing meeting:

> Rami Metal, representing Council Member Stephen Levin, reminded the community that when the original rezoning in 2005 happened, the community negotiated that the waterfront would not have power plants and that the compromise is these 30–40 story towers. . . .
>
> The question is—what can the community get . . . with respect to infrastructure, transportation, affordable housing and open space? . . .
>
> While it was stated very clearly that the purpose of the meeting was NOT to discuss rewriting the zoning, it kept coming up. One community member compared the new developments to "imitation Dubai," "Miami Beach" then even worse—"Williamsburg" and "LIC." [Long Island City] . . .
>
> [M]any attendees were looking for hope to downzone the area from the 2005 rezoning, especially in terms of the height of the buildings. They want to FIGHT THE TOWER! (Greenpointers, 2013)

This desire to "fight the tower" is in part the result of unmet promises from past developments. Part of the concession to the community for allowing such high towers was supposed to be access to the water, with a series of waterfront parks to be managed by the city. To date, however, almost none of this has come to pass, and many Greenpointers instead have to access the water (the East River) only through a hole in the

Figure 4.14. Greenpoint Landing. Photo by Winifred Curran (2018).

Figure 4.15. Greenpoint Landing under construction, with view of the Chrysler Building in the background. Photo by Winifred Curran (2018).

fence at the end of Huron Street (Curbed, 2013). Despite the successes of environmental activists in Greenpoint in achieving clean-up of the Creek and greater awareness in the community at large, it's possible that with rezoning of industrial land, the new barrier to the water will be a wall of luxury towers, blocking access to the water for all those who cannot afford to pay for this view.

Afterword

Ten years after our initial field trip to Greenpoint, we're still unwilling to predict the future.[3] We do, however, see more than residential towers and scrap metal barges when we tour the neighborhood. We now "see" the oil and toxic brew that lies beneath, but we also see the history of contestation and activism, of other battles fought by a dedicated group of residents. These residents battle on, sometimes for concessions, and sometimes for something bigger.

Notes

1. www.yelp.com/biz/newtown-Creek-nature-walk-brooklyn#hrid:pjJxw7w-fIJeitbT59EXBHg
2. www.aptsandlofts.com/featured-developments/48-box-condominiums
3. For a detailed update on the cleanup and neighborhood change, see Curran and Hamilton, 2018.

References

Brownfield Opportunity Area. (2012). *Newtown Creek final report*. Available at: www.gmdconline.org/images/Newtown-Creek-Final-Report-and-Appendix-2012.pdf [Accessed 3 Sept. 2016]

Curbed. (2013). *Northwest Greenpoint's quiet waterfront awaits new towers*. Available at: ny.curbed.com/archives/2013/07/03/northwest_greenpoints_quiet_waterfront_awaits_new_towers.php [Accessed 3 Sept. 2016]

Curran, W. (2004). Gentrification and the changing nature of work: Exploring the links in Williamsburg, Brooklyn. *Environment and Planning A*, 36(7), pp. 1243–1260.

Curran, W., and Hamilton, T., eds. (2018). *Just green enough: Urban development and environmental gentrification*. London, New York: Routledge.

Curran, W., and Hamilton, T. (2012). Just green enough: Contesting environmental gentrification in Greenpoint, Brooklyn. *Local Environment: The International Journal of Justice and Sustainability*, 17(9), pp. 1027–1042.

Gandy, M. (2006). Urban nature and the ecological imaginary. In: N. Heynen, M. Kaika, and E. Swyngedouw, eds., *In the Nature of Cities: Urban Political Ecology and the Politics of Urban Metabolism*, 1st ed. London: Routledge, pp. 62–72.

Greenpointers. (2013). *"A giant sandwich is landing on Greenpoint"—Notes on Greenpoint landing & 77 Commercial St ULURP meeting*. Available at: greenpointers.com/2013/07/02/fight-the-tower-a-giant-sandwich-is-landing-on-greenpoint-notes-on-greenpoint-landing-77-commercial-st-ulurp-meeting/ [Accessed 3 Sept. 2016]

Millington, N. (2013). Post-industrial imaginaries: Nature, representation and ruin in Detroit, Michigan. *International Journal of Urban and Regional Research*, 37(1), pp. 279–296.

New York City Department of Environmental Protection. (2012). *The Newtown Creek nature walk scavenger hunt*. Available at: www.nyc.gov/html/dep/pdf/newtown-sh-view.pdf [Accessed 3 Sept. 2016]

Newtown Creek Alliance. (2012). *Bioremediation workgroup inoculation bonanza*. Available at: www.newtownCreekalliance.org/2012/04/02/bioremediation-workgroup-inoculation-bonanza/ [Accessed 3 Sept. 2016]

Prudhomme, A. (2011). "The ripple effect": New book examines lasting impact of industrial pollution. *Huffington Post*. Available at: www.huffingtonpost.com/2011/06/07/rippleeffect-alex-prudhomme-freshwater_n_872039.html [Accessed 3 Sept. 2016]

Stern, S. (2012). Your guide to a tour of decay. *New York Times*. Available at: www.nytimes.com/2012/06/17/nyregion/mitch-waxman-tour-guide-to-decay.html?_r=0 [Accessed 3 Sept. 2016]

Warerkar, T. (2018). *New looks at Greenpoint Landing's 30-story rental*. Available at: ny.curbed.com/2018/6/27/17509718/greenpoint-landing-one-blue-slip-renderings-leasing [Accessed 13 Jul. 2018]

Chapter 5

From Sprawling Cowtown
to Social Sustainability Pioneer

The Sustainability Journey of Calgary, Alberta

Freya Kristensen

Introduction

The most remarkable feature of flying into the city of Calgary, Alberta, particularly if arriving from the west, is the rollercoaster ride of turbulence that you will probably experience as the plane descends over the Rocky Mountains and battles with the air currents. If you are lucky and have a smooth descent, you might be calm enough to observe the layout of the city and the unmistakable markers of sprawl—the looping, nonsensical maze of streets that culminate in lollipop-shaped cul-de-sacs—that have come to represent the City of Calgary. If you know Calgary, it might seem strange to have a case of urban sustainability from a city nicknamed "Cowtown." Calgary is perhaps best known for being the unofficial capital of the Wild West and for hosting an annual rowdy party known as The Stampede. It is precisely this surprise that makes Calgary so interesting. How is such a city tackling the complex issue of urban sustainability? On this field trip we will meet and interview several City of Calgary staff members to find out what kinds of policy related to social sustainability are being tested out here.

CALGARY'S ANOMALIES

In order to set the stage for our visits, I will describe briefly what makes Calgary such an interesting place in which to investigate social sustainability policy.

Calgary is known as an oil and gas town. However, while in 1965 half of its population was working in the oil industry, today that number has fallen to one in seven (Turner, 2012). Still, over 900 oil company head offices are located in the city (Sandalack and Nicolai, 2006). Calgary is a new town, with over half of its current residents having arrived after 1988 (Turner, 2012). Visiting Calgary, you get the sense that it was constructed rather hastily, with little thought to urban design. Highways are everywhere. One minute you might be calmly driving through a quiet neighborhood, and then suddenly, with little warning, be unceremoniously launched onto a mad eight-lane highway via the shortest on-ramp you have ever seen.

Calgary has been the fastest-growing city in Canada since 2006, yet has the lowest population density among Canada's big cities (Statistics Canada, 2012), a mark it has held since at least 1911 when it was the same size as Toronto with a tenth of the population (Sandalack and Nicolai, 2006). And, thanks to its oil wealth, Calgary has the highest per capita income among the large Canadian cities (Ghitter and Smart, 2009). The wealth of this population has led to a high demand for single-family homes and resulted in low-density neighborhoods, divided by highways and served by large commercial areas, a particular suburban form for which Calgary is known both nationally and internationally (Sandalack and Nicolai, 2006: 141).

Given the city's love of highways, you might be surprised to learn that Calgary not only *has* a transit system, but that it was the first system in North America to register for an ISO14001 certification—an internationally recognized program that measures environmental performance. The pride of this system, the CTrain, is a Light Rail Transit (LRT) that has its own dedicated roads in the downtown core and is entirely wind powered—a first in North America (Calgary Transit, 2015).

Calgary's mayor, thirty-nine-year-old Naheed Nenshi, is the first Muslim mayor in Canada. Campaigning on a platform of city densification, Nenshi has been in the process of trying to increase development cost charges for developers who insist on building on the outskirts of the city in order to reflect the true costs of urban sprawl (Gee, 2012). One of his more notable projects has been to publish a list of all of his external meetings on a public website, in an effort to increase transparency and accountability at City Hall. Mayor Nenshi and the Council's enthusiasm has been a driving force to continue the momentum for sustainability that began back in 2005.

Okay, key background covered—let's hop on the CTrain and head downtown.

Figure 5.1. The entirely wind-powered Calgary CTrain. Photo by Jocelyn Kabatoff.

Field Trip

CITY HALL

A short walk from the CTrain station, our first stop is City Hall, home of the Office of Sustainability. Created in 2010, "the Office" has several important responsibilities, including designing the City's sustainability direction and working toward meeting the targets defined in the major 2005 visioning process known as imagineCalgary. This was an ambitious project, aiming to elucidate a 100-year vision for the city, using the input of as many of the city's citizens as possible. Once the consultations were complete, more than 18,000 Calgarians had participated in the process, answering a set of five questions pertaining to the future of the city. The result was the Plan for Long Range Urban Sustainability (imagineCalgary Plan), a comprehensive set of goals and matching targets for a sustainable Calgary. The architects used a "systems approach" so they could include the various components of the city, such as the governance system, the economic system, the built environment, and more (The City of Calgary, 2007).

Figure 5.2. Calgary City Hall, home of the Office of Sustainability. Photo by Jocelyn Kabatoff.

The imagineCalgary Plan is one of two documents that lay the groundwork for sustainability in Calgary and guide the actions of the Office of Sustainability. The other is the Triple Bottom Line (TBL) policy, approved by council in 2005, which combines 350 of the City's policy statements into more than twenty themes. It is designed to help policymakers identify positive and negative implications associated with a new policy, and to this end includes questions under each topic area for the policymaker to answer. The TBL document is divided into four sections—economic, social, environmental, and integrated (smart growth)—though some of the policies overlap with others. The social aspect itself includes five key goals related to inclusivity and equal access, safety, cultural diversity, healthy living, and strong neighborhoods (The City of Calgary, 2011). The Office is responsible for reviewing and updating the TBL, a process underway at the time of this writing.

The Office of Sustainability acts as the secretariat for the imagineCalgary plan, and as such is charged with transforming the imagineCalgary goals into the 2020 Sustainability Direction, thereby linking imagineCalgary and the TBL to the City's three-year business plans and budgets and setting attainable 2020 goals. The 2020 Sustainability Direction has become the most important guiding document for sustainability in the city, laying out the major sustainability goals to be achieved over the next decade. Objectives and targets for the Sustainability Direction are listed under six "goal areas": Prosperous Economy, Sustainable Corporation, Smart Growth & Mobility Choice, Community Well-Being, Financial Capacity, and Sustainable Environment. Each of these goal areas is based on definitions contained within the imagineCalgary Plan as well as other relevant policies and plans (Office of Sustainability: 13).

Dick Ebersohn is one City of Calgary staff member who speaks about the critical role played by imagineCalgary in providing a foundation for sustainability efforts in Calgary. Gregarious and helpful, Ebersohn is a transplant from South Africa, having moved to Calgary in 2005 to work as a Strategic Planner with the imagineCalgary process. He spent three years working as a sustainability consultant for the Office of Sustainability, moving to a different city department in late 2012. I asked Ebersohn what the City's philosophy was when it embarked on the imagineCalgary process.

The idea behind, or the basis for, imagineCalgary was really to create a vision over the next 100 years that is reflective of the needs of Calgarians and not their wants, which is quite interesting because a lot of times we want to focus on wants.

And that's not always necessarily sustainable. The approach that imagineCalgary took was more of a systems approach, saying we're not just here to fix problems, we're really here to fix the system so that these problems basically start to disappear.

Ebersohn continued:

At the time of imagineCalgary, people were talking a lot about integrated thinking. What that means is that we want to understand what kinds of positive or negative impacts a particular decision or action can have on various aspects of life. So we have to start identifying leverage points in our system that will have a positive impact. And that was really the idea behind imagineCalgary: building on the assets that we have in our community, whether it's buildings, people, organizations, communities, or bringing those people, those brilliant minds together, to build something new. imagineCalgary has really influenced how the city has come to be today I think. So it wasn't just a municipal project and process. This was a city-led, community-owned process. The idea was that the city would invest in the community but the community would lead this. And it was truly a place where we were able to engage and I would say give capacity to the community to participate in a project. And we really built their leadership and we built on their leadership as such.

Housed in the City Manager's Office (a testament to the stature sustainability enjoys in Calgary), the Office of Sustainability is run by three staff people—one manager and two "sustainability consultants"—who oversee the implementation and integration of sustainability across all city business units (in Calgary, city departments are divided into "business units"). Being such a small team, the Office does not see itself as responsible for implementing sustainability across the city corporation, but rather to be a resource for sustainability information and to tie together the sustainability work going on within individual business units. This is done in several ways, including holding a monthly breakfast for sustainability champions in the city, which features a different City of Calgary staff member speaking about their sustainability initiatives; and promoting collaboration between city departments through facilitating sessions for project managers.

Christina Fuller, a sustainability consultant who works closely with the City Manager's Office, likes to talk about how sustainability is being integrated across the city corporation. She says that the Office is actively trying to move away from the idea that a particular business unit is responsible for one area of sustainability. Rather, everyone should be thinking about how their work affects the different aspects of sustainability. Speaking specifically about social sustainability, Fuller elaborated:

> I cringe at the idea of placing responsibility for social sustainability in one business unit, because that's not the systems thinking approach that we in the Office of Sustainability want to be encouraging. So for example, the transportation planner who is planning the bus route through a neighbourhood also is having a huge impact on social sustainability. Strictly from a responsibility perspective they may not view themselves as being responsible for the social side of sustainability but they certainly have a strong impact and contribute to making a strong neighbourhood and that kind of a thing.

THE ALBERTA TRADE CENTRE

Now that we understand how sustainability policy is created and directed at a very high level in the Office of Sustainability, let's see how policies related to the social side of sustainability are enacted on the ground. The next stop on our tour involves a rather unpleasant four-block walk along traffic-laden three- and four-lane throughways to the Alberta Trade Centre, which is home to Community and Neighbourhood Services (CNS), the business unit most closely responsible for policy and practice related to social sustainability at the City of Calgary. You'll notice during the walk that the iconic Calgary Tower is in full view; this red emblem of the city boasts the world's tallest 360-degree observation deck. Today we are visiting CNS as it contains a division called Family and Community Support Services (FCSS), which carries out "preventive social services" across the city. Perhaps the most notable achievement of FCSS in the last five years has been the development of a Social Sustainability Framework that sets priorities for how money for social services is spent across the corporation over the next ten years.

The Social Sustainability Framework (SSF) emerged as a result of both, introspection and proactive planning on the part of some FCSS staff members who began to question their role in delivering traditional social services in light of the City's move toward sustainability. Despite the effort by the TBL and the 2020 Sustainability Direction to integrate economic, environmental, and social systems in policymaking, FCSS staff told me that in reality the social aspect was, until recently, functioning completely distinctly from these broader corporate goals. As a result, about five years ago there began an effort among FCSS staff members to better define their department's priorities and more closely align with existing city goals and priorities related to sustainability. Although the council

Figure 5.3. The iconic Calgary Tower. Photo by Jocelyn Kabatoff.

ultimately decides FCSS's funding priorities, staff have a role in bringing forth recommendations to the council on what these priorities ought to be. From about 1989 until 2008, these funding priorities, established by the council, were lacking in strategic focus and were simply trying to meet FCSS's broad mandate of "prevention." As one social planner put it, "they were trying to cover just about every social issue anyone could think of that you might possibly call a prevention issue."

A major issue confronting FCSS staff was that every three years, coinciding with the election of a new mayor and council, new funding priorities were established. Since social issues are rarely resolved within the short timeframe of three years, this was a rather disruptive process. In an attempt to resolve this problem, FCSS staff decided to link their work to the broader policies and goals of the City of Calgary through creating

Figure 5.4. Alberta Train Centre, home of Community and Neighbourhood Services. Photo by Jocelyn Kabatoff.

a Social Sustainability Framework. The Framework identifies two major areas toward which to direct city resources: "preventing spatial concentrations of poverty" and "preventing social isolation." I talked with two social planners, Heather White and Katie Black, who played large roles in this process, in order to find out how the SSF came about and how it has affected sustainable development in Calgary.

FK: You both work for Family and Community Support Services, the division that conceived of the Social Sustainability Framework. Can you tell me a little bit about how you came up with the idea? Were you trying to solve a particular problem?

HEATHER: Family and Community Support Services is a funding program, providing funds for preventive social services here in Calgary. It's a unique program in Canada where we receive 80 percent of our funds from the province; the municipality contributes the rest for a total of just over $30 million. So we are somewhat unique within the city corporation because we have these provincial dollars that we use out in the community but we're city staffed and funded and we work here as city employees. The reason I'm giving you a bit of background on this is that a number of years ago we weren't seeing our provincial contribution keeping pace with the large increase in population. Our city is now over a million people and the funding program is forty-six years old and outdated. So we embarked on a priority-setting process, aiming to align our work with existing policy documents like imagineCalgary and the Triple Bottom Line.

KATIE: Until the Social Sustainability Framework was created, FCSS has tried to cover just about every social issue anyone could think of that you might possibly call a prevention issue. The problem was compounded by the fact that every three years there is a municipal election and council priorities changed. But of course it wasn't a very robust change process because not that much changes for social issues in three years. Homelessness might bubble up or something else might subside, but social change doesn't happen that rapidly. Our sense back in 2007–08 was that we really had an opportunity to do a better job of anchoring our priorities or suggesting that the council anchors its priorities in some other high-level documents and research that was emerging. We identified imagineCalgary as one of those documents, because it involved so many Calgarians in defining the 100-year vision of the city. Social well-being was a strong theme in the final document.

HEATHER: Through that exercise we began to recognize that across the City of Calgary, the social sustainability piece was very weak. It was very difficult to pin down. For example, when we employees bring any project proposal to council, the TBL policy requires us to speak about its potential economic, environmental, and the social impacts. What we found was that the social impact was almost always either marked "not applicable" or left quite vague. So this observation helped us to see that our priority should be to clarify what is meant by "social sustainability." This led us to embark on establishing what we eventually called a "social sustainability framework," which was approved by Council in 2008. So that was really an important time for us in our business unit as Community and Neighbourhood Services, and since that time we've worked quite closely with the Office of Sustainability to roll out what is that social sustainability piece, what does it look like, how do we embrace it as a corporation.

FK: The Social Sustainability Framework is focused on two key areas: social inclusion and strong neighbourhoods. How did you decide on those two aspects?

KATIE: It was due to two things. As Heather and I mentioned earlier, our starting driver was to fund preventive social services, and so we were looking at what's effective in the world of social issue prevention. We were particularly taken by the risk and protection prevention paradigm: the idea that prevention is about reducing risk factors and increasing or enhancing protective factors. Then we as a business unit had a discussion to identify our unique competitive advantage or our distinct value proposition as a municipality committed to preventive social services. So what makes us different from the United

Way or from a church with a strong social mandate or anything else? In that discussion we started thinking about what
else a municipality delivers, so where do we have synergies
or opportunities to ride in others' slipstreams or help each
other succeed? And because a municipality is a geographically
defined phenomenon—it exists in a certain patch of land—a
lot of municipal functions have to do with what happens in
people's geographic locations. How their garbage gets picks up,
where the buses drive, where the streetlights are located, where
we locate parks, etc. So that's where we turned our attention
to these ideas about spatial concentrations of poverty and
geographic considerations because the literature is pretty clear
about neighbourhood effects in social outcomes. That where
people live does make a difference to how they thrive or don't.
So we said OK, the literature is talking about neighbourhood
effects, the municipality has a strong neighbourhood and geographic bias, so let's marry those two in terms of the strong
neighbourhoods work, and then the social inclusion work was
just thinking about if we want to have a thriving city, where
every citizen is engaged and has an opportunity to participate
as he or she chooses to, then we know that there are barriers
that would have to be overcome. These barriers are defined
by people's circumstance as new immigrants, people living in
poverty, people who are isolated by virtue of family violence
or because they are seniors whose social network has gradually
died off or moved away. So that was the other place where
we said OK, we have a unique opportunity to use our invest-
ments in preventive social services to actually promote civic
engagement and citizen participation, but our piece in it will
be to reduce or prevent social isolation and to promote social
inclusion. Not necessarily to come out and vote, but just to be
full participants in life in community.

FK: Is there a benefit to labeling the work you do "social sustainability" versus something else?

HEATHER: I think the benefit is that it actually pulls it out.
We have said that we're a TBL organization for a while, but it
was a soft area and it was the area that people said was always

the hardest to measure. So for us to be able to pull it out and be the champions and speak about the importance of social sustainability, it's really captured people's imaginations. People intuitively know it's a really important piece, but they're not necessarily really sure what to do with that. It's really just helping people to operationalize that—to get people really thinking about how they can integrate the social piece into the work that they do.

KATIE: I think there are a lot of benefits to labeling the work "social sustainability." Most importantly, it positions us to take our rightful place alongside other sustainability discussions because I think social services activities in a municipal context have often existed a little bit on the margins, maybe in part because a lot of the work we do is actually with folks who live on the margins of our society. If other parts of the municipality can boil down their complex issues into a few key ideas that folks can get their heads around, but our complex issues are still kind of out there in a meandering, nonconcise format, we're just going to be left behind. So, having and calling it a "social sustainability framework" positioned it alongside other sustainability initiatives in the corporation.

Since its adoption, FCSS and Community and Neighbourhood Services (CNS) staff have worked closely with the Office of Sustainability to roll out the Social Sustainability Framework and have it understood and embraced across the corporation, because in effect, the Framework has extended beyond simply establishing funding priorities for FCSS. Since it aligns with the TBL and imagineCalgary documents, the SSF is relevant across the corporation and affects all business units in their understanding and implementation of social sustainability. In practice, as Katie and Heather mentioned, the SSF has started to clarify how social sustainability can be operationalized in City policies and projects across various business units. This is largely the job of the Office of Sustainability. As one staff member from CNS says:

We've worked very closely with the Office of Sustainability and it has really been our vehicle to bring that social piece out as much as possible because that's not really our core business—

ensuring that the rest of the corporation embeds social sustainability. That's really the Office of Sustainability's mandate.

There is evidence that across the city corporation, effort is being made to include the social dimension in decision-making processes. For instance, a Technical Advisory Committee (TAC) team model is used by some business units in the City, such as Land Use Planning & Policy (LUPP). In the TAC team model, representatives from different sections of the corporation will come together to talk about a project from various perspectives. The CNS represents the social sustainability perspective on these TAC teams. According to one social planner who regularly sits on such committees, in the case of LUPP, seeing projects through a social sustainability lens often results in new housing surpassing the minimum requirements of the Alberta Building Code. For example, in taking into account social sustainability goals, new housing often includes provisions to make them more accessible to seniors and those with disabilities.

In the case of the Transportation Department, there is an effort by the CNS representative to encourage the TAC team to consider the impact of new LRT lines on those living close to the new route, as it has been shown in Calgary that the price of rental housing increases dramatically when new transit routes are established. While social sustainability is often overlooked by those business units not using the TAC team approach, most are more amenable to the principles of social sustainability when trying to fulfill broader corporate policy in particular. These broad corporate policies (e.g., the 2020 Sustainability Direction) include substantial sections on what social sustainability means in the City of Calgary, making it difficult for business units to overlook.

In theory, the Social Sustainability Framework ought to be a well-referenced, guiding document for how to carry out the social dimension of sustainability across the corporation of the City of Calgary. However, in practice FCSS is still working on getting more recognition for social sustainability generally and specifically for the SSF. A central challenge confronts senior leadership and council in encouraging the use of the SSF; despite the city's efforts to think more holistically about sustainability, few staff not working directly in a social services role understand how the SSF applies to their work. It is the role of FCSS and CNS to work with senior leadership to workshop the SSF across the city corporation in order that all staff, from garbage collection to wetlands protection, understand how the SSF relates to their job. However, a key issue flagged by CNS is that senior leadership may not entirely understand the SSF and as such is not holding others to account in using it. This is a problem being tackled currently by CNS staff.

Despite these challenges, there have been some early successes. In rolling out the Strong Neighbourhoods aspect of the SSF, a limited budget meant choosing certain neighborhoods in which to work; it was simply not feasible for every neighborhood in Calgary to participate. FCSS ended up identifying eight particularly vulnerable neighborhoods on which to focus. By defining goals around what it means to be a "strong neighborhood" and identifying particular critical neighborhoods in which to do this work, the SSF has enabled business units from all over the corporation to come together to further the initiative. As Katie Black puts it:

> So rather than just going out in a shotgun manner—try a bit of this and a bit of that—the social sustainability framework is now sort of focusing discussions from many different business units or departments across the corporation to say, when we want to do stuff in neighbourhoods, let us use this model. Let us make sure that we're engaging with residents, that we're hearing from residents what's important to them and delivering accordingly.

Back to City Hall: Fair Calgary

Another way that social sustainability is being operationalized in Calgary is through a policy known as "Fair Calgary," which was created around the time of imagineCalgary and about two years before the Social Sustainability Framework. So while it is not a policy that emerged from either of those two processes, Fair Calgary has been an integral part of meeting Calgary's social sustainability objectives and is linked to the social leg of the TBL, specifically the "social inclusion" and "accessibility" aspects. Fair Calgary provides a "Fairness Filter Framework" and definitions of social sustainability–related terms (e.g., "equality"), alongside a number of guiding principles, which individual business units across the City are to consider in decision-making processes. More specifically, Fair Calgary is designed to reduce barriers for low-income, socially marginalized Calgarians. The Fairness Filter Framework is designed "to optimize the capability of Calgarians' participation in and use of The City's programs, services, facilities and public spaces within the resources allocated by

Council" (The City of Calgary, 2012b: 6). It is to be used as a guide for business units in determining how to ensure access to the city's programs for the greatest number of Calgarians.

For the last stop on our field trip of Calgary we will retrace our steps back past City Hall and reboard the CTrain to understand how Fair Calgary is improving the lives of low-income Calgarians. The most notable success enjoyed thus far by Fair Calgary has been in its application to the City of Calgary's transportation business unit, in a project known as "Fair Fares," which resulted in the creation of a means-tested transit pass specifically for low-income Calgarians. Creating this pass was not

Figure 5.5. The clock tower of Calgary's Historic City Hall, a historic landmark in the City. Photo by Jocelyn Kabatoff.

without its difficulties, however, and required some bargaining with the transportation business unit. Since business units have limited budgets and the transportation business unit in particular has a cost-recovery mandate, the new low-income bus pass would necessarily result in a revenue loss that would have to be recovered in some way. After a series of meetings, the outcome was that transportation would receive a budget increase and there would be a cost increase to the annual seniors' bus pass, from C$35/ year to C$35/month (this increase did not affect the annual low-income seniors' bus pass).

Another example of a Fair Calgary success has been the development of a single-entry point for people with low income to access city services. While not yet implemented, this will mean that all city programs for low-income people will be brought into line, under one entry standard (i.e., a common maximum yearly income). Although business units will still have the ability to develop secondary criteria for accessing these

Figure 5.6. Waiting to boarding the CTrain back to City Hall. Photo by Jocelyn Kabatoff.

programs, the single-entry system will enhance dignity and respect for low-income Calgarians by no longer requiring them to constantly prove their low-income status.

On board the CTrain, we meet Nancy, a single mother of two who works part-time and is considered low-income by the City. Since she does not own a car, Nancy relies on her subsidized transit pass to get her to and from her job at a downtown pharmacy. On the way to an afternoon shift, Nancy spoke to me about the impact that the Fair Calgary initiative has had on her life:

> Thanks to the work of Fair Calgary, I now spend less per month on my transit pass, which has been a real help. But I am looking forward to the new single-entry system because right now it's a lot of work for me to sign up my daughter for subsidized swimming lessons or get my son into summer camp with a discounted fee. Every time I go to access a city service I feel like I constantly have to show that I'm poor, which is really tiring. The new system will mean I only have to do this once and I then get access to all the City's subsidized programs and services. This will be a huge relief to me.

Efforts by those staff members working on Fair Calgary are working to resolve a persistent problem alluded to by Nancy: there is currently no consistency about the meaning of "low income" among the different programs and services offered by the City. A new city strategy released in May 2013, the Calgary Poverty Reduction Initiative, includes plans to introduce a standard means test for accessing city subsidies along with a slew of policies to reduce poverty across the city (The City of Calgary and United Way of Calgary and Area, 2013). CNS staff hope that efforts like the single-entry point system will ultimately improve participation rates in City programs and services among low-income Calgarians.

LAST STOP: BELTLINE AQUATIC AND FITNESS CENTRE

The Beltline Aquatic and Fitness Centre (BAFC) is located in the downtown core of Calgary. Built in 1954 with an intended lifespan of fifty years, the City is now assessing whether to spend the money to invest in the major upgrades necessary for BAFC to continue functioning. Not helping its case is the fact that BAFC has only a small clientele: in 2011 it brought in just

22 percent of its total operating budget. But what might be a clear-cut decision to close such an aging, underused facility in one city is not so simple in Calgary. A further examination of who is actually using Beltline uncovered that in fact it is a hub for many of the "vulnerable Calgarians" identified by the SSF: new immigrants, Aboriginal people, and low-income youth and seniors. Because of this discovery, CNS joined with the Office of Sustainability to conduct a Social Return on Investment analysis (SROI) in order to determine the worth of BAFC based on its social value. Most significantly, BAFC is used by a high number of low-income and immigrant youth who are classified as "at risk." Should BAFC be torn down, these youth who come to BAFC to play basketball after school and access other programs such as homework support and counseling would otherwise be on the streets (The City of Calgary, 2012a).

Typically, a decision on whether or not to tear down an aging facility is based on the amount of investment required to upgrade the building, weighed against the potential revenue that could be generated.

Figure 5.7. Beltline Aquatic and Fitness Centre, located in downtown Calgary. Photo by Jocelyn Kabatoff.

In the case of BAFC, it was determined that a best-case scenario value ratio would be 1:0.27; that is, for every dollar invested, a return of just twenty-seven cents would be generated. However, taking into account the social value wrapped up in reduced social isolation, better health outcomes, reduced gang activity, and higher high school completion rates, the value ratio grows to 1:0.99. The SROI predicts that this value will grow if effort is made to encourage more low-income seniors to use the facility as well as the more affluent newcomers to the area. The report suggests that the value ratio has the potential to increase to 1:2.39 if effort is made to expand programming to suit this new demographic (The City of Calgary, 2012a).

While the SROI made a strong case to upgrade BAFC, the City has yet to make a final decision about the facility. A City of Calgary staff member informed me that while the SROI is being taken into account in the decision-making process, a consultant has been hired by the City to "conduct a needs and preferences study through citizen engagement and develop recommendations to best meet the needs and interests of stakeholders regarding Inner City recreation." The process is expected to take six months, and as of this writing, the fate of BAFC is unknown. While it is true that in most cities the economic side takes priority, in Calgary there seems to be a real struggle to abide by the principles set out in the City's guiding sustainability documents. Fair Calgary and the Social Sustainability Framework have enjoyed some successes, but when it comes to decisions that require a large influx of cash by the City, the path forward is less clear-cut. The case of the BAFC demonstrates that even for a city with the best of intentions and all the requisite documents and statements in place, the economics are hard to avoid. The precarious future of the BAFC epitomizes the challenges faced when an attempt is made to truly integrate the core aspects of sustainability.

References

Calgary Transit. (2015). *Commitment to the environment.* Available at: www.calgarytransit.com/environment/iso14001.html [Accessed 3 Sept. 2016]

Gee, M. (2012). Naheed Nenshi's challenge: Making Calgary a livable city. *The Globe and Mail*, Available at: www.theglobeandmail.com/news/politics/naheed-nenshis-challenge-making-calgary-a-livable-city/article565256/?page=all [Accessed 3 Sept. 2016]

Ghitter, G., and Smart, A. (2009). Mad cows, regional governance, and urban sprawl path dependence and unintended consequences in the Calgary region. *Urban Affairs Review*, 44(5), pp. 617–644.

Office of Sustainability. *Calgary 2020: The city of Calgary's 10-year plan towards imagineCalgary*. Available at: www.calgary.ca/CA/cmo/Pages/The-2020-Sustainability-Direction.aspx [Accessed 3 Sept. 2016]

Sandalack, B. A., and Nicolai, A. (2006). *The Calgary project: Urban form/urban life*. Calgary: University of Calgary Press.

Statistics Canada. (2012). *Population and dwelling counts, for census metropolitan areas, 2011 and 2006 Censuses*. Available at: www12.statcan.gc.ca/census-recensement/2011/dp-pd/hlt-fst/pd-pl/Table-Tableau.cfm?LANG=Eng&T= 205&S=3&RPP=50 [Accessed 3 Sept. 2016]

The City of Calgary. (2007). *imagineCalgary plan for long range urban sustainability*. 1st ed. [pdf] Calgary: The City of Calgary. Available at: corymorgan.com/wp-content/uploads/2013/03/imaginecalgary.pdf [Accessed 3 Sept. 2016]

The City of Calgary. (2011). *Triple bottom line policy framework*. 1st ed. [pdf] Calgary: The City of Calgary. Available at: www.calgary.ca/Transportation/TP/Documents/Safety/Community-Studies/Triple-Bottom-Line-Policy-Framework.pdf [Accessed 3 Sept. 2016]

The City of Calgary. (2012a). *2020 sustainability direction annual report*. Available at: www.calgary.ca/CA/cmo/Pages/The-2020-Sustainability-Direction.aspx [Accessed 3 Sept. 2016]

The City of Calgary. (2012b). *Fair Calgary policy*. Available at: www.calgary.ca/CA/cmo/Pages/Triple-Bottom-Line.aspx [Accessed 3 Sept. 2016]

The City of Calgary and United Way of Calgary and Area. (2013). Enough for all: Unleashing our communities' resources to drive down poverty in Calgary. *Final Report of the Calgary Poverty Reduction Initiative, Vol. 1*. Calgary: The City of Calgary.

Turner, C. (2012). Calgary reconsidered: Six truths about the city that's no longer, simply, Cowtown. *The Walrus*, 9(5), pp. 24–37.

Chapter 6

The Greenest City Experience

Exploring Social Action and Social Sustainability in Vancouver, Canada

Marit Rosol and Cristina Temenos

Introduction

The City of Vancouver, Canada, has developed a reputation as a leader in urban sustainable practice and planning (Affolderbach and Schulz, 2017; Berelowitz, 2005; Punter, 2004; Rosol, 2015a). It is often cited as a poster child of urban sustainable development based on its densely populated downtown area, its walkable and mixed-use neighborhoods, and its apparently happy coexistence with its natural surroundings. Vancouver offers breathtaking views of the mountains, inviting beaches, and ample green space, including a mostly publicly accessible waterfront. The city is proud of its natural setting and its environmental activist history. Greenpeace was founded here, as was Canada's first Green party. Today, Vancouver is striving to be the "Greenest City" in the world, indeed one of the policy frameworks the city operates under is dubbed the Greenest City Action Plan.

We put together this tour on Vancouver sustainability policies in the summer of 2013 and 2014 as urban geographers from Germany and the United States who have both worked on Vancouver sustainability initiatives, as well as urban sustainability initiatives more broadly. Starting with the roots of neighborhood environmental activism in Vancouver, we take you along a policy tour that has been mapped onto the landscape of neighborhoods in East Vancouver. Along the way, we address, and perhaps raise more questions about, how a relatively young city like Vancouver has come to have such a glowing reputation for sustainability. How does the city itself implement sustainability policies? And how do its actions and resulting urban form reflect precepts and tenets of environmental, economic, and social sustainability? This route entails four "stops" that take us from the roots of environmental and neighborhood activism in the 1960s and 1970s to the Greenest City policy framework of today.[1]

Field Trip

THE CHINATOWN FREEWAY DEBATES: THE GEORGIA AND DUNSMIR VIADUCTS, STRATHCONA, AND HOGAN'S ALLEY

You might wonder why a tour of Vancouver's sustainability policies is starting beneath a freeway overpass. It's not technically a freeway overpass—because there's no freeway, just the overpass. We begin this tour by standing under an artefact of the past. The concrete roadway above us is the Georgia Viaduct, a remnant of a failed plan to bring a freeway through the heart of Vancouver in the 1970s. Public opposition to this plan is often credited with "saving" the city, its walkability, its neighborhood feel. In stories of Vancouver's success as a sustainable city, it is a defining moment.

Coupled with a middle-class preference for suburban development, a narrative of "urban decay" accompanied urban planning in North America from the 1950s onward. In Vancouver, the rationale for implementing large-scale urban restructuring projects was based on this narrative and undergirded by a stagnant economy, depopulation, changing—often racialized—populations, and increased crime and poverty. These modernist projects often consisted of highways, public housing developments, and modernist high-rise office buildings, while destroying historic neighborhoods and displacing (often poor and nonwhite) communities. While the depopulation and stagnant economies were not as severe in most Canadian cities as they were in the United States, urban planners, politicians, and economic stakeholders nevertheless worried about these tendencies (Ward, 1999).

Vancouver was no different; city planners and business stakeholders advocated for auto-centered development as a way of rationally moving people—increasingly traveling by cars—in and out of downtown; easily linking existing commercial centers; and increasing truck access to the main port (Liscombe, 2011; MacKenzie, 1985). The Georgia and Dunsmuir Viaducts, built in 1972, are the only completed part of a 1960 development plan, put forward by the Vancouver Board of Trade that advocated a forty-five-mile network of freeways linking up the metropolitan region (MacKenzie, 1985). The appetite for car-oriented development was so great that, with the 1960 Board of Trade plan still on the table, Project 200,[2] a Vancouver waterfront redevelopment was introduced around the same time. It included an "oceanview" freeway running along the scenic English Bay and the destruction of the oldest parts of the city—Gastown, Chinatown, and Strathcona—in favor of Modernist high-rise towers and a freeway exit leading commuters straight to their parking garages on the waterfront. However, Project 200 never came to fruition. In 1971, the federal government stated that money slated for urban redevelopment in the province of British Columbia would not be used for a freeway system in the Vancouver region.

Figure 6.1. Georgia Viaduct. Photo by Cristina Temenos (2013).

Why is it that both of these ambitious freeway plans (the Board of Trade plan and Project 200) didn't materialize as they did in so many other North American cities, leaving the Viaducts as one of the few traces on Vancouver's landscape? There are two dominant narratives in Vancouver planning histories: (1) there was not enough funding, nor regional planning strength, to allow a freeway plan to be built in the metro Vancouver region, and (2) citizens, through community groups such as the Strathcona Property Owners' and Tenants' Association (SPOTA), the Chinese Benevolent Association, the Architectural Institute of British Columbia, and the Citizen Council of Civic Development banded together and defeated the slum removal projects started in 1958, and the freeway developments that stemmed from them (Lee, 2007; Hasson and Ley, 1994: 112–136). What actually happened, as is often the case and as we show below, was a mixture of the two.

Led by student activist and neighborhood resident Shirley Chan, social planner Darlene Marzari, and community lawyer Mike Harcourt, collective action against the freeway plan involved community meetings, demonstrations on the steps of City Hall, the hanging of black banners throughout Strathcona, and engagements with other professional groups. As mentioned, Strathcona is the oldest residential neighborhood in Vancouver, and, walking east, the first thing you notice is the gardens in front of almost every house. In this neighborhood, lawns are spurned in favor of roses, wildflowers, and vegetables. Edible yards, considered a new North American trend in the past few years, have long been a staple of this community. Many of the Edwardian cottages we see today are the same ones that SPOTA members fought to save. The demands of the protestors were relatively simple and common sense by today's planning standards: consult the community before planning decisions are made; allow independent property assessments before buying out (mostly immigrant) homeowners in the neighborhood; consider alternative routes to bringing a freeway through the historic neighborhood.

By 1967, the "Chinatown Freeway Debates," as they were known, came to a head, with weekly demonstrations, and upward of 500 to 800 citizens crowding city council meetings to protest the destruction of Strathcona. On November 8, 1967, the federal minister responsible for housing, Paul Hellyer, toured Strathcona with Shirley Chan and Darlene Marzari. The experience of the place impacted Hellyer so much that the same week he froze federal funding for urban renewal projects across Canada, including funding that Vancouver City Hall was counting on to finance freeway construction (Harcourt and Cameron, 2007), the key success for the movement, effectivly putting an end to the development plans.

The Chinatown Freeway Debates marked the beginning of a paradigm shift in Vancouver planning. The victory against the freeways established a precedent of integrating community consultation into planning decisions—although in some cases community groups may still have to fight for adequate consultation and participation, as we will see in the later example of Little Mountain. In 1972, as a direct result of the freeway fiasco, the Non Partisan Association (NPA)—the probusiness political party in power for the past thirty years—was defeated in both mayoral and council elections. The newly formed Electors' Action Movement (TEAM) that won the election boasted Mike Harcourt (later Vancouver Mayor and Premier of British Columbia) and Darlene Marzari as new council members.

While the freeway system in Vancouver never materialized, the Georgia and Dunsmuir Viaducts still stand. A question not answered, or even addressed, in most accounts of the salvation of Strathcona is what happened to the roughly 3,500 people (Harcourt and Cameron, 2007: 35) who were displaced from Strathcona under the urban renewal begun in the 1950s? What happened when the viaducts were built? Looking around the corner, on Union St, we can see two small traces of what was on this land before 1972. The first is a small blue plaque, almost unnoticeable on the side of a building. It reads:

> Hogan's Alley was part of the ethnically diverse East End, centered between Prior and Union and Main and Jackson. It was home to much of Vancouver's Black community and included businesses such as Vie's Chicken and Steak House on Union and the Pullman Porters' Club on Main. The neighbourhood was a popular cultural hub before mid-twentieth century urban renewal schemes and the Georgia Viaduct Replacement Project demolished many of its buildings.

The first and only concentrated black community in Vancouver was, like many other North American cities, the greatest casualty of Vancouver's urban renewal scheme. While much of the black population had moved away from the immediate area of Hogan's Alley into the rest of Strathcona and the city in the decade before the 1967 demolitions, several cultural institutions such as the AME Fountain Chapel and Vie's Chicken and Steak House remained until at least 1980 (Compton, 2011). The kitchen of Vie's is the only remaining building of Hogan's Alley, and as we enter it, you can see it is now a place of homage to one of the neighborhood's most famous residents. The psychedelic sign out front reads, "Jimi Hendricks Shrine."[3] Inside the small dark space, the walls are decorated with photos of the musician and his family around Vancouver. What the photos show, if you look beyond the smiling people at the center, is a vibrant black community throughout Vancouver, and continuing to return to Hogan's Alley as a cultural center. In comparison to cities in the United States, the black community was (and is) relatively small in Vancouver. Yet this neighborhood boasted venues where musicians such as Louis Armstrong and Cole Porter played. Jimi Hendrix's grandmother sang in the choir of the Fountain Chapel. It was a neighborhood that disappeared in 1972, and did not receive formal recognition until the plaque we saw above was put up in 2011. In this sense, the great "success" of fighting off the freeways for the salvation of Vancouver's downtown livability was not without the casualty of an already walkable and culturally diverse, but also marginalized, community.

THE DOWNTOWN EASTSIDE AND THE ECODENSITY INITIATIVE

Continuing from Strathcona, we wind our way through Chinatown into the Downtown East Side (DTES), often designated the poorest urban postal code in Canada. Various condo redevelopments sit beside derelict Edwardian storefronts. Some are vacant, some are used for social housing, and much more recently some house the occasional fine-dining establishment that so often signals gentrification and radical neighborhood change. We now stop at Carnegie Community Centre to talk about a more recent political battle: lifting height restrictions in Chinatown and the DTES, ostensibly to foster sustainability through density. Density is a word that has been on the lips and fingertips of Vancouver politicians, planners, and community activists for years (Rosol, 2015a; Quastel, Moos, and Lynch, 2012). It was here, in the rooms of the former Carnegie Library, where activists and neighbors gathered in their protest against Condo development and the EcoDensity initiative of former NPA mayor Sam Sullivan (e.g., Carnegie Community Action Project, 2008).

The proclaimed goal of EcoDensity, introduced in 2006 and approved by Vancouver City Council in 2008, was the achievement of greater urban sustainable development through densification of existing neighborhoods to make Vancouver more environmentally sustainable, affordable, and "livable." Its aim was particularly to increase development options in low-density residential neighborhoods, effectively engaging sustainability as a hegemonic tool to force densification (City of Vancouver, 2006).

Anxiety over what EcoDensity would mean for peoples' daily lives led to open protest against the policy in a number of neighborhoods. From the beginning, the initiative had been accompanied by a lot of passion, controversy, and confusion, both of approval and concern, as well as mistrust and fear, that awkwardly separated and united individuals and interest groups in unforeseeable ways. Some praised it as the best tool to achieve a sustainable city; others contested it as the "greenwashing" of a developer's agenda. The analysis of the debate around EcoDensity shows the importance of discursive strategies, wording, and meaning (Rosol, 2013). Both proponents and critics agreed that, for proponents, EcoDensity was a way to "launder a dirty word [density]" (interview of senior planner by Rosol, 2008); for critics, the wording caused suspicion. The proponents of the initiative tried to push housing density by creating a

Figure 6.2. Photo of DTES / Carnegie Community Centre / condo developments. Photo by Cristina Temenos (2013).

discourse that fixes its meaning onto sustainability and other well-received concepts such as affordability and livability. Thus, EcoDensity can be seen as a prominent example of how environmental concerns are introduced to "neutralize environmental opposition by projecting a value-free vision of 'win-win-wins' between economic growth, social development and ecological protection" (While, Jonas, and Gibbs, 2004: 554).

However, the opponents challenged exactly this—the equivalence of density with livability, affordability, and sustainability. Instead of being able to turn the broad support of sustainability in Vancouver into a consensus over densification and increase the popularity of the mayor, proponents in the end needed to make concessions just to agree on some basic principles. On June 10, 2008, Vancouver City Council adopted the amended fourth draft of the EcoDensity Charter. Some initial actions were opposed by the oppositional councilors, but the motions were carried by majority (City of Vancouver, 2008b). In the end, opponents were successful in denying the mayor his success story by creating a huge controversy around the initiative. It took two years and four draft versions to just approve a charter (cf. Quastel, 2009: 717–718). It also cost Mayor Sullivan his office, as he was not nominated for reelection by his own party (Bula, 2008).

Here in the DTES, the EcoDensity initiative proposed added heights and density beyond existing zoning. This would entail demolishing existing (affordable) housing stock and building new high-rise condominiums. Activists from the DTES opposed the possibility of introducing condominium towers into their neighborhood, fearing further gentrification and loss of affordable housing. They feared displacement and homelessness in a neighborhood already under massive socioeconomic and development pressure (for a critical history of the neighborhood, see Smith, 2003). As the DTES is a neighborhood with an already remarkable density and a building height allowance up to four stories, comparable to many European cities, the reason for further rezoning is rooted in increasing land values and thus profits through rezoning. Housing activists argued that if affordability was the goal of EcoDensity, proactive measures would be needed, including preserving existing (rental and social) housing stock and governmental intervention toward new cooperative and social housing. Density alone would deteriorate affordability—especially in attractive inner-city locations like the DTES (e.g., Lee et al., 2008).

Despite quietly dropping the initiative after the election of a new mayor from the opposing Vision Vancouver party in 2008, EcoDensity still impacts the DTES. One legacy of EcoDensity in the DTES was the "Historic Precinct Height Study," aimed at pushing for additional density through height in the historic area of Vancouver, including the DTES (City of Vancouver, 2008a, 2010a, 2010b), as with EcoDensity more generally, using a sustainability policy as a pretext for supporting real estate interests. As a result of this study—which focused on built form and did not include associated social and economic effects—and despite sustained community opposition, height increases of up to fifteen stories were approved in Chinatown and the DTES in 2011, effectively preparing the rezoning of the DTES for condo towers. Activists, therefore, called it the "DTES Gentrification Package" (Markle, 2010; Blomley, Ley and Wyly, 2011; Walia, 2011).

How one of the alleged goals of EcoDensity—achieving affordability in Vancouver—is thwarted by other (housing) policies will be illustrated in our next example: the story of the Little Mountain housing complex, named after Vancouver's highest point in the adjacent Queen Elizabeth Park. Here again the demolition of affordable housing stock had been accompanied by rhetoric of higher density in the name of sustainability.

LITTLE MOUNTAIN

Outside the Carnegie Community Centre, we take the #3 bus south, traveling through typical low-density, primarily single-family housing neighborhoods. Soon we arrive at a nearly empty lot, a fenced-off building site that was once the oldest social housing complex in British Columbia: "Little Mountain" (for more information, see Rosol, 2015b).

This high-quality 224-unit social-housing complex was a response to a serious shortage of affordable rental housing in Vancouver. It was opened in 1954 after five years of political contestation by homeowners associations, the real estate board, business people, and some local councilors. Such social housing—the term "social" refers to the public funding for construction and the subsidized rents—became possible through an amendment to the National Housing Act in 1949 (Leone and Carroll, 2010; Hulchanski and Shapcott, 2004). Little Mountain was built with public, mostly federal, money on previously undeveloped swampland. It was not linked to urban renewal, and from the beginning it was a mixed-income community with a progressive rent scale determined at 20 percent of household income. Interestingly, none of the families who moved in as first occupants came from Strathcona, an area at the time known for its poor housing conditions and already a candidate for slum clearance (Thomson, 2010: 70–98).

Plans for redevelopment of Little Mountain became public through a newspaper article in March 2007. By May 2007, the dissatisfaction with the new development began to erupt. The protest began with a march along the adjacent Main Street, an increasingly gentrifying and trendy shopping area. Protesters also demanded a phased process—so people could stay longer in their homes—and secured relocation. Little Mountain tenants and their supporters formed the Community Advocates for Little Mountain (CALM) in May 2007.[4] They organized housing stands, that is, public rallies or pickets and street marches, attended meetings, spoke to politicians, wrote letters, and gave countless interviews. CALM used creative tools like street art, art-ins and "urban knitting," where boards sealing windows and fences were covered in yarn designs. Further, they sold mock shares of the BC Premier's house, and camped to protest

Figure 6.3. Little Mountain in 2013. Photo by Cristina Temenos (August 2013).

against displacement and demolition, as well as for the support of social housing and tenants' rights (for a detailed visual and written description, see Thomson, 2010: 172–206). The tenants of Little Mountain were not opposed to redevelopment or higher density per se; rather, they objected to the degree of densification, displacement, and lack of a consultation process—established in practice and in law during the Chinatown Free-way Debates—before relocation and demolition started. Their previously approved community vision, for example, rejected developments higher than four stories.

To prepare for the privatization of land, relocation started in March 2007, leaving only thirty households on the site in the fall of 2008 and only ten by September 2009. The BC government sold the land to a private developer in 2008. After the 2008 crash of the real estate market, the redevelopment of the site was stalled for a year, leaving houses boarded up and empty until November 2009, when the site was bulldozed. By the end of 2009, only four residents were able to remain after a long struggle for their right to stay put: a disabled woman, two blind senior citizens (both passed away in 2014), and a pensioner, who was evicted in November 2014. The last of the buildings, which housed the four residents, was demolished in December 2014. In the name of densification and to make room for at least 1,400 market condos, the old walk-ups have been torn down, there is almost no remnant on the landscape to remind us of the recent struggles of residents and housing activists. The developer promised to replace all 224 social housing units eventually, but only in number, not in size. Replacement units have only one or two bedrooms, rather than three-bedroom units and row houses, which are especially important for families. Replacing only the demolished units also supports the argument that gentrification and participation in the booming real estate market is the goal, not social equity.

In April 2013, more than three years after the site was bulldozed and six years after the displacement of a community began, construction finally started. Because of the advocacy of the remaining tenants and their supporters, an agreement by the BC government, the City of Vancouver, and the developer permitted a social housing building to be constructed ahead of the rezoning process for the rest of the site. The first fifty-three-unit social housing building was completed in 2015. Despite this success, years after displacing the low-income inhabitants of Little Mountain, only a tiny fraction of the original inhabitants will realistically be able to relocate at the site. In the meantime, 220 units of social housing have been lost, and as yet they have not been fully replaced.

What for, one has to ask? The official discourse emphasizes the "better use of the land" through denser redevelopment and the chance for a "mixed-income and diverse neighbourhood."[5] The goal was to "create a high quality, higher density, socially inclusive and environmentally sustainable community," to increase housing options in Vancouver, and generate funds for the development of social housing in Vancouver and elsewhere in the province (BC Housing and City of Vancouver, 2007: 2). According to a 2007 Memorandum of Understanding between the City of Vancouver and BC Housing, half of the money gained through the sale of the land was to be reinvested in housing in Vancouver (including the replacement of units at the site), and the rest used to finance social housing elsewhere in the province. This model, of which Little Mountain has been the test ground, is based on a new approach in BC housing policy established in 2007 that seeks to privatize postwar social housing and redevelop it as higher density and mixed tenure while also generating money for new projects (Thomson, 2010: 172).[6] Redevelopment has been justified here as elsewhere, in part, on the basis that social mixing will create more social capital for low-income families at Little Mountain. However, Little Mountain is a wonderful example of the level of social capital that existed, of the strong ties among residents, of their solidarity and social organization, ties that have been capped in the process of redevelopment (Thomson, 2010). Moreover, as research in many cities shows, the idea of social mix is often evoked when the actual plan is—often state-led—gentrification (Bridge, Butler, and Lees, 2012; Mösgen, Rosol, and Schipper, 2018).

In the case of Little Mountain, all the added density will be market units, and densification will not bring more social and affordable housing to the neighborhood. As David Chudnovsky, a former provincial elected representative from the left-leaning NDP and advocate for the current Little Mountain residents, criticizes:

They're privatizing an important asset of the people of British Columbia, in exchange for what? In exchange for simply replacing the 224 units of social housing that were here before. No increase, [. . .] Holborn [the developer] will build hundreds and hundreds and hundreds of units of condos that are expensive that don't speak at all to the real problem of the city, which is the crisis of affordability, for families, for poor people, for older people, for young people. (Cole, 2013a)

Thus and apart from the individual hardship the former inhabitants of Little Mountain had to go through, this example points to a broader problem: in a city desperate for affordable housing, it is incomprehensible why land owned by BC Housing is privatized rather than used for creating new affordable housing. Vancouver has the highest housing prices in Canada (Mendez, 2017; Somerville and Swann, 2008: 2, 7; Royal LePage, 2015) and an extremely low rental vacancy rate of under 1 percent since 2005. In this overheated property market, affordability is an urgent matter that affects not only low-income groups but more and more the middle class. Why not use land that belongs to BC Housing for exactly its purpose: providing housing for those who cannot afford it on the market? Why not use the increased density for providing *more* social and affordable housing? Instead of keeping and preserving public housing as one of the few tools that mitigate housing crises in metropolitan city regions, they are privatized by the very agencies that should preserve them and whose mandate should be to provide housing for the population that cannot afford market prices. Further, selling public land to private developers not only affects the housing supply today, but the government gives away an important tool and options for mitigating housing crises in the future. As one resident put it: "That's a lot of public land that is going to be sold at the expense of the future of this province" (Interview, 22 July 2008).

The Greenest City

From the former Little Mountain site, we head back to the edge of Strathcona, to Strathcona Park, and Cottonwood community garden. Here, we conclude our policy tour with a discussion of Vancouver's Greenest City Action Plan and recent redevelopment plans. On June 26, 2013, Vancouver's City Council approved a two-year, $2.4 million final planning phase of the Georgia and Dunsmuir Viaduct removal (Cole, 2013b). Vision Vancouver City Councilor Geoff Meggs stated: "We'll certainly right a historic wrong by removing the viaducts, which as we heard, once threatened to destroy both Strathcona and Chinatown" (Cole, 2013b). The removal of the viaducts, where we started the tour, is another lynchpin in Vision

Vancouver's Greenest City Strategy. Altogether, the removal of the viaducts will, in the eyes of city hall, do more than just "right a historic wrong," it will open seven acres of land partially owned by the city, and partially by private developers for condominium development, and will allow the city to address traffic-calming issues that are a direct result of the viaducts.

While there is general consensus in the city that the removal of the viaducts is beneficial for Vancouver, questions remain as to what motivates the city to do so, and whether this development will be socially just. It is estimated that up to 8,000 housing units could be developed, with only 22 percent, less than one third, designated affordable housing (City of Vancouver, 2011, 2018). This would help the city address another planning priority, homelessness. In 2014, Vancouver estimated 1,803 homeless people lived on its streets, and affordable housing in the community is both a city planning priority, and—as we saw earlier at Little Mountain—a focus for poverty activists in Vancouver (City of Vancouver and Eberle Planning and Research, 2012; GVRSCH, 2014). However, the city does not quantify what "affordable" means in the context of the viaduct removal, and subsequent real estate development. Considering a recent and often referenced "affordable housing" initiative by the City of Vancouver (the Olympic Village) resulted in Cooperative Housing Units starting at C$1,600 per month—when a one-parent family with two children received C$660 housing support on social assistance—significant questions remain about for whom "affordable" housing will be offered in a neighborhood that is rapidly gentrifying (Cole, 2010; MSDSI, 2008).

There have, however, been positive moves within this planning process. The Hogan's Alley Society comprised of former Hogan's Alley Residents and activists within Vancouver's Black community have been advocating a restorative justice process through the Eastern Core and North East False Creek planning processes. Discussions include locating a Black Cultural Centre within the former Hogan's Alley, as well as having meaningful input into the development and management of social housing in the North East False Creek plan. Discussions of creating a community land trust to manage the social housing units have been underway (City of Vancouver, 2018).

The redevelopment of the land will make way for a "greenway" with a park and bike paths into downtown, serving the new condo developments that the viaduct removal will allow to be built. In order to address the traffic-calming issues, the redevelopment will also need to reroute the traffic that travels along this busy entrance to the downtown core. To where though? The Strathcona Resident's Association has been advocating for the Eastern Core Planning Process, which is directing plans for the viaduct removal, to adequately deal with traffic concerns on Prior Street—the northern boundary of Strathcona Park—which, in its current form, does not. City Hall has proposed rerouting the traffic one block south, and widening the Malkin Connector as a possible solution (City of Vancouver, 2011). Widening the Malkin Connector would move the traffic from Prior Street to Malkin Avenue, the southern boundary of Strathcona Park. Cottonwood Community Gardens are located on the edge of Strathcona Park, and sit on a right-of-way for Malkin Avenue. It is this land in particular that the city wants to reclaim to pave over to widen the street. This route would lead through a neighborhood zoned for light industrial use, and often characterized as devoid of people or vibrant urban life. However, it is, in fact, the essence of a mixed-use community. Strathcona Park and Cottonwood community garden are placed on the boarder of Strathcona and Grandview neighborhoods. Surrounding the area south of Prior St, and north of the railroad tracks is cooperative, social, and market housing (some heritage) for those who access Cottonwood garden and Strathcona Park. Small businesses, both commercial and industrial, are peppered throughout the neighborhood. It is a neighborhood where people walk to work, children walk to school, and that has sustained itself for a hundred years. Yet, in order to become the "greenest city," in the name of sustainability, Vancouver city planners are ready to disturb an already established sustainable community. Questions about the nature of green redevelopment, urban planning, public consultation, and social inclusion have come to the forefront of the debates sparked by the viaduct removal. The Greenest City Action Plan highlights how "Strathcona neighbourhood residents stopped the construction of a massive freeway into downtown that would have levelled their community and altered the shape of the city forever" (City of Vancouver, 2009). Yet, residents are asking how the current city-favored plan maintains community cohesion and public consultation.

The EcoDensity initiative, as we explained above, was contested from its inception, constantly suffering claims of greenwashing development and, in 2008, Sam Sullivan's NPA party was defeated by Vision Vancouver, which won a majority of council seats on the promise of change. Soon after, City Hall announced a new sustainability policy: The Greenest City Action Plan, approved by Vancouver City Council in 2012. The ambitious (or hubristic) goal of this plan is to become the greenest city in the world by 2020 (for a critique, see McCann, 2013). It comes complete with targets and benchmarks to track progress and brings together the three tenets of sustainability under a green rubric. It is focused on building community through increasing green space, walkability, and bicycle access. Community gardens are a key component of this action plan. Everywhere you look in the city, new community gardens are popping up—in parks, along buildings, in empty lots (Quastel, 2009). Vancouver's climate allows for year-round cultivation, and most gardens have waitlists for plots. Cottonwood has a very organic feel, with many gardeners practicing permaculture gardening; here, between all the individual plots, there is the native garden, the Asian garden, and walking further along, the trees blocking the view and noise of the produce warehouses across Malkin Avenue continue on for the length of the garden. The garden was started in the early 1990s, one of the first in the city. According to board members, before the community garden was on this land, it was a dumping site; artefacts dating back to 1903 were found in the early days of Cottonwood (Driftmier, 2012). If

Figure 6.4. Cottonwood Community Garden. Photo by Cristina Temenos (2013).

you look up into those tall trees, you can see eagles' nests. It's amazing that in this neighborhood, surrounded by industry, a small colony of bald eagles makes its home within Strathcona Park.

As mentioned, traffic in the neighborhood, especially on Prior Street, has been a concern since the viaducts were completed in 1972. The Strathcona Resident's Association cites the problem of neighborhood separation from its community park and community gardens as one of the motivators to advocate for traffic-calming measures. Many community residents wonder what is the point of diverting the traffic in this way if the garden, the reason itself, is destroyed. At the meeting on the Eastern Core Planning Strategy on June 26, 2013, thirty-one people spoke on the issue of the report proposing plans for the viaduct removal. As a result, the approved two-year study on the viaduct removal was amended to specifically name Cottonwood and Strathcona community gardens as "existing assets" (City of Vancouver, 2011: 10) and directed the study to look for ways of enhancing them. This was a significant change from the previous report, which did not name them, and directed planners to look at ways of producing new assets.

Outlook

No one knows the future of Cottonwood Community Garden. The Eastern Core planning process is attempting to remove the last vestiges of the freeway and urban renewal plans that were defeated fifty years ago, and in the process, it faces many of the same community concerns that were present fifty years ago: equitable land use, meaningful community consultation, and (social) sustainability. Strathcona's legacy of community activism and multiculturalism has been a part of its identity for the past fifty years, and it is publicly acknowledged by the municipal government, academics, and public intellectuals (Harcourt and Cameron, 2007; Liscombe, 2011). But, as the current conflict around the viaduct removal shows, the struggle continues. In this sense, path dependencies, histories of development and environmentalism, and social struggle have shaped contemporary sustainability planning in ways that are both material and discursive (Temenos and McCann, 2012). While residents had to fight against modernist car-oriented planning in the 1970s, the new struggle—in the DTES, in Little Mountain, and in Strathcona—is against displacement of people and community facilities in the name of sustainability.

At the end of this policy tour, then, we might reflect on questions of sustainability and what makes a sustainable policy initiative. What does sustainability mean for the daily lives of Vancouver residents—especially for those who are living in some of the poorest postal codes of Canada, those who are displaced from a vibrant mixed-income community, and those who now face a highway through their community garden? How does the line of policy initiatives that we saw materially in the city reflect the priorities of those not concerned with Vancouver's reputation on the world stage? This in turn raises questions for the young city about the very notion of "green." Is Vancouver so environmentally friendly that it can claim its green status? Or has it already achieved "greenest city" status in another sense? Its policies demonstrate that Vancouver is still young and green—a fresh, clean, and curated city—but also quick to forget the lessons in social justice and housing affordability that mobilized Vancouver as an innovator in the field only thirty years ago.

Notes

1. See maps.google.com/maps/ms?ie=UTF&msa=0&msid=2094211555014 03938097.0004e43fc69a91b928a3f.
2. See the blog by Vancouver urban planner and politician Gordon Price pricetags.ca/2012/03/22/project-200-the [Accessed 1 June 2018]
3. While Jimi Hendrix grew up primarily in Seattle, he was as a child often taken to Vancouver to stay with his paternal grandmother, Nora Hendrix, and spent a year of elementary school in the city. In 2015, the shrine was moved to a downtown location on Homer Street due to redevelopment of the site.
4. See www.my-calm.info.
5. See www.vancouverlittlemountain.com/news/1425.
6. Mixed-income redevelopment of social housing is happening not only in Vancouver, but also in other Canadian cities, such as Regent Park and Don Mont Court in Toronto (Hackworth and Moriah, 2006).

References

Affolderbach, J., and Schulz, C. (2017). Positioning Vancouver through urban sustainability strategies? The greenest city 2020 action plan. *Journal of Cleaner Production*, 164, pp. 676–685.
BC Housing and City of Vancouver. (2007). *Memorandum of understanding between BC housing and the City of Vancouver regarding the redevelopment of Little*

Mountain. Available at: www.bchousing.org/resources/Housing_Initiatives/ Redeveloping_Housing/Little_Mountain_MOU.pdf [Accessed 3 Sept. 2016]

Berelowitz, L. (2005). *Dream city: Vancouver and the global imagination.* Vancouver: Douglas and McIntyre.

Blomley, N., Ley, D., and Wyly, E. (2011). Gentrification pushes out the poor. *The Vancouver Sun.* Available at: www.sfu.ca/~blomley/op-ed.pdf [Accessed 3 Sept. 2016]

Bridge, G., Butler, T., and Lees, L., eds. (2012). *Mixed communities: Gentrification by stealth?* Bristol: Policy Press.

Bula, F. (2008). The anatomy of Sam Sullivan's downfall. *The Vancouver Sun,* 14 June 2008.

Bula, F. (2012). Last-minute deal averts eviction for Little Mountain social-housing holdouts. *The Globe and Mail.* Available at: www.theglobeandmail.com/news/ british-columbia/last-minute-deal-averts-eviction-for-little-mountain-social-housing-holdouts/article4663485 [Accessed 3 Sept. 2016]

Carnegie Community Action Project. (2008). "Eek O'Density" packs theatre. Available at: ccapvancouver.wordpress.com/2008/04/04/eek-odensity-crowd-packs-theatre [Accessed 3 Sept. 2016]

City of Vancouver. (2006). EcoDensity primer: An introduction to building communities that are green, livable and affordable in Vancouver. Vancouver: City of Vancouver.

City of Vancouver. (2008a). EcoDensity initial actions. Available at: www.vancouver-ecodensity.ca/webupload/File/actions-FINAL.pdf [Accessed 3 Sept. 2016]

City of Vancouver. (2008b). Regular council meeting minutes. Jun 10, 2008. Available at: covapp.vancouver.ca/councilMeetingPublic/CouncilMeetings. aspx?SearchType=3 [Accessed 3 Sept. 2016]

City of Vancouver. (2009). Greenest city action plan. Available at: vancouver.ca/ green-vancouver/greenest-city-2020-action-plan.aspx [Accessed 3 Sept. 2016]

City of Vancouver. (2010a). Policy report development and building: Historic area height review—Conclusion and recommendations. 1st ed. [pdf] Vancouver: Director of Planning. Available at: former.vancouver.ca/ctyclerk/ cclerk//20100119/documents/rr2a.pdf [Accessed 3 Sept. 2016]

City of Vancouver. (2010b). Policy report urban structure: Historic area height review—Policy implementation. 1st ed. [pdf] Vancouver: Director of Planning. Available at: former.vancouver.ca/ctyclerk/cclerk/20110120/documents/ penv4.pdf [Accessed 3 Sept. 2016]

City of Vancouver. (2011). Administrative report: Viaducts and False Creek flats planning: Eastern core strategy. 1st ed. [pdf] Vancouver: Director of Planning. Available at: vancouver.ca/docs/eastern-core/core-strategy-council-report. pdf [Accessed 3 Sept. 2016]

City of Vancouver. (2018). The future of Northeast False Creek. Available at: vancouver.ca/home-property-development/northeast-false-creek.aspx [Accessed 13 Jul. 2018]

Cole, Y. (2010). Olympic village social housing units "tokenism," says Vancouver housing activist. *The Georgia Straight*. Available at: www.straight.com/news/ olympic-village-social-housing-units-tokenism-says-vancouver-housing-activist [Accessed 3 Sept. 2016]

Cole, Y. (2013a). Construction set to begin on first social housing units at Little Mountain redevelopment. *The Georgia Straight*. Available at: www.straight. com/news/371616/construction-set-begin-first-social-housing-units-little-mountain-redevelopment [Accessed 3 Sept. 2016]

Cole, Y. (2013b). Vancouver votes to proceed with two-year study of viaducts removal. *The Georgia Straight*. Available at: www.straight.com/news/396066/vancouver-votes-proceed-two-year-study-viaducts-removal [Accessed 3 Sept. 2016]

Compton, W. (2011). *After Canaan: Essays on race, writing, and region*. Vancouver: Arsenal Pulp Press.

Driftmier, P. (2012). Tearing down the viaducts: Green for all or green for some? [podcast]. Redeye Coop Radio 100.5 FM. Available at: thecityfm.wordpress. com/2013/04/17/podcast-tearing-down-the-viaducts-green-for-all-or-green-for-some [Accessed 3 Sept. 2016]

Greater Vancouver Regional Steering Committee on Homelessness. (2014). Results of the 2014 homeless count in the metro Vancouver region. 1st ed. [pdf] Available at: www.metrovancouver.org/services/regional-planning/homelessness/HomelessnessPublications/2014MVHomelessCountJuly31-14Results.pdf [Accessed 3 Sept. 2016]

Hackworth, J., and Moriah, A. (2006). Neoliberalism, contingency and urban policy: The case of social housing in Ontario. *International Journal of Urban and Regional Research*, 30(3), pp. 510–527.

Harcourt, M., and Cameron, K. (2007). *City making in paradise: Nine decisions that saved Vancouver*. Vancouver: Douglas & McIntyre.

Hasson, S., and Ley, D. (1994). *Neighbourhood organizations and the welfare state*. Toronto: University of Toronto Press.

Hulchanski, D., and Shapcott, M. (2004). *Finding room: Options for a Canadian rental housing strategy*. Toronto: CUCS Press.

Lee, J.-A. (2007). Gender, ethnicity, and hybrid forms of community-based urban activism in Vancouver, 1957–1978: The Strathcona story revisited. *Gender, Place & Culture: A Journal of Feminist Geography*, 14(4), pp. 381–407.

Lee, M., Villagomez, E., Gurstein, P., Eby, D., and Wyly, E. (2008). *Affordable EcoDensity: Making affordability housing a core principle of Vancouver's EcoDensity charter*. Available at: www.policyalternatives.ca/publications/ reports/affordable-ecodensity [Accessed 3 Sept. 2016]

Leone, R., and Carroll, B. W. (2010). Decentralisation and devolution in Canadian social housing policy. *Environment and Planning C: Government and Policy*, 28(3), pp. 389–404.

Liscombe, R. W. (2011). A study in Modern(ist) urbanism: Planning Vancouver, 1945–1965. *Urban History*, 38(1), pp. 124–149.

MacKenzie, K. (1985). *Freeway planning and protests in Vancouver, 1954–1972*. Unpublished master's thesis, Simon Fraser University.

Markle, T. (2010). Vision embraces NPA's gentrification plan for the downtown eastside. *The Mainlander*. Available at: themainlander.com/2010/12/10/visions-gentrification-plan-for-the-downtown-eastside [Accessed 3 Sept. 2016]

Mendez, P. (2017). Linkages between the formal and informal sectors in a Canadian housing market: Vancouver and its secondary suite rentals. *The Canadian Geographer/Le Géographe canadien*, 61(4), pp. 550–563.

McCann, E. (2013). Policy boosterism, policy mobilities, and the extrospective city. *Urban Geography*, 34(1), pp. 5–29.

MSDSI (Ministry of Social Development and Social Innovation). (2008). *Increases to income assistance rate tables*. Available at: www.sd.gov.bc.ca/factsheets/2007/increase_table.htm [Accessed 3 Sept. 2016]

Mösgen, A., Rosol, M., and Schipper, S. (2018). State-led gentrification in previously "un-gentrifiable" areas: Examples from Vancouver/Canada and Frankfurt/Germany. *European Urban and Regional Studies*, 37(4).

Punter, J. (2004). *The Vancouver achievement: Urban planning and design*. Vancouver, Toronto: UBC Press.

Quastel, N. (2009). Political ecology of gentrification. *Urban Geography*, 30(7), pp. 694–725.

Quastel, N., Moos, M., and Lynch, N. (2012). Sustainability-as-density and the return of the social: The case of Vancouver, British Columbia. *Urban Geography*, 33(7), pp. 1055–1084.

Rosol, M. (2013). Vancouver's "EcoDensity" planning initiative: A struggle over hegemony? *Urban Studies*, 50(11), pp. 2238–2255.

Rosol, M. (2015a). Governing cities through participation—A Foucauldian analysis of CityPlan Vancouver. *Urban Geography*, 36(2), pp. 256–276.

Rosol, M. (2015b). Social mixing through densification?: The struggle over the Little Mountain public housing complex in Vancouver. *Die Erde*, 146(2–3), pp. 151–164.

Royal LePage. (2015). House Price Survey: Second Quarter 2015. Available at: www.royallepage.ca/en/realestate/info-and-advice/market-reports-and-surveys [Accessed 3 Sept. 2016]

Smith, H. A. (2003). Planning, policy and polarisation in Vancouver's downtown eastside. *Tijdschrift voor Economische en Sociale Geografie*, 94(4), pp. 496–509.

Somerville, T., and Swann, K. (2008). Are Canadian housing markets over-priced? Centre for Urban Economics and Real Estate. Available at: cuer.sauder.ubc.ca [Accessed 3 Sept. 2016]

Temenos, C., and McCann, E. (2012). The local politics of policy mobility: Learning, persuasion, and the production of a municipal sustainability fix. *Environment and Planning A*, 44(6), pp. 1389–1406.

Thomson, T. M. (2010). The death and life of the little mountain housing project: BC's first public housing community. Unpublished master's thesis, University of British Columbia.

Walia, H. (2011). Vancouver approves Chinatown condo towers, prices out the poor. *The Vancouver Sun*. Available at: blogs.vancouversun.com/2011/04/20/vancouver-approves-chinatown-condo-towers-prices-out-the-poor [Accessed 3 Sept. 2016]

Ward, S. (1999). The international diffusion of planning: A review and a Canadian case study. *International Planning Studies*, 4(1), pp. 53–77.

While, A., Jonas, A., and Gibbs, D. (2004). The environment and the entrepreneurial city: Searching for the urban "sustainability fix" in Manchester and Leeds. *International Journal of Urban and Regional Research*, 28(3), pp. 549–569.

Chapter 7

Introducing Luxembourg

Ephemeral Sustainabilities

Constance Carr

Introduction

Wedged between Germany, France, and Belgium, Luxembourg is tiny and easy to overlook. Even many geographers have to google it first and zoom in to locate it. Yet, it's also, in all likelihood, an integral part of your life, in ways that neither you nor most Luxembourgers are even aware of. If you have sent any airmail to Europe lately, it probably landed in Luxembourg's cargo hub. If you have ordered anything on the European continent from Amazon or Apple Store, it was administered in Luxembourg. If you have purchased Nutella, a Kinder Egg, or a Ferrero Rocher, chatted on Skype, bought anything with PayPal, or downloaded a movie from Netflix, the headquarters of these corporations are in Luxembourg. If you have a bank account at a major bank, it probably has some pseudo-unsecret functioning in Luxembourg. If you have anything at all to do with the European Union, Luxembourg is one the main cities that hosts the administration. It is ironic that, while most have never heard of it, Luxembourg's spatiality is an important node on material global flows of various kinds, and it always has been. The Celtic and Roman early history of present-day Luxembourg can be interpreted as a regional integration, as can later medieval political constellations when the territory of Luxembourg was swapped between ruling royal families

137

(Péporté et al., 2010). After national independence in 1839, cross-border political economic constellations emerged as Luxembourg's steel production industry linked to the German Custom's Union (*Zollverein*). Later, the borders were redrawn again after the French-German war and the two World Wars. Postwar cross-border cooperation also unfolded with Benelux. Cross-border relationships were also institutionally affirmed by the creation of the Summit of the Greater Region (Niedermeyer and Moll, 2007). Luxembourg's permanence is apparently simultaneously nowhere and everywhere—ephemeral. This tour is designed to expose the contradictions of this condition to you, and then to consider sustainability.

I take you on this field trip as someone who immigrated to Luxembourg in 2010, hired by the Department of Geography and Spatial Planning of the University of Luxembourg, and funded by the *Fonds National de la Recherche*, to conduct research on domestic processes sustainable spatial development (research projects named SUSTAINLUX and SUSTAIN_GOV). This tour of Luxembourg is based largely on that research. The goal of this tour is to introduce you to the unusual features that characterize this small state, and then challenge your imaginations of sustainability. There are assumptions of territory and membership in most lay notions of sustainability. Yet, precisely these two components are in short supply in Luxembourg. The question therefore is, what is sustainability in conditions of the ephemeral, and moreover, who does it serve? To borrow a term from Madanipour, the ephemeral is anything but "weightless" (2011). A walk through the City of Luxembourg can show the real and concrete manifestations of a national collective capitalizing on its nodal position in the European Union, the banking industry, global business development, and research and development. This field trip is designed to show you the real geography of how a small state continually recreates itself in flows whose drivers and engines are often beyond its jurisdiction.

I should note that I am not going to give you a tour of the sustainability initiatives. There are, indeed, a variety of cross-societal groups that have been working on various projects to address emissions reduction or mobility or a variety of other socioeconomic and/or environmental problems (Carr, 2011). "L'Empreinte Écologique du Luxembourg" showed that if the entire world lived like the average Luxembourger, twelve planets would be required (Conseil Supérieur pour un Développement Durable and Global Footprint Network, 2010: 6). "Partenariat pour l'environnement et le climat," is a cross-societal initiative to look at ways of reaching climate control goals. Other nongovernmental milieu include, but are not limited to, Friends of the Earth Luxembourg (*Movement Écologique*), Greenpeace, Caritas, Climate Alliance Luxembourg, Action Solidarité Tiers Monde, and the University of Luxembourg, the University of Luxembourg's Sustainable Development Working Group, and the Global Development Rights Framework Luxembourg. Further, a comprehensive list of businesses, active in Luxembourg on the topic of sustainable development in some way, shape, or form, can be found at the website of the Movement Écologique—the organization that hosts annual eco-fairs at the LuxExpo on Kirchberg. At the fair, a wide-ranging variety of actors present their work. Together, these organizations form an extensive network of trade and commerce whose primary objective is the creation and distribution of products that support the objectives of sustainable development defined as the recognition of closed ecosystem circulatory systems and the protection of natural resources (Movement Écologique and Oekozenter Lëtzebuerg, 2010). These organizations are worthy of mention and are proof that sustainability has arrived in Luxembourg (Carr, 2013a). Nevertheless, I want to avoid any voyeuristic academic tour. Furthermore, they all rest on something deeper, and that is the ability to maintain the cornerstones that support them.

Our field trip begins in the City of Luxembourg, on Kirchberg specifically, which is the seat of European Institutions and a number of banks. We will then search out more banks and big business in the Old City and the neighboring party district of Clausen. Thereafter, we will head southward to the new Campus Belval of the University of Luxembourg, before circling back to the Ministry of Sustainable Development and Infrastructures (MDDI) that houses the National Department of Spatial Planning (DATer). These fields will show you the cornerstones of Luxembourg's national sovereign niche strategy that is primarily orchestrated in the City of Luxembourg, and that contrasts with the old, rural, and autonomic municipal life of its citizens, which will be seen at the end of the tour. On our last stop, we can reflect on sustainability over organic champagne on the Mosel River that forms the border between Luxembourg and Germany.

Cornerstone One: the European City

Notwithstanding the observation that calling Luxembourg one of the capitals of the European Union is a highly contested act (Chilla, 2011: 61), offering the plateau of Kirchberg for the institutions of the European Union and hosting its workforce was one of the first pillars of the current sovereign niche strategy of Luxembourg. While clearly the majority of EU offices are located in Brussels, one can find a number of EU institutions on the plateau including the European Investment Bank, the European Investment Fund, the Court of Justice, the European Court of Auditors, the Secretariat of the European Parliament, the Translation Centre, the Euraton Supply Agency, and a European School. Some institutions are also scattered in the City center and elsewhere, such as the Maison de l'Europe or the Euroforum (Chilla, 2009). This labor force is 11,000 strong, second to Brussels, where the number of individuals working in the EU institution is roughly 30,000 (Chilla, 2011: 78). These numbers exclude the families of those individuals.

The decision to bring the European institutions to Luxembourg was made in the 1950s. Ten years before the Treaty of Brussels was signed, Luxembourg held a competition to design a bridge over the Alzette that would connect the Kirchberg with the Old City (Figure 7.1). Expecting to

Figure 7.1. The "Red Bridge" straddling the Alzette Valley and connecting the Kirchberg Plateau with that of the Old City. Photo by Constance Carr (2012).

build a "European City" (*Europastadt*) of 50,000 workers, the Luxembourg government expropriated the formerly agricultural 360-hectare plateau. Of course, given the limited square meters of Luxembourg, there was only a limited number of properties to choose from. That at least was the rational discourse (interviews with government officials, July 2011). Moreover, the arrival of the European institutions was a matter of national significance: municipal boundaries, zoning restrictions, and statutes did not apply, and it was given broad development possibilities (Chilla, 2011: 78). At that time, located outside the city limits and separated from other neighborhoods by the Alzette River valley, the plateau functioned as a sort of exclave: a property serving a particular economic purpose toward the improvement of the state's budget.

In the 1950s, the resident population hovered around 300,000. Fifty thousand new immigrants would have posed significant demands on the existing social arrangement and infrastructure. Today, with a population of just over half a million, the work force of the European Union remains a significant economic engine for the nation—even though the "European City" never transpired (Chilla, 2011). The well-paid work force can afford higher-priced homes and commodities, driving up real estate prices and consumption in general.

Cornerstone Two: Banking District

Aerial views of the plateau show that the European institutions take up only a small fraction of the land originally designated (Chilla, 2011). The built environment that exists today (in 2013) reflects the shift to Luxembourg's second economic pillar, the banking sector. On the plateau, one will also find the Deutsche Bank, Oppenheim, BayernLB, BHW Bausparkasse, BGL BNP Paribas Wealth Management, Clearstream Banking, Commerzbank, DekaBank, EFG Bank, Fortis Banque, HSH Nordbank, UniCredit Luxembourg, Hypo Pfandbrief Bank International, Internaxx Bank, IKB Deutsche Industriebank, SaarLB, Natexis Private Banking, Nordea Bank, Credit Suisse Fund Service, Northern Trust Global Services, State Street, The Bank of TDW & BGL, and the WGZ Bank. More banks are located in the Old City, which is our next stop. Before leaving Kirchberg via the Red Bridge, however, take note of LuxExpo and the otherwise ample office space, and the Findel Airport just behind the plateau. We will return to these again when discussing business development.

The Old City (Figure 7.2) is clearly the banking and business center of the city and nation. Above, only twenty-two banking firms were named. Another hundred or so are located downtown, concentrated primarily along the Boulevard Royal, Avenue de la Liberté, the Boulevard Joseph II, and the few cross streets that link them. In 1994, the highest point was reached with a total of 222 banks (Schulz and Walther, 2009). Consolidations, fusions, and mergers in the later years reduced that figure. As of 2009, the absolute number was 156 (Schulz and Walther, 2009). With this concentration of financial activities, Luxembourg is ranked sixteenth among global financial centers and fifth European-wide (City of London and Z/Yen Group Limited, 2010: 28).

The financial center is not only characterized by banking and investment services but also comprises a variety of insurance companies, legal services, auditing and consulting firms. The finance industry, inclusive of the firms supplying complimentary services, employed about 47,000

Figure 7.2. Old City located on the plateau (upper half of picture), and the the neighbourhood of Grund in the Alzette Valley (lower half and in foreground). Photo by Constance Carr (2012).

workers in 2006 (Schulz and Walther, 2009). Many of these firms located in the neighborhoods of Grund (see Figure 7.2) and Clausen, fostering upscaling and gentrification in neighborhoods that were formerly working class. This upscaling has also contributed to an influx of entertainment and gastronomy industry in these neighborhoods, such as the revamping of an old brewery to house clubs and restaurants (Figure 7.3).

Together, the financial and associated service industries constitute 40 percent of the nation's gross domestic product (Schulz and Walther, 2009). Tax revenues from these industries thus form an important cornerstone of Luxembourg's national budget. Surprisingly, the financial crisis of 2008 affected Luxembourg less severely than other financial centers. This is likely due to the specific forms of banking that are common in Luxembourg, which have little to do with the subprime crisis. Still, the crisis ignited fears that the banking sector could no longer continue as a central strong pillar of Luxembourg's economy. When asked about the

Figure 7.3. Revamping of an old brewery in the neighbourhood of Clausen, in the Alzette Valley. Photo by Constance Carr (2012).

biggest challenges facing Luxembourg, many SUSTAINLUX interviewees immediately referred to Luxembourg's ability to adapt or how Luxembourg will restructure (see table 7.1). This widespread uncertainty has thus fed a need to pay more attention to different sources of national revenue: the third and fourth pillars of Luxembourg's economy.

Cornerstone Three: International Business

I will discuss Luxembourg as an attractive place for international business development first, although it is likely the most recent and least reliable cornerstone. I will touch on it here because most of this is located in the City of Luxembourg, where we currently stand. As mentioned in the introduction, some of the giant international companies have settled their headquarters in Luxembourg. Figure 7.4 shows the cobblestone laneway that houses the elusive headquarters of Amazon Europe. While there is an increasing number of big names, a multitude of smaller businesses can also be identified. Many of these exist as mailbox companies: firms that have little more than an address in Luxembourg. It is not uncommon to

Table 7.1. Quotes from SUSTAINLUX Interviewees Concerning the Challenges that Luxembourg Faces

"How well Luxembourg manages to become less dependent of its financial sector. That's for sure that's the biggest [challenge]."

"I wonder if the financial center, in its current form, still has any legitimacy [and] if that motor isn't there, then all the [spatial] development processes turn upside down."

"I think it is really a major challenge for us to develop other fiscal incomes in order to make it possible to become independent."

"The biggest challenge is our banks because they change. We are depending on them—39 percent. Imagine that one year they are not making a profit: Then we collapse. We are too much depending from our banks. [. . .] For me, these are the vast dangers here in Luxembourg."

"It is also very clear that in the very future, we cannot rely on 40 percent of the national tax income coming from the banking center."

Figure 7.4. Home of European Amazon headquarters. Photo by Constance Carr (2012).

find dozens or even hundreds of mailboxes in the foyer of office buildings that serve as addresses for company headquarters. Many businesses are located in the downtown Old City districts, and their relocation to Luxembourg is fostered by the internationally competitive low level of taxes demanded by the national government. Ultimately, a nation requires less tax revenue when their primary expenditures are those of a welfare state that serves a mere half million.

Since the financial and Euro crisis, more and more businesses have taken up residence in Luxembourg. Moreover, an increasing number is taking up more floorage. This has put a lot of pressure on an already tight real estate market. Developments such as the Cloche D'Or, an office complex that offers over 490,000 square meters of office space, are indications of the new product that Luxembourg has to offer: office space (Hesse and Carr, 2013; Hesse, 2013). Similarly, LuxExpo, on the Kirchberg plateau, is an exhibition and congress center that has 33,000 square meters of showing space, and nine conference rooms. These developments are also arising near major transport arteries. Cloche D'Or sits next to a major highway cloverleaf south of the City, and as you may remember from earlier, LuxExpo is right next to the Findel Airport. These are signs of an emerging cornerstone that Luxembourgian officials may be in the process of developing. Time will tell if this takes foot.

Cornerstone Four: The Knowledge Economy

The last cornerstone of the economy is the so-called knowledge economy (Hesse, 2013: 22), of which the newly founded University of Luxembourg is a central part. The university was founded in 2003, and the research areas of focus reflect, at least in part, Luxembourg's niche strategy: international finance; security, reliability and trust in information technology; systems biomedicine; European and business law; and education and learning in multilingual and multicultural contexts. These programs of study are designed, on one hand, to attract an international research community, and on the other hand, to expand possibilities of postsecondary training for the domestic work force. At the moment, research is divided across three campuses located in different parts of the country.

In 2014, many of the research units along with a variety of other smaller independent research institutions planned to relocate to Belval

Figure 7.5. Belval Campus. Photo by Constance Carr (2018).

Campus, at the time under construction. As a former coal and steel production plant of Arcelor Mittal, Belval is a classic example of a brownfield reconversion site. The new science city hereby fulfilled the goal to find a use for a property that housed an industry in continual decline. It was also an example of what Hesse has called the Kirchberg Syndrome: the tendency to engage in projects in enormous dimensions relative to the size and capacities of the small state (2013). On a property of 125 hectares and the construction of 1.3 million square meters of floorage, Belval will be host to 7,000 new inhabitants and between 20 and 25 thousand workers (Hesse, 2013). The ambitions are indeed reminiscent of Europa City. At the same time, they are signals of the commitment that Luxembourgian officials are making toward the development of a new sector in the domestic economy. This is also confirmed in the local media coverage on the topic.

The Managing Bodies

We can now turn back to Place de l'Europe on the Kirchberg plateau, where the Ministry of Sustainable Development and Infrastructure (*Ministère du Développement durable et des Infrastructures*, MDDI) is located. It occupies one of the taller buildings on Kirchberg, and from the offices of the higher floors, one can view a large portion of the country and possibly beyond. Looking westward, the impression is one of a small historical city in the foreground and green hills rolling off into the horizon in all directions. While one may view a handful of construction cranes in the foreground, one is not left with the image of intense urbanization. Rather, in a an almost spooky way, it can be interpreted as symbolizing the ability of the national government to govern from above while preserving the nestled, green and pristine, and cozy little nation community.

The MDDI is one of nineteen Ministries of the Luxembourgian government, and thereby, of course, not the sole body coordinating development in the country. However, the objective of the four departments of the MDDI is to work together toward the implementation of a transversal politic of sustainable development. These are the Department of Public Works, the Department of Transport, the Department of the Environment, and the Department of Urban and Regional Planning. The latter two are the specific bodies that generate integrative and sustainable development strategies. Respectively, they produced the "National Plan for Sustainable Development," (*Programme National pour un Développement Durable*,

PNDD) (Ministerium für Nachhaltige Entwicklung und Infrastrukturen and Spangenberg, 2011) that identified emerging problematic trends in Luxembourg framed within the three pillars of sustainable development, and the "Directive Program for Urban and Regional Planning" (*Programme Directeur de l'Aménagement du Territoire*, PDAT) (Ministère de l'Intérieur, 2003) that concerned sustainable development with respect to the spatial arrangement of development. While it is clear that these documents targeted polarization trends in Luxembourg with respect to growth conditions of a tight housing market, automobile dependence, and social fragmentation, they can also be interpreted as an attempt to steer political economic and spatial development according to national agendas. As seen above, this entails managing the small state's economic dependence on international and European interrelations.

It may be worth noting at this point that, with the exception of one electoral period, the Christian Social People's Party (*Chrëschtlech-Sozial Vollekspartei*, CSV) has held office since World War II. National programs thus reflect that social political economic agenda, and not necessarily those of other voices that are seldom represented at that governing level. The municipalities are one such voice, as the CSV is underrepresented in municipal administrations. Rather, the Democratic Party (*Demokratesch Partei*, DP), the Greens (*déi Gréng*), or the Luxembourgish Socialist Workers Party (*Luxemburger Sozialistische Arbeiterpartei*, LSAP) often hold municipal office. Moreover, the 106 municipalities enjoy a high degree of municipal autonomy. Municipal Councils retain significant regulatory powers that include police regulations, infrastructure for primary education and child care facilities, water supply, sewage, road maintenance, looking after civil registries, and administering social assistance. Until 2004, they also oversaw the planning and urban development, which was further bounded by individual private property rights. In 2004, Parliament decided that the municipalities should further oversee the completion of official city plans (*Plan d'Aménagement General*, PAG) and zoning laws (*Plan d'Aménagement Particulier*, PAP). The national government, however, would have control of the approval process.

The national government thus faces the challenge of negotiating a consensus for its agenda with the municipalities. Instituting the PAG and PAP process was one attempt. It is also claimed that the PDAT, once passed in Parliament, will anchor sustainable spatial development in law. However, ten years have passed since their making. A revised PDAT is on the horizon, but legal enforcement is yet to arise. This is, in part, attributed to the highly fragmented character of the nation, where municipal institutions are reluctant to forfeit their autonomous rights in order to adhere to an agenda that does not necessarily reflect their own. It thus remains unclear how the national government's vision of sustainable development will be realized—and if it is even desirable.

Private property, one of the hallmarks of Luxembourgian land use, is another piece of the puzzle worthy of mention. According to my interviewees, it was decided sometime after World War II that private property was the path toward the greatest level of individual and group satisfaction. Further, while land values are very high in Luxembourg, private landowners remain the gatekeepers to land use. Even though the national government ultimately decides how land should be designated, landowners must want to sell if anything is to happen at all. As it is, globalpropertyguide.com lists Luxembourg as the sixth most expensive city in Europe in terms of apartment price per square meter. According to www.athome.lu, the website with the largest listings of home sales, over 5,000 single-family homes and 9,300 apartments are up for sale, more than half of which are in the planning stages. If all the planned housing units were realized in a short period of time, prices would likely go down, and the stability of the high-price market would probably be disrupted. Developers thus play an important mitigating role, as do the mayors, who decide which properties may be turned into building land, and the national government, which approves those decisions. While this characterizes land use in Luxembourg, it is not a game that is, by any means, unique. In Portugal, 200,000 million Euros were earned from the conversion of 100,000 Ha of rural land into urban space (Bingre, 2013). Unfortunately, corresponding figures for Luxembourg have not yet been published. This is a process that is anything but transparent, and its trajectory can barely be foreseen. It is, therefore, difficult to know how sustainable development strategies of any sort will proceed.

Ephemeral Sustainability?

Our final stop concludes our tour. At a winery along the Mosel River, we can rest and reflect on the subject of sustainability in Luxembourg. It's a lovely spot: the scenery is green, the wine is organic, and the grapes are grown on century-old vine fields that Romans carved out of the mountainsides. Given the rather rural landscape of the immediate vicinity, many might not agree that I just gave you an urban tour. Yet, just as Diener and colleagues demonstrated how the entire Swiss landscape—from St. Gallen to Saas-Fee—is integrated into one urban system, so is Luxembourg (2013). The residents, from the Ardennes to the Mosel Valley system, all depend on the economic building blocks set by the national government. We can thus think about how the five cornerstones have contributed to the standard of living in Luxembourg. We can then consider what sustainability means in Luxembourg, who it is for, and what some of the dilemmas are that lie therein.

More than a few of my interviewees noted that Luxembourgers were, in general, quite satisfied and do not feel the need to change anything. The fact seems to be that, for a large majority of the population, the real and concrete life inside Luxembourg is good. Forty percent of the Luxembourger citizens are very well-paid employees in the public sector (Chambre de Commerce, 2012). Public school teachers, for example, rank among the best paid in their profession—public primary school teachers earn more than double the OECD average (OECD, 2007). Another 50 percent of citizens do not need to work at all (Chambre de Commerce, 2012). Every resident in Luxembourg is well insured through the intact and cushy welfare state. The problem is, consequently, that Luxembourgers do not feel the need for a sustainability correction. Despite any, or perhaps because of, internal strife, the cornerstones of the economy have functioned well, and have generated a state budget that other nations only dream of. What then is there to change? Those with decision-making capacity do not seem to see a problem.

Yet, if there is one thing that research in Luxembourg shows, it is how profoundly intertwined in, and reliant on, external and international flows a nation can be (Affolderbach, 2013; Becker and Hesse, 2010; Bousch et al. 2009; Carr and Hesse, 2013; Chilla, 2011; Chilla and Schulz, 2011; Leick, 2009; OECD, 2007; Wille, 2012). The cross-national urban agglomeration of Luxembourg thus raises some questions of sustainability, particularly with respect to the pillar of social sustainability: Who may be the beneficiaries of Luxembourgish sustainability? Mirroring the labor statistics of Luxembourg citizens are those of residents and commuters. According to the Chambre de Commerce, the number of jobs has doubled, and the number of cross-border commuters has almost quintupled over the past twenty years (2012). Seventy-five percent of business entrepreneurs do not have citizenship. In the private sector, that number is at 71 percent. Overall, 43 percent of residents have only landed immigrant status. There is thus a clear social stratification, where citizens are more privileged than residents, and both of these are privileged over cross-border laborers. This third group is also growing, as Luxembourgers who are unable to afford the high-priced housing emigrate to the border regions (Affolderbach and Carr, 2014; Becker and Hesse, 2010). This social stratification is relevant because it raises questions of "who," as there is a clear advantage for those at the top of the hierarchy; however, it also raises spatial issues. Should sustainability objectives target places within a certain jurisdiction, such as the nation-state of Luxembourg (and the demos within)? Or should Luxembourgian politicians target beyond their borders as well? Beyond the border, of course, would normally be the jurisdiction of the neighboring state; there is thus a contradiction and dilemma.

A look into literature on the political economy of small states or island states is illuminating to understand Luxembourg (Grydehøj, 2011). It is small indeed, and bordered by a national boundary. It also resembles an island, to which people either escape, get stranded on, or, indeed, rescued from. The problems that affect small states are unique and often overlooked in the literature (Lorig and Hirsch, 2008). One condition is their apparent ephemerality. When confronted about the complex set of issues facing Luxembourg with respect to sustainability within the context of the SUSTAINLUX research (Carr and Hesse, 2013; Carr, 2013b)—performed as a Delphi-like qualitative research methodology—sustainability was, in part, seen as the small state's broader response to change in a volatile set of political economic conditions. Yet, even if the strategies are successful and the result seems to be a luxurious paradise to outsiders, there is still a grain of suffering that comes along with the knowledge that the success is transient and volatile. In such an environment, it is difficult to develop reliable, long-term strategic plans, or coherent structures of democratic participation, as the stakeholders, too, are in flux. While the current political economic conditions are relatively new, the fleetingness is not. Its importance on international flows may be growing. It may also be short-lived. As a result, nobody knows what will happen in the next five, ten, or twenty years.

The Brundtland Report, *Our Common Future* (United Nations, 1987: 54), hallmarked for the first time sustainable development as a worthy international objective, and it became a moniker and framework that would be further developed in later meetings, such as in Rio de Janeiro (United Nations, 1992), the Johannesburg Summit (United Nations, 2003), and the Framework Convention for Climate Change (United Nations Framework

Convention on Climate Change, 1992), to name a few. Luxembourg, too, followed suit, and sustainable development was placed at the forefront of development policy initiatives. Many of the examples named in the introduction aim to respect the three pillars of sustainability (Carr, 2011). The ability for Luxembourg to follow up on its international commitment, however, depends on its ability to subsist, and this is anything but easy. The only thing that is clear is that Luxembourg will have to continue to adjust and morph according to wider international political economic flows. It is illusory to assume that Luxembourg could shut its borders and self-subsist. One participant in the Delphi-round even commented that it was precisely this ability to react and morph that characterizes Luxembourg's advantage (Carr, 2013b). Will the banking sector slowly or suddenly collapse, leaving Luxembourg with a 40 percent reduction in its GNP? Will European politics continue to scale upward and concentrate in European Union establishments (which would likely be good for Luxembourg), or will the Euro crisis continue, weakening those establishments? Will business continue to flourish? Will the knowledge sector take hold? Will Luxembourg find a way to buffer the change and protect its cornerstones? Or will it find another source of income altogether? These are open questions. Time will tell. Sustainability, eager as it might be, will simply have to wait.

References

Affolderbach, J. (2013). Negotiating border regions: Retail development in Luxembourg and the greater region. In: P. Gilles, H. Koff, C. Maganda, and C. Schulz, eds., *Theorizing Borders through Analyses of Power Relationships*, 1st ed. Brussels: Peter Lang, pp. 125–148.

Affolderbach, J., and Carr, C. (2014). Blending scales of governance: Land-use policies and practices in the small state of Luxembourg. *Regional Studies*, 50(6), pp. 944–955.

Becker, T., and Hesse, M. (2010). Internationalisierung und Steuerung metropolitaner Wohnungsmärkte: Das Beispiel Luxemburg. *Informationen zur Raumentwicklung*, 5(6), pp. 1–13.

Bousch, P., Chilla, T., Gerber, P., Klein, O., Schulz, C., Sohn, C. and Wiktorin, D., eds. (2009). *Der Luxemburg Atlas—Atlas du Luxembourg*, 1st ed. Calbe: Hermann-Josef Emons Verlag.

Carr, C. (2011). Luxembourg sustainable spatial development policy: General milestones and circuits, working paper 2. Luxembourg: Institute of Geography and Spatial Planning of the University of Luxembourg.

Carr, C. (2013a). Discourse yes, implementation maybe: An immobility and paralysis of sustainable development policy. *European Planning Studies*, 22(9), pp. 1824–1840.

Carr, C. (2013b). Report of stakeholder workshop, working paper 5. Luxembourg: Institute of Geography and Spatial Planning of the University of Luxembourg.

Carr, C., and Hesse, M. (2013). Implications of results, working paper 6. Luxembourg: Institute of Geography and Spatial Planning of the University of Luxembourg.

Chilla, T. (2009). Luxemburg in Europa: Prominente Position eines kleinen Staates. In: P. Bousch, T. Chilla, P. Gerber, O. Klein, C. Schulz, C. Sohn, and D. Wiktorin, eds., *Der Luxemburg Atlas—Atlas du Luxembourg*, 1st ed. Calbe: Hermann-Josef Emons Verlag, pp. 14–15.

Chilla, T. (2011). *Punkt, Linie, Fläche: Territorialisierte Europäisierung. Habilitationsschrift*. Saarbrücken: Universität des Saarlandes.

Chilla, T., and Schulz, C. (2011). *Raumordnung in Luxemburg—Aménagement du territoire au Luxembourg*. Luxembourg: Binsfeld.

City of London and Z/Yen Group Limited. (2010). Global financial centres 7. Available at: 217.154.230.218/NR/rdonlyres/661216D8-AD60-486B-A96F-EE75BB61B28A/0/BC_RS_GFC7full.pdf [Accessed 3 Sept. 2016]

Conseil Supérieur pour un Développement Durable and Global Footprint Network. (2010). *L'Empreinte écologique du Luxembourg*. Available at: www.myfootprint.lu/ [Accessed 3 Sept. 2016]

Diener, R., Herzog, J., Meili, M., de Meuron, P., and Schmid, C. (2013). *Switzerland—An urban portrait*. Basel: Birkhauser Verlag AG.

Grydehøj, A. (2011). Making the most of smallness: Economic policy in microstates and sub-national island jurisdictions. *Space and Polity*, 15(3), pp. 183–196.

Hesse, M. (2013). Das „Kirchberg-Syndrom": Grosse Projekte im kleinen Land. Bauen und Planen in Luxemburg. *DISP—The Planning Review*, 49(1), pp. 14–28.

Hesse, M., and Carr, C. (2013). Integration vs. fragmentation: Spatial governance for land and mobility (extended abstract). In: M. Hesse, G. Caruso, P. Gerber, and F. Viti, eds., *Proceedings of the BIVEC-GIBET Transport Research Days 2013*, 1st ed. Luxembourg: BIVEC-GIBET, pp. 379–381.

Leick, A. (2009). Suburbanisierung: Wenn die Stadt ins Umland wächst. In: P. Bousch, T. Chilla, P. Gerber, O. Klein, C. Schulz, C. Sohn, and D. Wiktorin, eds., *Der Luxemburg Atlas—Atlas du Luxembourg*, 1st ed. Calbe: Hermann-Josef Emons Verlag, pp. 52–53.

Lorig, W., and Hirsch, M. (2008). *Das politische System Luxemburgs: Eine Einführung*. Wiesbaden: VS Verlag für Sozialwissenschaften.

Madanipour, A. (2011). *Knowledge economy and the city: Spaces of knowledge*. London, New York: Routledge.

Ministère de l'Intérieur. (2003). Programme Directeur D'Amenagement du Territoire. Le Gouvernement du Grand-Duché de Luxembourg. [online] Available at: www.miat.public.lu/publications/amenagement_territoire/index.html [Accessed 3 Sept. 2016]

Movement Écologique and Oekozenter Lëtzebuerg. (2010). *Gesamtregister Aussteller 2010 Registre des Exposants 2010*. Available at: oekofoire.oeko.lu/ [Accessed 3 Sept. 2016]

Niedermeyer, M., and Moll, P. (2007). SaarLorLux—Vom Montandreieck zur 'Großregion.' In: H.P.P. Dörrenbächer, O. Kühne, and J.M.M. Wagner, eds., *50 Jahre Saarland im Wandel*, 1st ed. Saarbrücken: IfLiS, pp. 297–321.

OECD (Organisation for Economic Co-operation and Development). (2007). *OECD territorial reviews: Luxembourg*. Paris: OECD Publishing.

Péporté, P., Kmec, S., Majerus, B., and Margue, M. (2010). *Inventing Luxembourg: Representations of the past, space and language from the nineteenth to the twenty-first century*. Leiden & Boston: Brill.

Schulz, C., and Walther, O. (2009). Finanzplatz Luxemburg. In: P. Bousch, T. Chilla, P. Gerber, O. Klein, C. Schulz, C. Sohn, and D. Wiktorin, eds., *Der Luxemburg Atlas—Atlas du Luxembourg*, 1st ed. Calbe: Hermann-Josef Emons Verlag, pp. 130–133.

United Nations. (1987). Report of the World Commission on Environment and Development: Our Common Future. Available at: www.un.org [Accessed 3 Sept. 2016]

United Nations. (1992). Earth Summit Agenda 21: The United Nations Programme of Action from Rio. Available at: www.un.org [Accessed 3 Sept. 2016]

United Nations. (2003). Johannesburg Plan of Implementation: World Summit on Sustainable Development. Available at: www.wsscc.org [Accessed 3 Sept. 2016]

United Nations Framework Convention on Climate Change. (1992). *United Nations: Climate Change*. Available at: unfccc.int [Accessed 3 Sept. 2016]

Wille, C. (2012). *Grenzgänger und Räume der Grenze: Raumkonstruktionen in der Großregion SaarLorLux*. Brussels: Peter Lang GmbH.

Chapter 8

Montpellier Écocité

From Growth Machine to Sustainability?

David Giband

Introduction

Welcome aboard this streetcar! Be sure you've got your e-ticket: no coins or tickets here. Use your smart phone, tablet, or laptop to validate your ticket in the Montpellier public transportation system. Let me guide you through the *Écocité* (Eco-city) of Montpellier, France, named "De Montpellier à la mer" ("From Montpellier to the sea"). I have to tell you that it will be a virtual visit. The project, to be completed by the year 2020, will be one of the most ambitious urban sustainable districts in the country (Table 8.1). It seeks to transform a part of the eastern Montpellier suburbs into a "nature city," one of a new generation of eco-tech cities and an urban laboratory open to citizen participation for social and environmental well-being. Before leaving, take your time and please have a look at the official Écocité website and videos.[1] I'm David Giband, geographer at the University of Perpignan, and your guide today. The tour will take us from Montpellier to the sea along the new streetcar line number 3, the easiest way to discover the Écocité. On our way, we will have four stops to explore this vast project (see roadmap, Figure 8.1, pg. 156).

Table 8.1. Some Indicators about the Ecocité

Housing units in eco-construction	15,000
Public housing units	37,500
Inhabitants expected	50,000
Offices (in square meters)	300,000
Renewable energies	80%
Ecocité Area (in acres)	900
Park and recreation areas (in acres)	500

Source: Ville de Montpellier, 2015.

Field Trip

Montpellier Écocité

Écocité is a national label given by the French Ministry of Ecology to nine urban sustainable development projects after a competition launched in 2009. Montpellier Écocité was the first to be labeled and is presented as a pioneer in the national Écocité program. It is a joint project of the Montpellier metropolitan authority, the French state, a public bank (*Caisse des dépôts et consignations*), research centers (*Pôle mondial de l'eau*, CIRAD), four local municipalities,[2] and major private companies involved in environmental business (Veolia), computing (IBM), health (Sanofi), sewer and water supply (BRL, ERGIS eau), and energy (ERDF). The objective is to build "tomorrow's digital eco-city"[3] on the basis of new public–private partnerships.[4] In this attractive city (each year 6,000 newcomers settle in the town; Table 8.2) located in the south of France, newcomers (50,000 inhabitants are expected) will live in social and generationally mixed neighborhoods built according to soft mobility and eco-technology principles. On the other hand, the project proposes to transform a ten-mile commercial area—consisting of low-quality shopping

Table 8.2. A Young and Growing City

Population (metropolitan area), 2011	457,839
Population under 35 years old	50%
Average annual growth rate (population, 2006–2011)	1%

Source: Ville de Montpellier, 2015.

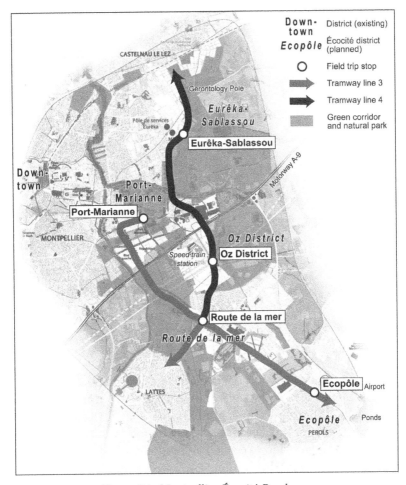

Figure 8.1. Montpellier Écocité Roadmap.

malls[5] and fallow agricultural land along both sides of the highway connecting Montpellier to the Mediterranean Sea—into an urban sustainable development laboratory (Figure 8.2). The challenge is to set the standards for further urbanization by remodeling sprawling suburbs according to the concept of sustainability. This "living lab"[6]—as it is called by its promoters—is an ambitious project: "The goal is to conceive a model city for the 21st century: participatory, innovative and smart."[7] Three major principles form the basic structure of the whole project: an interconnected and smart city, soft mobility, and a new way of living together. In this

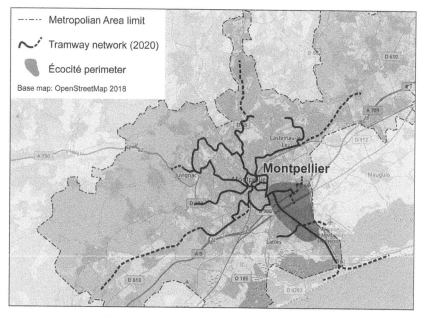

Figure 8.2. Location of Montpellier Écocité.

"nature city," urbanization is organized around streetcar stops, with large open spaces, public facilities, and new smart services. The guiding idea is to create an urban environment founded on a "networked nature city" where streetcar lines link "islands of urbanization" separated by natural parks and green corridors. Écocité has been described as a sustainable and digital mode of urbanization where eco-technologies "will draw tomorrow's model city." Eco-technologies figure at the heart of the project ("a smart Ecocity," says the press kit),[8] concerning three major domains: flood regulation, water supply, and energy economy and transfer. The purpose is to design a city fully adapted to the Mediterranean climate (with regular floods in spring and fall, and heatwaves in the summer). In order to respond to this challenge, many technological solutions will be implemented (use of solar energy, smart systems for energy performance, free energy exchanges between districts), helping to build a zero-carbon Écocité. A smart grid will optimize energy management, producing, consuming, and distributing energy according to a free-exchange deal between users and producers in the Écocité area. When an important energy user, such as the speed train station or the airport, has an energy surplus, it will redirect it to other users in the area (housing, office, or retail buildings) without any fee.

Four new districts, located between green corridors and natural parks, form the Écocité and lead the way to its urbanization: Route de la mer, Oz, Eurêka-Sablassou (also named "Pôle gérontologie"), and Écopôle (see Figure 8.1). In all of these four districts, urban planners and city officials point to the rise of a new urban way of life characterized by ecology of proximity, positive densification, and social use of smart technologies. Ecology of proximity refers to new social relationships built on daily interaction and routines between neighbors who share the same environment and take part actively in governance and sustainability. Positive densification has to do with both a more compact sort of urbanization around streetcar stops and positive externalities expected through the construction of low-energy buildings and districts. In the Écocité, urbanization is concentrated around a network of soft mobility hubs (streetcar stops, bicycle and pedestrian paths) according to transit-oriented development (TOD) techniques used in North America and Europe. Networking is also an argument in favor of more compact urbanization in a region where urban sprawl traditionally prevails. Eco-technologies, widely used and promoted in this Écocité, are envisioned for social use. For instance, energy monitoring and performance are intended as a benefit for the occupants of each building and neighborhood. Écocité is viewed as an urban technical laboratory for eco-technologies that serve people. As a smart city, it reinforces innovation and shares capacities of information in order to optimize and rationalize the use of natural and energetic resources and to enrich the services offered to citizens.

A Trip by Streetcar to the "Route de la Mer": Écocité, Smart City

Let's now move to 2020! We are leaving Richter streetcar stop in Port Marianne, a large eco-district built between 1989 and 2009 at the periphery of the city in order to open the way for further extensions from the east side of Montpellier toward the Mediterranean Sea. Port Marianne, violently contested in the 1990s (it was seen as an annexation of suburban municipalities by Montpellier), is today considered as the starting point of the Écocité. Right now, we are moving down the avenue Raymond Dugrand to the "route de la mer" district (see Figures 8.1 and 8.2), the first stop on our virtual trip. This avenue was named in honor of the former deputy

mayor, Raymond Dugrand (1977–2001), a geographer and the kingpin of
Montpellier urban development in the 1980s and 1990s. Here, streetcar line
3 functions as the backbone of the Écocité for six kilometers (Figure 8.3).
It serves as the main axis of the metropolitan soft mobility network, linking
old and new Montpellier, connecting streetcar lines with pedestrian and
bicycle paths, and serving as a guideline for further urbanization in this
strategic area. The avenue Raymond Dugrand has been cited as a model
for a more generally interconnected city, linking all kinds of transportation:
speed train (arriving in the north in the new speed train station of the
Oz district), streetcar lines, bicycles, and pedestrian paths. This network
connects the avenue to surrounding new residential areas and also to car-
friendly routes to the airport on the south side of the Écocité. As Jean-
Pierre Moure, president of the Montpellier Metropolitan authority in the
2010s, once said in a local newspaper, "this avenue has to maximize all
kind of surface transportation." Along this avenue, the landscape has been
reshaped. See how ugly shopping malls have been replaced by mixed-use
buildings (Figures 8.4 and 8.5)! A pedestrian-friendly environment using a

Figure 8.3. Street car line 3, flagship of the Écocité. Photo by David Giband (2018).

Figure 8.4. The suburban mall landscape. Photo by David Giband (2018).

Figure 8.5. Mixed-used buildings under construction. Photo by David Giband (2018).

"rambla" style for sidewalks and public spaces has replaced huge parking lots used by former shopping malls. This is the first time in France that a commercial corridor has been transformed into a public space devoted to soft mobility. "Violently urbanized in the 1970s"—according to Bernard Reichen, the architect in charge of this restructuring—the road to the sea was basically conceived as a major route to bring tourists to the city, with service facilities and retails along a highway, making urban sprawl easier.

EURÊKA-SABLASSOU: LIVING LAB, SOCIAL LAB

Let's move on to our second stop: Eurêka-Sablassou (a district devoted to gerontology), an illustration of how the social is to be conceived and understood in a sustainable Écocité. Here promoters are fostering social and intergenerational mixes for a new sort of urban life and social relationships. According to the president of the metropolitan authority, the Écocité design relies on "innovative and sustainable practices serving people" in order "to prepare a human and user-friendly city in which the citizen is the true actor of the city transformation" (Moure, 2016). Concretely, the social is considered in terms of mixed housing programs (a quarter of all housing units, i.e., about 15,000 apartments) and as a bunch of architectural and technological innovations serving the whole population as a "living lab" designed in cooperation with big companies (like IBM, Veolia). First, the social refers to the "social use of new eco-technologies." This "living lab" offers technical solutions to local sustainability issues, mainly in the areas of flood regulation (alert by SMS), water and energy supply (monitoring by a smart grid), and soft mobility. The social appropriation of these eco-technologies will define new relationships, create solidarity, and foster a new sense of place based on the self and on the local management of sustainability issues (i.e., flood alerts and energy monitoring).

Second, since the 1980s and the implementation of the "politique de la ville" (national program for the renovation of social housing neighbor-hoods, or "la banlieue"), the social has referred to a social mix, following national urban policies. Not surprisingly, social mix is here understood as a mix of different kinds of housing in the same neighborhood. Each real estate program has to include a certain amount of subsidized public housing (usually 25 percent). Rather than a mix of people from different origins, social classes, or backgrounds sharing the same neighborhood, the social is understood here in arithmetical terms. This leads to confusion between social mix and housing mix—or between people and types of housing. This leaves little room for considerations such as social diversity or social practices relating to places and housing. The theory is that a housing mix will generate a social or intergenerational mix.

Here we are! Let's get off at this stop. In Eurêka-Sablassou, a "new concept" drives sustainable social urban planning: the vertical mix. Vertical mix refers to a traditional type of building organization where stores are located on the first floor and apartments of different sizes and status (public, private, and intergenerational) on the upper levels. This is supposed to be socially fair and just, increasing social interaction and fostering a new sense of place. This sense of place has disappeared in French residential suburbs, where individualism and small houses reign. Encouraging a vertical mix is seen as a way of reviving a Mediterranean type of city. However, the vertical mix as a social or intergenerational mix, core of the Eurêka-Sablassou district philosophy, sounds more like a real estate project focusing on specific customers: seniors, aging, and disabled people (with clinics, exclusive condominiums, and gated communities). Let me point out that a third of all newcomers in Montpellier are retired people looking for a sunny and convenient place to live. On the first floor of these buildings you won't find small stores recalling a street-corner society, but small franchise retail complexes using new commercial marketing tools. Curiously, advertisements in local newspapers do not point out intergenerational mixing but instead underline the high-energy performance of the high-rise buildings for luxury condominiums.

The Inheritance of George Frêche: From Urban Growth Machine to the Écocité

You wonder if Écocité is a new project? Well, not exactly. It continues an urban master plan dating from the late 1970s when mayor George Frêche (1997–2004), in the manner of bossism, set out to transform a medium-sized city into an "innovative metropolitan area," with the aim of connecting the city to the sea ten miles away. Beginning with the construction of the Antigone district (1977), and later with the Port Marianne district (1989), Frêche prepared the ground for transforming Montpellier into an urban growth machine, multiplying architectural projects and new neighborhoods designed by star architects, such as Ricardo Bofill (Antigone district), Zaha Hadid (archives building), Jean Nouvel (new city hall), Massimiliano and Doriana Fuksas (school of hotel management), and many others. Since that period, urban planning has fostered technological, architectural, and urban innovation, following an urban growth strategy that seeks to attract research centers, high-tech firms, and creative classes to this celebrated French Sun Belt city. Discovering Montpellier Écocité after the 2009 competition, the national press described Montpellier as "the city where architects never sleep" (La tribune des métropoles, 2012: 4). This underlines an urban growth strategy deeply rooted in the image of an urban and architectural laboratory. In 1985, George Frêche referred to "Montpellier, the gifted city." So you can easily understand that communication is not only an important part of the Écocité project—it is embedded in a strategy and urban image dating from the 1980s. This strategy has accompanied contemporary urban change and has constantly shaped the local urban image, from a discourse valuing a "gifted city" to another discourse centering on an "eco-model city" at the turn of the twenty-first century. In the 1980s and 1990s, image, environmental issues, and representation already played an important role. Moreover, Écocité is a continuation and expansion of some former contested operations, such as Port Marianne, intended to connect the city to the sea. Écocité renews the urban image emphasizing quality of life, a Sun Belt location, and a creative city open to innovation. Please look at Figures 8.6 and 8.7.

Far from the official text highlighting a "model city for the 21st century," many voices are opposed to a project that is seen as a communication tool for city leaders. They criticize weak citizen involvement, poor sustainability, and gentrification. According to the local ecologist party, Europe Écologie Les Verts (EELV), "citizens have been faced with a fait accompli." Dialogue and citizen involvement have been lost in communication actions intended to create a "zero protest Écocité" (a joke referring to the concept of a "zero carbon Écocité"). Despite the election of the former deputy mayor, Hélène Mandroux,[9] as new mayor for the period 2004 to 2014, megalomania and lack of consideration for citizen participation continued to characterize urban governance in Montpellier. This situation has remained unchanged since then. Today, mayor Philippe Saurel[10] (former socialist candidate), is also described by opponents as an autocrat. The local political scene, from the conservative party to EELV and the left-wing parties, has regularly pointed out this lack of democracy. The emphasis on public consultation and the use of interactive promotion tools do not hide what is considered as a "pure real estate project," a project with the aim of housing newcomers in high-tech neighborhoods and expensive condominiums, creating the image of a "nonstop innovative city."

Figure 8.6. A billboard valuating the quality of life. Photo by David Giband (2018).

Figure 8.7. Eurêka, research and business park. Photo by David Giband (2018).

Approaching the Oz District:
A New Home for the Creative Class

Environmentalist groups and neighborhood coalitions have brought up most of the criticism. Ecologists specifically target the Oz district, which is considered as a "pure real estate and speculative action"[11] with the goal of attracting new gentrifiers. But let's return to the streetcar and I will explain as we travel to our third stop, the Oz district. The Oz district is considered a masterpiece of the Écocité project. Presented as a new approach to urban and sustainability issues in Mediterranean cities, it promotes the idea of "urban comfort," emphasizing both high-quality landscapes and citizen involvement. This vast new district will be devoted to nature and business: of the 900 acres of land, 500 will be used for parks and recreational spaces (see Table 8.1). Besides a new speed train station, low-energy buildings containing apartments, stores, and offices are to be located inside green parks and natural corridors. Landscapes of high quality, with natural parks and green corridors, and preserving bio-diversity, are the keystone of "new hybrid urban forms" that will establish new relationships between city and nature.

The Oz district focuses on low-energy buildings, but also on expansive condominiums. Private investors like to compare Oz to New York City Central Park, both because of the park landscape and because of the expected population: managers, executives, researchers, and the like. Thus, the future inhabitants of the Oz district are expected to be people with a high income. Close proximity to the speed train station[12] and an attractive and exclusive environment is complemented by *Wizard of Oz* imagery, especially the emerald city, depicted in the novel as a green city. If you take a look at the advertisements on one of the promoters' websites,[13] you will notice that Oz is called "a new neighborhood in the American style." This is clearly a reference to the American way of life (in a suburban style) rather than to a dreamed-of emerald city. Oz is a place where future inhabitants are considered as active consumers in attractive surroundings, and not primarily as citizens concerned for their environment. This is described as a new "urban attitude."[14]

On a larger scale, the imagery produced for the Oz district suggests a new kind of town for a new kind of citizen: digitally connected, using eco-technologies and fostering soft mobility. These images are far from the expectations of the local people, especially humble people. We need to recall that Montpellier, despite being described as a southern boomtown, is actually one of the most fragmented and poorest towns in France. According to the national census bureau, in 2013, the average per capita income was one of the lowest in the country: €23,726 in Montpellier compared to the national average of €31,000. At 13 percent, the unemployment rate is higher than the national average of 10 percent (Institut National de la Statistique, 2016; see Table 8.2). These social and economic facts contrast with the expensive condominiums proposed for sale or rent in the Oz district and with a real estate strategy that focuses on the creative class.

Envisioned as part of a broader metropolitan economic plan (named "Montpellier unlimited"),[15] many neighborhood groups (for example in the suburban city of Lattes) see Oz, and more generally Écocité, as a commodification process in which big companies in partnership with local authorities aim to promote their technologies and their economic interests, behind an "ethical project." With its strong political support, technological dimensions, and fostering of collective interests, Écocité leaves little space for discussion and contestation. Collectif tramway,[16] an association of streetcar users, was inaudible when it criticized the huge amount of money spent on recruiting star architect Bernard Reichen, and the lack of public meetings at the planning stage of streetcar line 3. "The innovation is only technological, not social," according to the president of Collectif tramway, who underlines a (poor) social vision restricted to a quota of 25 percent for social housing. The social part of the project was modeled on the basis of administrative norms that many opponents said were disconnected from people's true needs. Moreover, it seems that the social housing in all of the four districts is not "so social" after all. Rents are expected to be between 20 and 30 percent higher than in other social housing complexes in the city, denying access to a large part of the population.

You will probably argue that the use of new eco-technologies means new forms of social life. But the use of eco-technologies promoted here (i.e., energy monitoring) is restricted to those inhabitants with sufficient education and appropriate knowledge. The new neighborhoods are mainly for newcomers from the so-called "creative class" rather than local low-income people.

SUSTAINABLE IMAGE OR COMMODIFICATION?

From an environmental point of view, many ecologists qualify Oz as a "useless project," wondering for example why the speed train station is not located in the city center. Such a central location would have reinforced

Montpellier's centrality in the sense of a more compact city. Instead, its suburban location and connection to motorways favors urban sprawl. The ecologists also complain that a so-called "sustainable district" is crossed by a motorway (the A-9, one of the most congested motorways in France) and by a high-speed train line, and that it is located close to a noisy international airport. "Where is sustainability?" they ask on their blog.[17] The answer is probably to be found in an urban growth pattern that strongly supports real estate activities. This also explains why cars have not really been swept out of the area. Indeed, soft mobility principles here do not exclude highway and motorway developments. Facing the protests—and powerful lobbying—of shopping mall owners and real estate investors who were afraid that the soft mobility framework would reduce retail customer traffic, the urban planners decided not only to plan spaces for cars but also to enlarge the motorway A-9 connecting Écocité to the airport and to downtown Montpellier. The arguments used here relate to the importance of economic development, employment, and the impossibility of relocating retail activities inside the metropolitan area. In 2012, the vice president of the association of shopping mall owners warned the city officials that Écocité could not be realized without their full assent. "For 30 years, la route de la mer has been the main commercial center in the region for retail stores devoted to furniture and leisure activities [. . .] our requirements are very specific: huge parking lots, easy access to motorways. Écocité is a good political and urban planning project. But it is not yet a commercial project in line with our goals and constraints."[18] The vice president of the Montpellier chamber of commerce added: "Écocité is a unique project. Professionals (retail owners) won't let it happen without being an active part of it. For the moment, it seems to us it is too much centered on urbanism."[19] Of course, franchise stores have been transformed from ugly shopping malls into fancy stores located inside new low-energy buildings. But, nevertheless, it seems that we are far from early visions calling for new modes of consumption that limit the use of cars and the monopoly of franchise shopping malls.

Underlining this paradox, some other groups criticize the financial costs of the speed train station[20] and the megalomania of the whole project, which does not really fit with the size of Montpellier, and recalls late mayor George Frêche's famous delusions of grandeur. Since the Frêche era, urban planning issues seem to have been concerned with large and contested projects: opera houses, sailing ports, technoparks, and the like. We may remember debates about Port Marianne in the 1990s, questioning the benefits and criticizing the megalomania of this eco-district.

Toward a More Participatory City?

At the core of the Écocité discourse, the "participatory city" raises many questions. It seems that the participatory city concept mainly refers to communication tools and to the use of new technologies for spreading information about Écocité and its different projects. Indeed, participation is understood in a very passive way, as invitations to local inhabitants to attend public meetings and to agree with proposals, not leaving much space for further debates or counterproposals. At these meetings, the information is presented in the style of sophisticated institutional communication, diffusing an image of a better urban future[21] and observing how the artwork on streetcars by fashion designer Christian Lacroix represents a step toward a better future! These meetings are complemented by digital communication tools. Let me mention the metropolitan authority website—called "urban conversation"[22]—which is devoted to discussions of the Écocité. On this website, the debate between citizens and the public authorities in charge of the project is reduced to a "conversation" between peers on specific topics, far distant from polemics, annihilating criticism, conflict, and protest. Conversation is associated with politeness or urbanity, and excludes polemics. It turns conflict regulation on specific topics or projects between a public authority and a group of local actors into a very general (digital) conversation. By resorting to innovative digital technologies and social networks, Écocité leaders have removed debate from the public sphere and placed it in a digital and sanitized (Web) sphere. In other words, local public debates and protest are diluted in a digital arena where citizens are "peers talking to peers" and can comment on controlled images and projects.

At Oz, and more generally in the whole Écocité area, voices contesting, or even just questioning, social or environmental benefits are hardly audible. Most of the time, antagonistic citizens and political groups are denied their legitimacy. They are suspected of acting as political partisans against a consensual and highly ethical project. Who can be opposed to a project initiated in the name of social and environmental well-being, essential for further generations? But contestation is not limited to local activists. The former mayor of Lattes, one of the suburban cities inside the Écocité perimeter, was one of the first to express his concern and to question Écocité governance and benefits. Facing a project that changes the physiognomy and will affect the social composition of his city, he denounced a metropolitan project where the voices of small towns were marginalized. He has also recalled that the metropolitan governance lacked democracy and functioned in the case of Écocité as a "techno-cratic structure" mirroring (reluctant) small towns. He clearly established a link between Écocité governance and the bossism or autocratic urban governance of former Montpellier mayor George Frêche: a kind of met-ropolitan governance strongly supported by the French state, encouraging metropolitan concentration in the name of decentralization policies.

Behind all these protests, one question remains unanswered: instead of urbanizing the periphery why don't the metropolitan authorities improve urban central districts? Many of these districts lack facilities, retail stores, and public transportation. More density in urban central districts can be regarded as a strength, as in popular social housing neighborhoods like La Paillade or Le Petit Bard.

Maybe the answer is to be found in the urban planning process. Indeed, more than a model city, don't you think we are observing here the implementation of a new kind of urbanism inherited from the bossism system of the 1970s? An urbanism in which sustainable and environmental values and issues are systematically used to achieve public and private goals, to promote a competitive and attractive city, to strengthen the image of an innovative city, and to reduce public dialogue to communication tools (see Figures 8.5 and 8.6)? An urbanism characterized by permanent competition for eco-technological innovativeness, leading to a technological overbid, focusing on solutions promoted by private companies (depending on green economy growth), instead of spending public money on poor and dilapidated neighborhoods? An urbanism rooted in a long tradition of municipal bossism characterized by big urban renewal projects, and a communicative machine producing the image of a "gifted city," always one step ahead of the others? An urbanism used to suppress public protest by autocratic regulation, in which megalomania is part of the strategy and urban image?

Conclusions at Écopôle: Écocité, an Urban Archipelago or a Fragmented City?

I won't answer all these questions. We should now move on to our final destination near the end of the streetcar line: Écopôle (the fourth stop on our trip). Actually, this is a very strange place. Reading the promoters' flyers, one can imagine Écopôle as a green business park with different ways of organizing offices and retail stores in a preserved natural environment. We can observe big parking lots, wide avenues designed for cars and poorly designed buildings. Let's stay here a little longer. Before flying back home, just have a look at the beautiful view beyond Écopôle, with the ponds and the sea. If you turn and look back, the picture is a bit different, a fragmented urban landscape. In less than twenty years, Écocité has established a pattern of urbanization that local urban planners call an "urban archipelago." This spatial metaphor was basically used to justify doubling the size of Montpellier, linking the city to the seashore in an urban fragmented pattern, symbol of a model city (forcibly) incorporating the small municipalities of the eastern suburbs. This image echoed the socially mixed programs forecast for this Écocité. Planners and promoters consider an archipelago kind of urbanization as the most efficient answer to sustainable and social issues in the Montpellier area. Écocité neighborhoods are depicted as islands that concentrate urban growth, limit negative effects, and are interconnected by soft mobility networks and eco-technological tools preserving biodiversity. According to local urban planners, these islands or neighborhoods are the physical spaces where a new kind of citizenship can be invented. Density, soft mobility, and socially and intergenerationally mixed buildings produce a special neighborhood ambiance resulting from a new way of living together. The use of eco-digital technologies, focusing on proximity, is connected with the hope of changing behavior and social relationships. But other local actors (such as environmentalists) argue that in an archipelago, the islands remain isolated from each other. As islanders do not automatically share the same problems, they can easily gate themselves off from each other. Indeed, islands can be the physical ground for social separation, leading to urban fragmentation. This is particularly true in a city known for its speculative real estate market. Such a conception risks helping islanders to create gated communities far away from the socially diverse neighborhoods of the old city. Let me formulate this plainly: are we facing a brand new sustainable urban archipelago or a fragmented mode of urbanization turning its back on the traditional city for good?

Notes

1. See www.youtube.com/watch?v=KaYoYdnpKqU.

2. Montpellier and three surrounding municipalities: Lattes, Perrols, and Castelnau-le-Lez.

3. Philippe Sajhau, vice president of IBM Smart Cities, quoted in www. acteurspublics.com/2013/04/04/montpellier-prefiguratrice-des-ecocites.

4. For instance, IBM will finance the Montpellier smart city program devoted to model and monitor uses, regulation of energies in the Écocité, and the risk of flooding.

5. With 250 stores covering 2,000,000 square feet.

6. This term suggests that Écocité is an urban laboratory in real time.

7. H. Mandroux, mayor since 2004, quoted in Le Monde Web edition: www.planete-plus-intelligente.lemonde.fr/villes/montpellier-l-ecocite-experimente-l-architecture-durable_a-13-2589.html

8. In Écocité/Cité intelligente, press kit, October 12, 2012.

9. Candidate for the local socialist party, like George Frêche.

10. A former socialist candidate and self-proclaimed heir of George Frêche, he has successively supported the left, the green, and the liberal parties in local elections.

11. Read their blog at www.resistons.net.

12. From this new train station you can reach Paris in three hours, Barcelona in two hours, and Lyon in two hours.

13. Watch the promotional video at www.wat.tv/video/oz-montpellier-prgramme-immobilier-62ior_61wl5_.html.

14. See urbanattitude.fr/oz-grand-projet-montpellier-nature-urbaine/#!prettyPhoto/0.

15. www.montpellier-unlimited.com

16. collectiftramway.free.fr/index.html

17. montpellier.eelv.fr/?s=%C3%A9cocit%C3%A9

18. Patrick Harrot, vice president of the retail owners, city of Lattes, inter-viewed on July 20, 2012; see www.montpellier.cci.fr/pages/open_window.php?horsarbo=&4144.

19. Ibid.

20. €135 million.

21. See www.mobilicites.com/fr_actualites_montpellier-presente-sa-collection-de-tramways-printemps-ete_0_77_1812.html.

22. www.monagglo2020.com

References

Institut National de la Statistique. (2016). *Agglomération (unité urbaine): Montpellier*. Available at: www.insee.fr/fr/ppp/bases-de-donnees/donnees-detaillees/duicq/uu.asp?reg=91&uu=34701 [Accessed 3 Sept. 2016]

Moure, J.-P. (2016). *Ecocité, un modèle de ville durable*. Available at: www.montpellier3m.fr/medias/fichier/dp-ecocite_1314807892909.pdf [Accessed 3 Sept. 2016]

La tribune des métropoles (2012). L'Écocité de Montpellier. Unsigned article. *La tribune des métropoles*, p. 4.

Chapter 9

Building Ecopolis in the World's Factory

A Field Note on Sino-Singapore Tianjin Eco-city

I-Chun Catherine Chang

Introduction

In September 2011, I flew to China to attend the Binhai Forum. This Chinese international eco-city conference, an annual event that had started in 2010, was held at the Sino-Singapore Tianjin-Binhai eco-city (Tianjin eco-city hereafter). The Tianjin eco-city is a new ecological friendly town built from scratch at the coastal Binhai New Area in Tianjin city, and has served as a national eco-planning model for other Chinese cities.

I got off my flight at Beijing Capital International Airport in the evening and was greeted by two volunteer college students who would be accompanying me to the conference hotel. On our way to ground transportation, they started making real estate sales pitches. "Tianjin eco-city is actually very close to Beijing! It will only take you thirty minutes on high-speed train to get there," one of them told me. The other followed: "If you do business, you know, you can buy a house in Tianjin eco-city and run your business in Beijing." They even prepared brochures of the properties in the eco-city as part of my conference packet. When we reached our limo, a green building expert from Australia and another urban sustainability consultant from the UK had already been waiting. There were some sporadic exchanges about our professions on the

173

ninety-minute ride, but the conversation was mostly dominated by the students introducing new highway and train systems that would make Tianjin eco-city within the commuting distance of Beijing. The goal of these transportation infrastructures, one student told us, was that "the eco-city can be the living place for those 'good residents.'" Although she did not elaborate, I believe what she meant by "good residents" were well-off Chinese or international elite who could afford the rather expensive properties at the eco-city.

Amid the sales pitches, I began wondering: is the most prominent Chinese eco-city merely another real estate development project? In theory, an eco-city is supposed to be a sustainable community fitted into the biosphere, friendly to the ecological conditions, self-sufficient in resource consumption and economy, and socially sustainable, that is, inclusive of various livelihoods (Register, 2002: 174–176). Recent literature on eco-cities, nevertheless, suggests that major eco-city developments in the world tend to create privileged "enclaves," where the air is fresher, the sky is the bluer, the city is greener—but only the rich can afford to live there (Hodson and Marvin, 2010). Sitting inside the limo as the conversation continued on the topic of who would be the first group of residents to move in, I started to picture Tianjin eco-city, the national exemplar of ecological urbanism in the world's factory: how green, glamorous, and privileged can this place be?

It was not green or glamorous. We approached the eco-city in the late evening. Looking out of the window, I could barely see anything. It was dark: no skyline, no street lights. Every once in a while, we passed enormous factories. Some were still running, but others seemed abandoned. And even in the dark we could tell that there were no beautiful trees or neatly manicured lawns. Finally, the limo pulled up in front of a modern high-rise hotel surrounded by industrial buildings. "You are now in the industrial park of Binhai New Area," the students told us and showed us the location on a map. Sounding confused, the British sustainable consultant asked, "So where is the eco-city?" One student pointed at the other side of the road: "At the east end of the industrial park, there."

I looked in the direction she pointed. Under the moonlight, several slim, gray shadowy buildings rose into the sky afar, much like giant chopsticks standing against the backdrop of the Bohai Gulf. This was the Tianjin eco-city, a city to be built inside one of China's largest industrial belts, the Bohai Rim at the nation's northeast. That was also the city that carried the Chinese dream of greener urban living.

Eco-City Rising from the Waste Land

Since the 1990s, reviving the rust belt of Bohai Rim has been a priority on the regional development agenda of the Chinese government. Compared to the prosperous southeastern coastal China, economic development in Bohai Rim has stagnated since the market reform. In order to revitalize this region, the government set the goal to build new towns and establish high-value industries. Upon this background, and with a national movement to build eco-cities since the mid 2000s, the Chinese Premier Wen Jiabao and the Singapore Prime Minister Lee Hsien Loong signed the "Framework Agreement on the Development of an Eco-city in Tianjin, China" on November 18, 2007. After three working meetings in early 2008, China and Singapore planners finalized the master plan and began the construction of the Tianjin eco-city on September 28. The master plan was jointly designed by the China Academy of Urban Planning and Design, the Tianjin Urban Planning and Design Institute, and a Singaporean planning team (led by its governmental Urban Redevelopment Authority). The objective of the project was to build an environmentally and economically sustainable city equipped with green urban planning features to be the home of burgeoning biomedical and computer software industries.

There was also a larger ambition behind this eco-city development. Since the market reform, China has experienced urbanization at an unprecedented rate, and is expected to grow another 350 million people over the next twenty years (Woetzel et al., 2009). In order to accommodate the fast-growing urban population, there was an urgent need for the Chinese government to build more cities in a managed fashion in order to avoid common problems stemming from rapid urbanization. Those cities, according to China's eleventh Five-Year Plan, would contribute to a "resource-conserving and environmentally friendly society," that is sustainable, "ecologically civilized" and "scientific oriented."[1] Under this vision, Tianjin eco-city was set up as the national model of sustainable urban development. Its large-scale urban eco-solutions were to be replicable in other places in China, and even beyond its borders (Sino-Singapore Tianjin Eco-city Investment and Development Company, n.d.).

To ensure replicability, the initial planning expert panel of Tianjin eco-city decided that the project would not seek to showcase state-of-the-art green technology at all costs, but instead established a financially feasible model for most cities in China and developing countries to imitate (Wang, 2009: 3–4). This meant that the Tianjin eco-city did not set out to have zero carbon emission or zero waste design, as an ideal eco-city would, as technologies involved in such self-sufficient design would be too costly. Further, as a model, Tianjin eco-city must be able to address the environmental challenges that most Chinese cities and cities in the developing world confront. Specifically, land shortage and water shortage were the two prime challenges identified by the initial panel.[2]

These goals are reflected in the choice of location. The eco-city is planned on a rural area about 150 kilometers from Beijing, and 40 kilometers from Tianjin, another major city, with more than seven million residents. The project site is on non-arable, saline-alkaline soil with little vegetation; clean water supply is severely limited because the water bodies have been polluted by industrial waste. The Chinese government deliberately chose this site to demonstrate the potential of eco-city development. It began the eco-city construction by cleaning up the polluted water bodies, improving soil quality through replacement and cultivation methods, and installing water treatment facilities to recycle used water and increase the clean water supply.

SPATIAL DESIGN

According to plan, Tianjin eco-city will house 350,000 permanent and 60,000 temporary residents in an area of 34.2 square kilometers by 2020, which makes it a medium-size city by Chinese standards. The projected population density is relatively high: 1,198 persons per square kilometer—about the same as in the Tianjin city center and double that of nearby urban areas. The spatial design of the city is structured along transportation corridors, including subway and light rail lines, and roads that are between four to eight lanes wide. Tianjin eco-city emphasizes public transportation and plans to expand itself through transportation-oriented development. Meanwhile, the eco-city also seeks to be friendly to pedestrians and cyclists by setting up public transportation nodes within 400 meters for all residents (Sino-Singapore Tianjin Eco-city Administrative Committee, 2009; Baeumler et al., 2009: 10).

These visions are integrated under the aggregated public housing model originated from Singapore and adopted by the Tianjin eco-city. The basic units in this model are city blocks, otherwise known as "eco-cells." Each eco-cell is a square area 400 meters long at each side and meant to accommodate about 8,000 residents. Within this area are four to five high-rise residential towers (each between twenty to thirty stories high), green space, pedestrian walkways and bicycle lanes, and basic facilities. Four or five of the eco-cells constitute an "eco-community," which shares a community center, elementary school, and other types of public service facilities. Lastly, four or five eco-communities form an "eco-district," which has a suburban business center. The Tianjin eco-city is expected to have four such eco-districts surrounding an eco-island for recreational use in the center, all linked by transportation corridors (Baeumler et al., 2009: 18–19).

ENERGY, WATER, AND SOLID WASTE

In theory, an eco-city should be self-sufficient in its energy supply and consumption. The pragmatic approach adopted by Tianjin eco-city, however, leads it to target a fairly conservative goal of supplying only up to one-fifth of its total energy use from on-site renewable sources such as wind turbines and solar panels. The rest is expected to come from two combined heat and power (CHP) plants outside the eco-city that will gradually shift to clean coal as its power source. On the consumption side, Tianjin eco-city also plans to manage its energy demand through green buildings. All of the buildings are expected to meet China's national green building standards, and additional incentives are offered to acquire certification from the more stringent LEED and Singaporean Green Mark standards (Baeumler et al., 2009: 27–47).

The much-featured water issue in Tianjin eco-city highlights the use of nonconventional water sources. By 2020, at least half of the water supply is expected to come from rainwater harvesting, seawater desalination, and reclaimed wastewater. Other water will come from conventional water treatment plants in nearby areas. Sewage will be treated at a wastewater treatment plant financed and constructed by the World Bank. Storm water, on the other hand, will be collected by a separate system, reused or discharged into water bodies after appropriate treatment (Baeumler et al., 2009: 65–77).

As for solid waste, the Tianjin eco-city aims to achieve a 60 percent recycle rate. A pneumatic trash-collection system is to be set up in residential and business facilities for better urban hygiene, and work in conjunction with the conventional door-to-door collection system. Collected solid waste will be further consolidated at eight waste transfer stations across the eco-city and transported away to treatment, incineration, or landfill facilities. Tianjin eco-city also seeks to do away with waste pickers, who play an informal but substantial role in solid waste recycling across China, by limiting waste collection and recycling to formally contracted workers (Baeumler et al., 2009: 78–90).

Economic Sustainability and Development Phrases

Tianjin eco-city also emphasizes economic development. Specifically, it seeks to focus on service industries and become an educational and R&D center for environment-related technologies. It aims to attract investment from computer software, animation, and pharmaceutical companies, and to expand tourism and education-based services. The ultimate goal of such economic development is to create sufficient employment opportunities that will, along with other industries at the adjacent Binhai New Area, establish the eco-city's population and economy.

Tianjin eco-city plans construction and economic development to occur in phases. The first phase was scheduled between 2008 to 2010, with the goal of completing a small start-up area of four square kilometers to house a population of 85,000 and host initial companies. The second phase seeks to finish the basic layout of the eco-city, including major infrastructure, public facilities, and a transport network linking it with Tianjin-Binhai New Area and surrounding regions between 2011 and 2015. The third phase, set between 2016 and 2020, will focus on developing the north and northeast districts to create mixed-use areas of residential housing, businesses, and industries. It is expected that the eco-city will be fully developed, with the urban economic base firmly established, by 2020 (Baeumler et al., 2009: 10, 24). The total construction cost will exceed CN¥10 billion (approximately US$1.6 billion), which will be split equally between the Chinese and the Singaporean governments. Returns are expected from the public infrastructure investment, taxes and revenues, and residential and commercial real estate development (Baeumler et al., 2009: 101–113).

From Planning to Implementation: The Reality

On the last day of the conference, I went on a field trip with a group of conference attendees. The conference arranged volunteers to take us to the eco-city on a shuttle. Tianjin eco-city was surrounded by a manmade river, like a large moat protecting the city from the factories in the nearby

Binhai New Area. The only connection between the Binha New Area and the eco-city is a long bridge known as the Rainbow Bridge, linking the brown past and the green future of the area.

There was very little development going on in the Binhai New Area. But at the eco-city side of the bridge, we saw more than thirty towers rising to the sky. The project site was clearly undergoing massive transformation. Countless cranes were running on the ground or operating at the top of buildings. Some towers seemed completed and ready for move-in. At first glance of the start-up area, the eco-city looked like a typical Chinese residential town development: concrete high-rise buildings, large city blocks, four- to six-lane roads, characteristics that many people would find hard to associate with the "city-in-a-garden" slogan repeatedly cited by the Tianjin eco-city planners during the conference.

Figure 9.1. Tianjin Eco-city at the first glance. Photo by I-Chun Catherine Chang (2011).

But on further inspection, we discovered unusual features. For example, wind turbines of various sizes crossed the city: giant ones at the river bank, and three- to four-story structures next to the residential towers. The traffic lights and street lights were powered by solar panels. We saw no utility poles. Manhole covers on the pavement indicated multiple pipelines underground. There were storm water collection pipes, wastewater collection pipes, and electricity and cable lines. The landscaping of the city was more organized compared to most Chinese cities. In fact, it looked just like Singapore, with a touch of green-tech features.

Still, there were no signs of actual residents. According to the master plan, the city was expected to house 85,000 people when phase one was completed. But when I walked around the city a few months after that deadline, it was like being in a ghost town. I saw only some construction workers being transported on trucks into several uncompleted buildings, and a contractor leading three workers to work on landscaping. I chatted with this contractor and learned that they were planting new trees

Figure 9.2. Wind turbine, solar powered street lamp. Photo by I-Chun Catherine Chang (2011).

to replace the old dying ones. Many trees needed to be replaced once to twice a year, he said, because the soil was still too alkaline, and water supply was still limited for trees to grow. To deal with this issue, Tianjin eco-city has a list of landscaping plants more adaptive to the eco-city's ecological conditions; these plants may be native to China but are not native species of this region.[3]

Surrounded by residential towers in the center of the start-up area are Tianjin-eco city's government building and the animation center—a building dedicated to attracting and hosting related companies. The volunteers led us to the animation center and proudly explained that an animation firm had set up a branch here and a film post-production company would be moving in soon. They introduced us to several demonstration rooms, each of which showed different stages of animation production. But the tour ended there. We walked around freely inside the building, only to find that more than half of it was empty. I also looked outside, noticing only a few cars in the employee parking lot.

Back at the Tianjin eco-city's government center, student volunteers and the center's staff guided us around the miniature city model and distributed information brochures. I was given a brief introductory booklet of the eco-city's master plan, a booklet, and some flyers advertising the eco-city's real estate as well as the surrounding environment. I sat down at a corner and skimmed through them. According to the master plan introduction, 20 to 50 percent of the city's housing units would be affordable housing for low-income families. But nothing about affordable housing was mentioned in the advertising materials. Instead, the material was full of texts and images promoting the high-quality education, international business centers, convenient transportation options to Beijing, advanced hospitals, the parks, the river, and the lake, all of which are exclusively available to the eco-city's residents. On one of the flyers, the property was featured as "the gateway to the privilege of sustainable living." It was apparent that the real estate development was targeting middle-class family and business elites, selling the eco-city as a privileged green space.

An Eco-City Built for Whom?

As we waited for the shuttle for the return trip, a volunteer guide came to sit down and had a chat with me. She was a graduate student of a local university, and her parents lived in an old village center in the nearby Hangu area. I was interested in her perspective, as one of the locals, on the eco-city. "Would your family want to move here?" I asked. "Of course we want to! All the public facilities and the urban hygiene are in much better condition than the old community we live in. But we can't afford to move here. My parents don't earn enough." Her father works in an elementary school, and her mother holds a part-time job in a local grocery store. In her own words, they are just an "ordinary" family.

It was no surprise that "ordinary" families can't afford to live in the Tianjin eco-city. The real estate flyers I received indicated that the price of a condo unit in the eco-city ranges from CN¥ 12,000 to 16,000 per square meter. According to the volunteer, that is at least double the price of nearby old buildings. To make things even more difficult, the units in the eco-city are generally more spacious. So the actual cost of replacing an old house in the nearby villages with a unit in the eco-city would be even higher.

Another "ordinary" person I met on that afternoon told me a similar story. After the conference field trip, I took a taxi to explore the vicinity of the eco-city. The taxi driver was friendly and talkative, in his mid-thirties, and lived in the nearby Tonggu area. We started our conversation with where I was from and what I had come here for. "Oh, the conference, I know," he seemed excited, "every year this time, I can run much more trips between here and the [Tianjin] city." "How about other times?" I followed up. "Sometimes there are visitors who come on learning trips [to learn about the Tianjin eco-city], but otherwise nobody comes here." This was not quite what I expected to hear, so I pushed him for an explanation. "Nobody comes because [moving to] this place is too expensive for us, and there are also no [regular] jobs we can do."

Following that conversation, he told me how excited he had been several years ago when Tianjin eco-city was first announced. "I thought it would bring us a lot of decent jobs, a lot of people, and a place where I can escape to from old crowded street blocks in Tonggu," he drove the taxi down the rainbow bridge, "but I learned over these years that those companies [in the eco-city] only want people who can use computers, do complicated things. Those are things I can't do." He talked as if he was not qualified to live in the eco-city. If he was not qualified, most local Tianjin people would not be qualified, either. The Tianjin eco-city aims to create employment opportunities in software, green technologies, and pharmaceutical industries. But in an area dominated by blue-collar workers, how many of these employment opportunities can really benefit the local people?

As the taxi driver drove further from the bridge, I started to notice two-story temporary housing units on either side of the road. These were prefabricated units largely manufactured in factories and transported over. Each unit was very small. There were no trees or lawn, only yellow dust covering these housing units. I asked the driver what these housing units were for. "They are for migrant workers who came here for the eco-city construction." This was the place where those who built the eco-city lived. And we both knew these migrant workers, along with their temporary housing, would disappear once the eco-city is completed. Those who built the city will not be able to stay in the city.

Figure 9.3. Migrant workers' temporary housing. Photo by I-Chun Catherine Chang (2011).

Note after Return: The First Group of Residents

Since 2012, the Tianjin eco-city has made several attempts to increase the number of residents, most noticeably by encouraging employees of the Sino-Singapore Tianjin Eco-city Administrative Committee (SSTECAC; the eco-city's current governing body) to move their families into the city. Meanwhile, the SSTECAC also promoted a new income tax deduction initiative to attract professionals and high-income executives.[4] According to the policy, those who purchase a condo in the eco-city can have all of their income tax returned that year. The real estate companies, on the other hand, have lowered their prices from the initial range of CN¥ 12,000 to 16,000 per square meter to the current range of CN¥ 8,500 to 14,000. Other incentives the SSTECAC now promotes include free twelve-year education, free hospital visits, and free public transportation. Ironically, none of the schools and hospitals have been completed, and only four bus routes run with very low frequency (as of the end of 2013). The light rail and subway system still exist only in the eco-city's master plan.

Tianjin eco-city continues to attract new companies to move in and hopes these new companies can help increase its residential population. The eco-city subsidizes companies to hire professionals and executives at a rate of CN¥ 10,000 for each hire. By the end of 2013, there are about a thousand companies registered in the eco-city, but most of them are small businesses with limited numbers of jobs to offer. In addition, some of the registered companies do not have a physical office set on site. Currently, there are twelve completed buildings in the start-up area, and several office buildings are open for use. There are about 2,000 households, with approximately 4,000 people registered in the eco-city. However, many of these "residents" don't actually live here. Some apartments are bought only for investment. Even if all 4,000 "residents" lived here, the number would still be far below the projected 85,000. Ironically, more than 6,000 migrant workers come into the eco-city every day for construction, according to the Tianjin SSTECAC, but they are not provided housing inside the city.

Tianjin eco-city is no longer a ghost city, as I first saw it in 2011. But lives for the small number of residents remain far from the original vision. One portrait of the current living conditions can be found in a joke circulating among residents since early 2013: "[We] get around by walking, see doctors on Baidu,[5] spend the weekends on the couch, and enjoy our vacations on the Internet (*chū mén kào bù xíng, kàn bìng kào bǎi dù, liù rì kào shā fā, jiǎ qī kào wǎng luò*)." This joke vividly portrays current issues for Tianjin eco-city: low population density and lack of transportation options, medical service, and entertainment. These are also common issues that trouble many new-town developments. Whether Tianjin eco-city can overcome these issues and really turn into a green eco-polis, only time will tell.

Notes

1. Further information about China's eleventh five-year plan is available at english.gov.cn/special/115y_index.htm.

2. Interview with a leading planner of Tianjin eco-city in November 2011.

3. For a full list of the landscaping plants, see Sino-Singapore Tianjin Eco-City Administrative Committee, Sino-Singapore Tianjin Eco-city Water Management Guidelines (Tianjin: SSTECAC 2009, 22–37).

4. Details of the "Sino-Singapore Tianjin Eco-city Policy Incentives for Recruiting Special Talent (zhōng xīn tiān jīn shēng tài chéng yǐn jìn jǐn quē rén cái de yōu huì zhèng cè yì jiàn)" are available at www.eco-city.gov.cn/eco/html/zwzc/zcfg/20121130/8256.html.

5. Baidu is the most popular Internet search engine in China.

References

Baeumler, A., Chen, M., Dastur, A., Zhang, Y., Filewood, R., Al-Jamal, K., Peterson, C., Randale, M., and Pinnoi, N. (2009). Sino-Singapore Tianjin eco-city: A case study of an emerging eco-city in China. Washington, DC: World Bank.

Hodson, M., and Marvin, S. (2010). Urbanism in the Anthropocene: Ecological urbanism or premium ecological enclaves? City, 14(3), pp. 298–313.

Register, R. (2002). EcoCities: Building cities in balance with nature. Berkeley, CA: Hills Books.

Sino-Singapore Tianjin Eco-city Administrative Committee. (2009). Master plan of Sino-Singapore Tianjin eco-city 2008–2020. Tianjin: SSTECAC.

Sino-Singapore Tianjin Eco-city Investment and Development Company. Sino-Singapore Tianjin eco-city: A practical vision for sustainable living. Tianjin: Sino-Singapore Tianjin Eco-city Investment and Development Company, pp. 3–4.

Wang, S.-M. (2009). China rushes to build green cities (zhōng guó qiāng jiàn lü sè chéng shì). Common Wealth Magazine. Available at: www.cw.com.tw/article/article.action?id=39624 [Accessed 3 Sept. 2016]

Woetzel, J., Mendonca, L., Devan, J., Negri, S., Hu, Y., Jordan, L., Li, X., Maasry, A., Tsen, G., and Yu, F. (2009). Preparing for China's urban billion. Brussels, San Francisco, & Shanghai: McKinsey Global Institute.

Chapter 10

Sustainable Empire?

Michal Kohout

Disappointed

For the past ten years that I have lived in the Inland Empire (IE) I felt depressed about returning here after a long winter or summer vacation. I could not explain that feeling until a few months ago, when I concluded that it was disappointment. Here is one of the most beautiful places in the world, a spectacular interplay of mountains, valleys, and deserts all bathed in constant sunshine and moderate climate. An ecosystem that is in finely tuned balance between arid summers and modestly wet winters. A place of immense diversity and resilience; an ecology governed by catastrophism—the idea that change comes suddenly and unexpectedly.

Yet over a short history of human settlement, particularly after the Gold Rush, I see the place as devastated. Huge tracts of land have been converted into car-centered suburbs built using the raw materials provided by the mountain forests and alluvial fans in the valleys. Native vegetation has been exterminated and replaced by lawns and other imported exotics that are deemed more aesthetically pleasing than the ugly "brown" chaparral. The desert has been colonized by agriculture and later resorts, and retirement communities built on massively subsidized water resources from the Colorado River and the State Water Project. Accompanying the wholesale war on nature, I also grew aware of turbulent social conflicts pitting the descendants of Midwestern settlers against their Native American

and Mexican predecessors and newcomers, mostly from coastal communities. I see the IE as the battleground between conservative politics of
white entitlement from Orange County and progressive politics of social
justice from Los Angeles County. What disappoints me is that both are
committed to continuing the IE's growth machine legacy. What may be
worse is that while the region has grown dramatically in population, its
growth in civil society organizations has not kept up, therefore leaving
most decision making here to unelected technocrats and consultants who
tutor overwhelmed and underprepared public officials.

The way I saw it, the raging battle scarred the landscape and the
people who live here, and made the IE a dumping ground for all the vices
and worst practices coming from the coast. I was disappointed because I
could see no alternative to this way of living with nature and each other
here. Worst of all, the people living here seemed to appreciate the status
quo, and actually enjoy their quality of life. Every year, the university
where I work runs the only regional survey about the quality of life in the
IE. Despite the recent recession, over 75 percent of those surveyed think
the region is a good place to live (CSUSB, 2013). They give the following
reasons for their satisfaction: "good area, location and scenery" (34% of
the respondents), "good climate/weather" (20%), "not crowded" (7%), and
"affordable housing" (6.5%). Crime is by far the residents' biggest concern
(19%, followed by lack of job opportunities, traffic, and air pollution, all
between 8–10%). Most people are very happy with the police (70%), parks
and recreation facilities (65%), and shopping amenities (68%), but not so
happy with schools (46%), public transportation (47%), and street maintenance (35%). They show surprising confidence in their elected officials
(60%) despite the fact that voter turnout in local elections is very low, as
is public involvement in local politics, particularly among newcomers who
flood into the region (Ramakrishnan, 2007). This contradiction almost
turned my disappointment into despair until I was handed a new class to
teach, which gave me an opportunity to dig deeper into what was going
on in the region that was now my home.

Starting five years ago, I began asking my students to first analyze
regional development and later sustainability in the IE. Together we began
to follow a gentle shift in the local politics of the growth machine as the
2007–2009 recession hit our region harder than most. With official unemployment peaking at 15 percent, local officials began to wonder if the IE
could rely on its historical model of serving as a bedroom community
and storage facility for its powerful and more economically diversified

Figure 10.1. Inland Empire as San Bernardino and Riverside Counties.

neighbors on the coast. I started attending conferences where local planners, government officials, academics, and even some boosters began to
reflect critically on the short term, growth-at-all-costs practices. My students' work on community organizations and measures of sustainability
made me aware of the growing number of social justice and community
organizations that were also challenging the status quo. Eventually sustainability became a common term in the IE, and as in many places around
the world, its definition and implementation is sometimes a very narrow
defense of the status quo or a way to positive social and environmental
changes. In my class, we have begun to keep track of these changes and
their outcomes. Although this has moved me from the brink of despair,
I must confess I'm still disappointed, as most recent events point to the
return of the growth machine (Medina, 2012). Our only hope is that

growing social and environmental awareness will offer alternative choices for our regions' residents.

The Past in the Present

To connect the IE's past to its present challenges and future prospects there are no better guides than Carey McWilliams and Mike Davis, so pick up their books to read as you make your way here. Nobody understood the initial conflict in Southern California between nature and incoming migrants from the American Northeast and Midwest better than McWilliams. The journalist and labor lawyer observed that the newcomers annihilated Southern California's native vegetation and topography in their quest

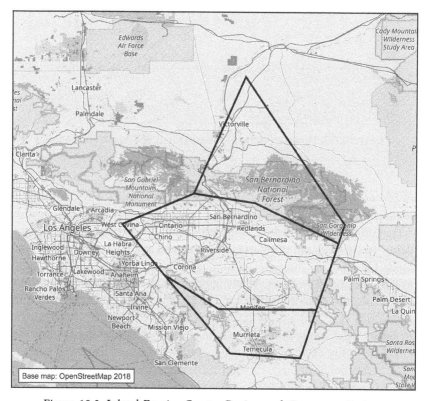

Figure 10.2. Inland Empire Greater Region and Consensus Region.

to imitate the landscapes they left behind. McWilliams (1946) chronicled their failures caused by droughts and dramatic natural events such as fires, floods, and landslides. And while he noted that most newcomers began to thrive in their new home because they made significant adjustments to their mindset and practices, he remained skeptical that a genuine transformation of mind and habit ("structural adaptation") was really taking place. McWilliams also exposed the social conflict that stained California's glowing image as a place of hope and plenty for everyone. In his books on agricultural production and Mexican immigration, McWilliams (1939, 1949) documented how the Golden State's agricultural wealth production relied on the exploited armies of immigrant (mostly Mexican) labor. His fearless advocacy on behalf of the exploited and excluded inspired the progressive movement in California and laid the groundwork for the struggle against ingrained prejudice and a powerful political and business establishment that stood in the way of inclusiveness and participation, key components of social sustainability.

Mike Davis, a native of the IE, picked up where McWilliams left off. Like McWilliams, Davis is unconvinced that structural adaptation is taking hold in Southern California. Instead, he documented a growing schism between the political and business establishments' stubborn belief in environmental uniformitarianism—gradual, predictable change—and the scientific community's growing awareness of California's true natural dynamic: catastrophism—sudden, unpredictable change. Davis (1990, 1998) tied the persistent and purposeful misrepresentation of Southern California's nature to established and immensely popular and profitable suburban development policies. He argued that a predictable and subjugated nature was essential to accommodate rapidly growing urban populations in vast automobile suburbs. The sudden and unexpected natural events, such as earthquakes, fires, floods, and droughts, are deemed momentary departures from the normal trends in climate and geomorphology by politicians, media, and the public. In fact, these "acts of God" are a natural reset that allow communities to remake themselves by receiving public natural disaster funds. Davis argues that in most cases this erases undesirable urban land use and displaces unwanted people. Although his *Ecology of Fear* was hammered by critics as a doomsday manifesto that few living in Southern California identify with (e.g., Waldie, 1998), the reality is that he got the basic relationships between nature and society, and within society in the region, right. Perhaps conceding to his critics' arguments that people actually like living here, Davis offered a more nuanced view in an article about the IE in *The Nation* (2003). He sees it as a place of opportunity and inclusion for the working- and lower-middle-class people streaming into its vast territory. He argues that the frontier character of the IE allows for people to start fresh, get work, buy a house, and settle in safe and diverse communities that don't have the baggage of class and racial segregation and discrimination still smoldering in Los Angeles and Orange counties. Maybe Davis is overly optimistic about the lack of discrimination but statistics on residential segregation, which show IE cities to be much more integrated by class and race than cities in coastal counties, prove his point (CensusScope, 2010).

The Growth Machine is Born

Our first stops connect the history of the region to its present. In the past, the region was seen as a blank slate to be filled by ambitious entrepreneurs and their ideas of transforming nature and society. The frontier had reached the Pacific coast and now bounced back east into the regions bypassed in the headlong rush across the continent. Inland California was now the new frontier, and places like the IE soon attracted interest and the investment of prominent businessmen from everywhere. Growth

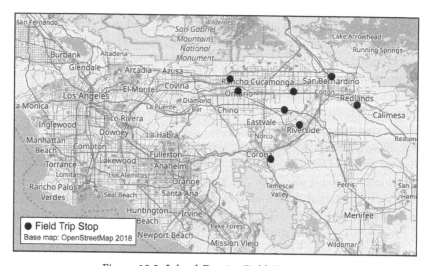

Figure 10.3. Inland Empire Field Trip Stops.

became the rallying cry for the headlong rush into the region. But growth would be impossible without first securing stable supplies of water. Later, that water would fuel stages of growth that were at first a revolutionary mix of agricultural prosperity and urban amenity, and, still later, the more familiar industrial blue-collar suburbs. Much of this historical background explains why many people today think the region is a great place to live. The past constructed the pervasively powerful ideal of political autonomy based on likeminded communities of property owners who prized individual rights over greater social responsibility or government role. This ideal was carved into the landscape in the form of the nation's first agricultural suburbs marketed to willing settlers by powerful developers and entrepreneurs who staked out the region.

Once you land in Ontario, we can head to the nearby remnants of Guasti Winery. In 1917, it was the largest vineyard in the world, with over 5,000 acres under cultivation. At that time, San Bernardino County had more acres of wine grapes than Napa and Sonoma counties have today (Straight, 2012). The hot dry summers and shallow underground water sources proved a perfect combination for grape vines first planted here by Spanish settlers. The vast tracts of unsettled land also proved perfect for ambitious social visionaries like Secondo Guasti, who built a company town around his vineyard complete with housing for workers, post office, bakery, firehouse, inn, and a church copied from his hometown in Italy. While Guasti became a heroic figure in local history, he perpetuated the regions' patterns of paternalism and social stratification by hiring white, mostly Italian, workers full-time and using mostly Japanese and Mexican workers for seasonal or part-time work (Cinotto, 2012). Today, a few of Guasti's vines still bear fruit, which is made into sacramental wine, but his town is now mostly gone. What remains will be restored for the city of Ontario by a developer who acquired the land and plans to build office and mixed-use space. It will become a monument to one of the region's historic figures, and one of the contributors to the regional growth machine model originated by the man whose statue stands in front of our next stop in front of Upland city hall.

Erected in 2005, the statue of George Chaffey pays homage to the father of the IE's growth machine. Chaffey came to Southern California from Canada, bought up land in the IE, and founded the Model Colony of Ontario in 1882. He created an "agriburb:" a suburban growth machine that combined modern urban amenities (cable rail, good roads, electricity, piped water, education, and cultural facilities) with natural amenities (clean

Figure 10.4, 10.5 & 10.6. From grapes to warehouses, remains of the world's largest winery, and plans for its future. Photos by Michal Kohout (2014).

air, sunshine, and irrigated land for high-value crops) (Sandul, 2010). Chaffey and his partners established a mutual water company to guarantee each landholder with irrigation water, and guarantee themselves endless profits for supplying it. Then they connected the IE's growing agriburbs to the rest of the country by railroad and ensured that the rapidly growing citrus industry had ever-expanding markets to supply. According to Mike Davis, the IE was the largest continuous "citrus forest" in the world by 1940. But it was not an agricultural hinterland to LA's urban heartland. Chaffey's statue faces Euclid Avenue, which epitomized the comforts of urban living including electrification and streetcars. In fact, cities in the original Ontario colony were among the first in the West to have electric lighting (Sandul, 2010). The agriburb was a mass-marketed glossy suburban ideal featuring the social amenities that have had broad mass appeal to this day: the right to land, labor-saving technology, entrepreneurial opportunity for all, and community cooperation rather than government rule (Davis, 1990: 384).

Today, the agriburbs and the citrus forest are almost gone, but our next two stops recall their past glories and hidden social conflicts. Our first stop is the Parent Navel Orange Tree in Riverside, one of the two original trees from which the citrus forest rose. Navel orange trees were imported from Brazil by the US Department of Agriculture and propagated in its hothouses. Later, a USDA official sent cuttings to his former neighbors who had moved to Riverside (NPR, 2009). Next, we're off to the California Citrus State Historic Park, with its interpretive trail within a 186-acre citrus orchard featuring many of the species grown in the state. But most important perhaps is the design of the park itself, based on an early twentieth-century landscaping style, with open spaces for play and picnicking and paths for strolling. The idea behind these early city parks was that people should have access to such places "to relax and restore their spirits" (McKinney, 2012). Our next stop is the Redlands Public Library to check out their *Citrus, Labor, and Community* collection, which details the lives of Mexican residents, some of whom worked for the local growers. Unfortunately, there's very little evidence here of the social relations between growers and their workers. Much of that history would have been erased by the boosterism of the era, if not for writers like McWilliams and Gilbert Gonzalez. They and later others documented the social relations of segregation and exploitation that sometimes exploded into violent struggles between minority (Chinese, Japanese, Filipino, and Mexican) workers and their white bosses. Today, this legacy of seeing some jobs as the domain of a disposable, mostly immigrant labor force still looms as a major obstacle to the socially sustainable practices of inclusiveness and solidarity. We will return to this issue on our last stop of the tour in Ontario, visiting with the Warehouse Workers United and heading to Dream Street, where the freshly minted suburban landscape reproduced "citrus forest" social relations in construction a vital and volatile IE industry.

For now, we head to Fontana and California Steel, which sits amidst the hulking remains of what once was one of the largest steel plants in the United States. The arrival of Kaiser Steel to the IE during World War II signaled a transition of the region from an agriburb to an all-American blue-collar suburb. The steel mill attracted a wide range of immigrants, who made the IE a more diverse place. Although Fontana started out as an agriburb, like many other cities in the IE, its fortunes took a sudden turn when Henry Kaiser, an enlightened New Deal capitalist, opened the first fully integrated steel plant west of the Rockies. Kaiser developed a high-road approach to worker productivity in his Bay-area shipyards. To gain maximum output from his workers without losing productivity to illness, injury, or turnover, he subscribed his workers to a prepaid medical plan, encouraged unions, and provided worker housing and transportation (Davis, 1990). Kaiser selected Fontana because of its autonomous water supply, ready-made power supply, good railroad connections, and because he felt the social engineering of agriburbs would supply a contented workforce (Davis, 1990: 390). As Fontana grew, attracting migrants from all over the United States and overcoming initial racial conflicts, it became a relatively tightly knit blue-collar community with many formal and informal organizations started up by the mill workers. Using Robert Putnam's (2000) terminology, we can say Fontana was rich in social capital, meaning high levels of community cohesiveness and participation. But not everything was rosy. Pollution from the plant destroyed the citrus forest, and Kaiser's bullying of the county supervisors over tax assessments continued the historical trend of the people's representatives serving business interests.

The residential boom set off by postwar mass migration to California butted up against the pollution spewing from the steel mill. Environment and the economy clashed with residential developers siding with environmentalists who challenged the mill and its workers (Davis, 1990). Then in the early 1980s, after years of neglect, the mill was sold and thousands

Figure 10.7 & 10.8 California Steel, formerly Kaiser Steel in Fontana. Photos by Michal Kohout (2014).

of workers laid off. Corporate raiders reduced the integrated mill into a slab-processing facility competing with Korean and Chinese imports. Fontana seemed doomed, but it recovered rapidly by welcoming and subsidizing developers to re-create master planned communities from LA and OC (Davis, 1990). The growth machine quickly changed gears from industrialization to construction. Fueled primarily by the dramatic influx of newcomers rebounding from the west coast, IE cities were flooded by new home buyers looking for more affordable copies of the coastal suburban dream. As a postscript, Fontana wasn't the only place that had to find another way to grow. During the 1980s and 1990s, the region lost about 25,000 union jobs mostly due to closures of Kaiser Steel in Fontana, and the Santa Fe depot and Norton Air Force base in San Bernardino. Yet by the late 1990s, the region started to grow dramatically, and its population and job growth continued until the bottom fell out in 2007.

Dirt and Dirty Jobs: The Growth Machine Lives On

Before we head to our next destinations that showcase the present situation in the IE, let's take a break to absorb information from several regional studies and one ambitious regional vision that has since been derailed by the most recent economic bust.

When the national media wrote about the IE during the boom and subsequent bust in the housing market, they focused on what we locally call the "dirt thesis," meaning there is a lot of land for new houses and that local governments, desperately competing for revenues, rubber stamp every housing, strip mall, and warehouse construction project. Of course, they found thousands of willing homeowners and businesses spilling into the region mostly from the nearby coastal communities. This mass migration of mostly lower-middle-class workers priced out of the real estate markets in Orange and Los Angeles counties drove the overheated construction and mortgage financing industries that collapsed when the housing bubble burst. The dilemma this process seems to produce is how to allow people the opportunity for economic and social advancement through home ownership in more integrated and safer cities, while avoiding the volatile economic conditions that threaten their newly acquired economic and social standing.

More systematic studies of the region outline these challenges and offer solutions that in most cases put great emphasis on a particular version of social sustainability that is often presented as human capital required for economic development. One study refers to the IE as a "failed geography" where environmental and social challenges threaten to undermine the optimism of the migrants who are settling the region (Kotkin and Frey, 2007). The studies concur that the IE growth machine creates opportunities for prosperity but also threatens their sustainable reproduction by neglecting looming environmental and social challenges such as pollution and subpar public education. The planners, business leaders, and consultants are justifiably obsessed about IE's undereducated population and lack of entrepreneurial initiative. Some propose solutions that would import the desired human capital by luring companies to the region with low taxes, low rent, and low-cost labor. Others propose addressing the problem by calling on local companies to team up with schools and colleges to help produce the workers the region needs now and in the future. Still others propose a regional remodelling into a high-tech hub by bulking up its research capacity and education institutions, emulating regional models from near (San Diego) and far (North Carolina) (Tornatzky and Barreto, 2004).

Part of the explanation for the regions' challenges are state-wide shifts in the political economy that have sharply divided the haves and have nots. In 1978, Californians passed Proposition 13, dramatically reducing cities' property tax revenue and forcing municipal governments to turn to sales taxes, user fees, and funds they collect for the state that may or may not be returned as their primary sources of revenue. Growth at all costs became the only means of survival for many IE cities. In 1986, Californians also passed Proposition 62, which mandates a two-thirds council majority to pass a general-purpose tax increase, further reducing local revenue sources. In addition, the Reagan administration began a trend of cutting federal funding to cities. All of these factors left cities in California competing for dwindling resources and heavily dependent on local sales tax revenue. In fact, one argument goes that the cities' sprawl is caused by building so-called "power centers," big box retail shopping plazas near highways, which gets them more sales taxes but also attracts more residential sprawl (Schmidt, 2014). Cities across the state have dramatically different fiscal capacities to meet their service demands. In the IE, some cities, particularly in the more affluent western portion of Riverside county, have low taxes and low services by choice, while most others have low services because they are constrained by low income (Joassart-Marcelli, Musso, and Wolch, 2005). The financial situation has become so unstable that during the most recent bubble-to-bust cycle, four new IE cities incorporated but are now struggling to avoid disincorporation, and San Bernardino went bankrupt.

These growth machine dynamics are difficult to overcome considering some of the future demographic and political trends. For one, many migrants from coastal counties that fuel the IE population growth are undereducated workers attracted by low-cost housing, thus reproducing the same patterns that the previous studies lament. This migration means that by 2015 the IE will be almost majority Latino, another crucial factor since this population is underrepresented in the region's political establishment and governance. By 2015, Latinos will represent 48 percent of the adult population of the region but only 34 percent of the registered voters. By contrast, whites will represent 35 percent of the adult population but 48 percent of registered voters (Johnson, Reed, and Hayes, 2008: viii). The local businesses boosters have also noticed this dynamic, highlighting the fact that Latinos will be replacing the current high-skill workers and managers in the region, while stressing the constant need for blue-collar, so-called "dirty jobs" (Husing, 2013). However, the biggest threat the boosters see to continued access of Latinos to "dirty jobs" are environmental regulators who are not concerned with creating jobs. This takes us back to the growth machine dynamic of economic imperatives being packaged as populist social justice to remove environmental barriers to growth. But that may be just one part of the story.

Green Valley Now! Big Plans Going Nowhere

Now that we learned more about the region and its challenges, we head to Corona to see how one entrepreneur harnessed the boundless optimism of IE's residents to try to change the region based on some of the suggestions pushed by the above studies. Our stop is the award-winning Dos Lagos multiple-use development built on a brownfield. Its developer, Ali Sahabi, who has a reputation as a builder of sustainable communities, was the main force behind the Green Valley Initiative (GVI) formed in 2007. Using his contacts at USC, he commissioned a plan to restructure the economy of the region. His plan attracted much attention, and many government and business stakeholders throughout the region signed on to the vision put forth by the report. Much of the report outlines similar challenges presented in previous studies: undereducated population, jobs housing mismatch causing excessive commuting, environmental degradation, lack of high-value jobs, fewer resources due to budget cuts at the state and federal level, and competition from coastal communities. However, the report adds one challenge the other studies did not: poor regional perception and lack of regional identity (USC, 2007). Specifically, the report blames poor urban design and planning for a lack of social interaction, leading to a lack of identity and social cohesion in the region (USC, 2007: 26). The remedies are rebranding the region—changing its name from the IE to Green Valley, and linking this to new environmentally conscious practices, such as promoting the use of green building practices, including higher-density walkable communities (smart growth) like Dos Lagos (USC, 2007: 41). Unfortunately, I can't show you any GVI projects because it no longer exists. In fact, there are no IE-wide sustainability projects, so for now Dos Lagos will have to do.

From Corona, we can head to Riverside to the University of California and its Center for Sustainable Suburban Development, which started with seed money from Ali Sahabi of Dos Lagos fame. Its advisory board includes community members, many of them representing powerful educational and government institutions in the region. So far, the Center is developing three main projects, one of which is to study the IE logistics sector as a sustainable economic activity. While still in Riverside, we can head downtown to walk around and contemplate Green Riverside, the city's sustainability plan put into operation in 2009. Developed by the city's movers and shakers as part of an "innovative growth strategy for the city," it defines sustainability as the environmental component of the overarching quality of life. Using a publicity campaign called "Seizing Our Destiny," the city's political, technocratic, and business elites survey the public on their quality of life. There is a "Green Accountability Performance Committee" that includes "wider community" members aside from business, faith, professional, and educational organizations. The committee has met thirteen times in the last five years, but there's no record of who is on the committee nor what they discussed. The city also hired a consultant who developed the "Thousand Points of Strength Index," which has 474 indicators that nobody can see or evaluate because they are proprietary (Green Riverside).

Nearby San Bernardino, which declared bankruptcy in 2013, also has a sustainability plan, funded by a federal Energy Efficiency Conservation block grant. Nobody's heard of this plan, a mishmash of environmental and energy indicators created by technocrats. Although there is something called "green infrastructure," which includes farmers' markets and community gardens, the bulk of the plan is focused on the grant's priorities, such as reducing solid waste, greenhouse gases, water quality and wastewater treatment, and land use issues including transportation (CARES). Maybe we made a couple of wrong turns here. Let's head to Redlands.

Unlike its larger neighbors, Redlands has made some significant strides in getting the community involved in its sustainability plan. Actually, it's the community in Redlands that got itself involved. Redlands is the only IE city that has a citizen's group helping to implement the city's sustainability plan. A year after the city's sustainability plan went into effect, the community realized nothing was happening because it wasn't funded. In 2012, they formed the Redlands Sustainability Network to start acting on the plan's goals. They have organized events around growing your own food, using native plants, conserving water, and creating a vision about the city's sustainability. The network's about 200 volunteers formed "action groups" on issues they designated as important to their community: energy, land conservation, green homes, sustainable food, transportation, sustainable business, and water conservation. Unfortunately, it seems they're having some difficulty in getting people to serve in some of these groups. Nonetheless, the network continues to organize events and the annual Redlands Sustainability Festival.

Dreaming of a Just Future

Redlands is a relatively wealthy city where community involvement is perhaps more commonplace. Its neighbors also have a history of community involvement, though much of it today isn't organized around sustainability; rather, the rallying cries are for justice and inclusion. In Jurupa Valley, one of the newly incorporated cities in Riverside County, now threatened with disincorporation, is the office of the Center for Community Action and Environmental Justice (CCAEJ). Run entirely by women activists, CCAEJ is a grassroots organization whose work is "grounded in 'place,' " meaning they fight for justice in their communities by organizing the people who live there (CCAEJ, 2016). Active since 1978, the organization has been fighting against the air-quality impacts of the rapidly growing logistics (goods movement) industry in the region. They have shown that air pollution from traffic around old and new warehouse locations and rail yards is disproportionately affecting poor people of color. They mobilized massive health studies and investigations after writing their own reports that have shown the direct health impacts on the people in communities close to the San Bernardino rail yards (Willon, 2011; CCAEJ, 2010). Taking a tour of the large Burlington Northern/Santa Fe (BNSF) facility helps us understand that the problem is urgent. While the railroad officials point out the nonpolluting CNG haulers and cranes, there are still many idling diesel locomotives and lines of idling diesel trucks waiting for their loads.

Just about a mile from the rail yards is our next stop, the Libreria del Pueblo, located in a mostly deserted downtown San Bernardino shopping mall. This one-stop migrant help center started by a local Catholic priest is part of a strong immigrant rights movement that has spread across the region. Spurred by local anti-immigrant activities that sow seeds of suspicion, scapegoating, and outright hatred in IE's communities, the immigrant justice movement has grown stronger as the Latino community began to fight back. The Libreria is part of the Justice for Immigrants Coalition (JFIC), a broad network of community groups that have been effective in fighting against aggressive immigration enforcement and anti-immigrant politics that threaten families and communities in the region. The JFIC also helps people understand their rights and empowers them to become citizens, both literally (process their citizenship application or register to vote) and figuratively (realize they have the right to use their voice). I have marched with the Coalition for immigrant rights, and its success is inspiring, but they are vigilant of the smoldering anti-immigrant prejudice that flares up into politics and policies in the region (e.g., Kohout, 2009)

Dream Street in Ontario is our next stop because it showcases the challenges faced by the IE. The complexity and contradictions of social sustainability are played out here, as photographer Doug McCulloh (2009) documented the rise of a working-class subdivision. The fact is that most people who live and are moving to this region want to buy houses in suburbs such as these, but many who build them cannot afford them. On the one hand, McCulloh documents the deep satisfaction of the new homeowners who feel very empowered starting a new life in a brand-new house. On the other hand, he documents the deeply marginalized and alienated workforce that built the subdivision (2009). Most of them cannot hope to buy the homes they helped to build, and many do not even feel a part of the society where they live and work because they are undocumented immigrants. McCulloh (2009) gets contractors to talk about their privileged standing in society because they're white and were once unionized skilled tradesmen. Now they subcontract crews of unskilled Latinos who don't even earn minimum wage. The whites see all Latinos as undocumented, and the Latinos think the whites are exploiting them. Each believe that's just the way it is. There's a growing awareness of the dynamics of exploitation, but little hope. The institutions that counteracted those dynamics have been slowly making a comeback.

On our way back to the Ontario airport, we come to our last stop on the tour, the headquarters of the Warehouse Workers United (WWU). For the past five years, this group of worker and union activists have been organizing warehouse workers in the IE. The idea is simple: if workers get better pay and safer working conditions, the quality of life in their communities will improve dramatically. The logistics sector (mainly warehousing and transportation) has become a major economic player in the region, but the transnational corporations and local entrepreneurs that operate warehouses here treat workers as disposable objects by not paying fair wages and endangering their health. Several years ago, I heard workers testify that companies switched from hourly wages to piece work to cut labor costs, that they forced workers to buy their own safety equipment, and that they made them perform illegal acts, such as erasing expiration dates off cans of pet food that would be resold. In most cases, employers try to insulate themselves from their legal responsibilities by hiring workers through temp agencies, which rebrand the workers as independent contractors responsible for their own fates. But the workers and their allies are fighting back by documenting the abuses and mounting legal challenges against high-profile companies, such as Walmart and Schneider Logistics, who have been fined by the state for labor law violations and ordered to stand trial for wage theft, along with the temp agencies they hired to shield them from their obligations. In addition, Warehouse Workers United makes the case that one of the region's largest economic engines does not serve our communities well by exploiting its residents. The IE has become the fastest-growing and largest warehousing region in the nation because it is the transshipment point for goods coming to the ports of Los Angeles and Long Beach, which handle more than 40 percent of all US imports (Thompson, 2013). Even though the industry is extremely vulnerable to downturns in US consumer demand, which hammered the region during the last recession, it has become rooted in the region because of its availability of land and labor. And while the industry's boosters claim it offers a path to middle-class prosperity, the

WWU counters that most workers struggle to stay above poverty, and temps barely reach poverty wages (DeLara, 2013). The workers themselves say that the jobs would be good if they paid decent wages and provided some benefits. Scores of academics and activists agree on advocating for economic and social policies that focus on dramatically increasing the wages of the working poor as a way to boost regional quality of life (e.g., National Employment Law Project).

Parting Thoughts

As we pull up to the terminal drop off at Ontario airport, I hand you a sheet of paper with my parting thoughts. It's hard to be disappointed with a place that holds so much hope to many people who come here to make a fresh start and to improve their lives. There are many places in the IE that have bad schools, bad air, bad traffic, bad government, bad jobs, and bad luck, but for many it's better here than in the places they left behind. Perhaps the places they moved into aren't rich in social capital, the cooperation and cohesiveness that Robert Putnam (2000) feels is such an important part of building communities. And perhaps they don't have much power in the sense that Martha Nussbaum (2011) wants us to have to be truly autonomous in making life choices. Perhaps the growth machine, run by a small group of elite technocrats, politicians, and business leaders, is still good at selling the suburban dream. But many people are happy here because you can more or less do what you need to do to get ahead or to stay afloat. It is still a frontier: a place where the desperately hopeful come to find a cheap place to live and stretch their meager paychecks or their social assistance. At one point, the ex-mayor of San Bernardino lamented that the reason his city was ranked the second poorest in the nation was because it attracts poor people. He was saying the region was poor because it attracts poor people, but it makes them too. But there's no shame being poor in one of the poorest places in the country. The poor live together, and that's why there's less segregation in the IE. Maybe the question to ask is how good could people have it here? Certainly, they could have it much better. People want higher pay, better education, lower contamination, and more time to spend with their families. They are also realizing there is no way to get there unless you have strong communities and real power. They know they must tame the growth machine.

References

California Resources for Sustainability. *City of San Bernardino sustainability master plan.* Available at: cares.ucdavis.edu/resource/city-san-bernardino-sustainability-master-plan [Accessed 3 Sept. 2016]

California State University, San Bernardino (2013). *Inland Empire annual survey.* San Bernardino: CSUSB.

CensusScope. (2010). *Segregation.* Available at: www.censusscope.org/segregation.html [Accessed 3 Sept. 2016]

Center for Community Action and Environmental Justice. (2010). *Pollution in San Bernardino: The BNSF intermodal rail yard San Bernardino, CA.* 1st ed. [pdf] Riverside: CCAEJ. Available at: www.engagegrassroots.org/uploads/3/7/3/2/37323423/san-bernardino-1-24-small1.pdf [Accessed 3 Sept. 2016]

Center for Community Action and Environmental Justice. (2016). CCAEJ's official website. Available at: www.ccaej.org [Accessed 3 Sept. 2016]

Cinotto, S. (2012). *Soft soil, black grapes: The birth of Italian winemaking in California.* New York: NYU Press.

Davis, M. (1990). *City of quartz.* London: Verso.

Davis, M. (1998). *Ecology of fear: Los Angeles and the imagination of disaster.* New York: Vintage Books.

Davis, M. (2003). The Inland Empire. *The Nation.* Available at: www.thenation.com/article/inland-empire [Accessed 3 Sept. 2016]

DeLara, J. (2013). *Warehouse work: Path to middle class or road to economic insecurity?* 1st ed. [pdf] Los Angeles: USC Program for Environmental and Regional Equity (PERE). Available at: dornsifecms.usc.edu/assets/sites/242/docs/WarehouseWorkerPay_3_web.pdf [Accessed 3 Sept. 2016]

Gonzalez, G. (1994). *Labor and community: Mexican citrus worker villages in a southern California county, 1900–1950.* Urbana: University of Illinois Press.

Green Riverside. *Riverside sustainability plan.* Available at: www.greenriverside.com [Accessed 3 Sept. 2016]

Husing, J. (2013). *Growing importance of the Inland Empire Hispanic community.* Available at: hwww.johnhusing.com/QER%20Reports/QER%20Jan%20 2013%20web.pdf [Accessed 3 Sept. 2016]

Joassart-Marcelli, P., Musso, J., and Wolch, J. (2005). The fiscal consequences of concentrated poverty in Southern California cities. *Annals of the Association of American Geographers,* 52(2), pp. 163–183.

Johnson, H., Reed, D., and Hayes, J. (2008). *The Inland Empire in 2015.* San Francisco: Public Policy Institute of California.

Justice for Immigrants Coalition. *Justice for Immigrants Coalition of inland southern California.* Available at: justiceforimmigrantscoalition.org [Accessed 3 Sept. 2016]

Kohout, M. (2009). Immigration politics in California's Inland Empire. *Yearbook of the Association of Pacific Coast Geographers*, 71, pp. 120–143.

McCulloh, D. (2009). *Dream street.* Berkeley, CA: Heyday.

McKinney, J. (2012). *Day hiker's guide to California's state parks.* Santa Barbara, CA: The Trailmaster.

McWilliams, C. (1939). *Factories in the field.* Berkeley: University of California Press.

McWilliams, C. (1946). *Southern California: An island on the land.* Layton, UT: Gibbs Smith.

McWilliams, C. (1949). *North from Mexico.* New York: Praeger.

Medina, J. (2012). As California's warehouses grow, labor issues are a concern. *New York Times.* Available at: www.nytimes.com/2012/07/23/us/in-california-warehouse-industry-is-expanding.html [Accessed 3 Sept. 2016]

National Employment Law Project. *Living wage and minimum wage.* Available at: www.nelp.org/site/issues/category/living_wage_and_minimum_wage [Accessed 3 Sept. 2016]

National Public Radio. (2009). *Who put the navel in navel oranges?* Available at: www.npr.org/templates/story/story.php?storyId=103250589 [Accessed 3 Sept. 2016]

Nussbaum, M. (2011). *Creating capabilities: The human development approach.* Cambridge, MA: Harvard University Press.

Putnam, R. D. (2000). *Bowling alone: The collapse and revival of American community.* New York: Simon & Schuster.

Ramakrishnan, K. (2007). *Survey of political and civic engagement in the Inland Empire.* Riverside: University of California.

Sandul, P. (2010). The Agriburb: Recalling the suburban side of Ontario, California's agricultural colonization. *Agricultural History*, 84(2), pp. 195–223.

Schmidt, A. (2014). A disincorporation story: Are new cities in California, like Jurupa Valley, a thing of the past? *Boom California*, 4(1). Available at: www.boomcalifornia.com/2014/01/riverside-county-disincorporated/ [Accessed 3 Sept. 2016]

Straight, S. (2012). Spirits of Guasti. *Boom California*, 2(4). Available at: www.boomcalifornia.com/2013/03/spirits-of-guasti [Accessed 3 Sept. 2016]

Thompson, G. (2013). The workers who bring you Black Friday: My Life as a temp in California's inland empire, the belly of the online shopping beast. *The Nation.* Available at: www.thenation.com/article/177377/holiday-crush?page=0,0 [Accessed 3 Sept. 2016]

Tornatzky, L., and Barreto, M. (2004). *Economic development and knowledge economy in California's Inland Empire: Progress or stagnation?* Los Angeles: Tomas Rivera Institute at University of Southern California.

University of Southern California. (2007). *Green valley initiative.* Los Angeles: University of Southern California Center for Economic Development, School of Policy, Planning and Development.

Waldie, D. J. (1998). Pornography of despair. Review of *Ecology of Fear* by Mike Davis, 1998. *Salon*. Available at: www.salon.com/1998/09/21/feature_15/ [Accessed 3 Sept. 2016]

Willon, P. (2011). Air quality regulators to study health effects of San Bernardino rail yards. *Los Angeles Times*. Available at: Articles.latimes.com/2011/jun/09/ local/la-me-air-quality-20110609 [3 Sept. 2016]

Chapter 11

Middle-Class Family Enclavism and Solidarity from a Distance

Notes from a Field of Contradictions in Dortmund, Germany

Susanne Frank

The Right House in the Wrong Place

In the cold winter of 2006, we began flat or house hunting in Dortmund. I had accepted a position as professor of Urban and Regional Sociology in the School of Spatial Planning at Dortmund University of Technology. Our daughter was four years old, our son only a couple of months. We knew the city of Dortmund hardly at all, and were fully open as to which residential area we would live in. The only condition was that it should not be too far from the university or the railway station, since my husband would continue to commute to his job in a distant German city and spend only three days a week at home with the family.

After a short while, we were offered our dream house: a charming old house, affordable and perfect in size and style, with a small garden, yet in a very urban area: the Nordmarkt, part of the Dortmunder Nordstadt. We were pleased to see that the environment was multicultural; coming from Berlin, this was what we were used to.

Our sobering up began when we happily reported this jackpot to the staff of the Turkish hotel where we were staying, which was located in the Nordstadt's pedestrian area—and met with complete incomprehension. We were told that the Nordstadt was a rough "problem area" we should definitely avoid—for the sake of our children. If he had the financial means, said the receptionist, himself a Nordstadt denizen, he would immediately relocate his family to the "better" parts of Dortmund in the south.

Perplexed, but still optimistic and keen to learn more about the neighborhood, we went out on a pub crawl in the evening and tried to strike up conversations with the people around us. The result was disillusioning: we talked to about a dozen very friendly and open residents, but not one of them encouraged us to move into the area. The opposite was the case: the unanimous advice was that if we had small children, we should settle in a more family-friendly and less dangerous area. We were told stories of crime, drugs, rival gangs of youths, and feelings of inse-

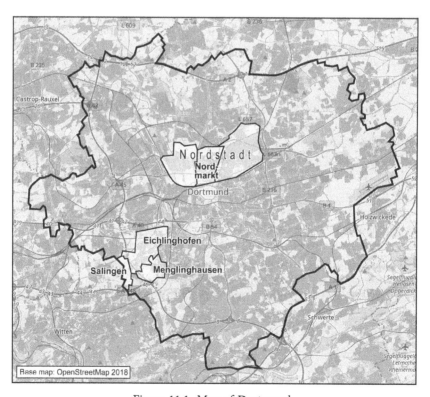

Figure 11.1. Map of Dortmund.

curity. Above all, we were alerted to the poor quality of the local schools and to their status as breeding grounds of "deviant behavior." A teacher of Turkish origin, working at the secondary school opposite "our" house, put it bluntly: "If you want your children to become drug addicts and learn how to use weapons—welcome to the neighborhood! Our schoolyard is a center of these activities. They will never leave children alone who live directly opposite."

Exploring the Nordmarkt Neighborhood

These reactions aroused the urban sociologist in me. Of course I was familiar with debates on the deepening and sharpening of sociospatial polarization, segregation, and exclusion throughout Europe. Pockets of poverty and deprived neighborhoods can be found even in the most successful service cities—to which Dortmund, the former capital of the coal, iron, steel, and brewery industries, certainly did not and does not belong. I learned how closely the formation of the Nordstadt was bound up with the rise of Dortmund as an industrial city in the second half of the nineteenth century. It had emerged as a working-class residential area along with the development of railway lines, coal pits, steelworks, and the port. Attempting to organize the ensuing chaos, in the 1860s, the municipal architect designed a rectangular street grid with representative ornamental squares ("*Schmuckplätze*"). The biggest three, Steinplatz, Nordmarkt (after which the neighborhood was named), and Borsigplatz (where, by the way, Borussia Dortmund, the famous football club, was founded in 1909), have become the centers of the district. When walking around the next day, we discovered a wealth of impressive buildings from various eras, and especially from the Art Nouveau period. However, large parts of the Nordstadt were destroyed by air attacks during World War II. The postwar architecture is mostly plain and pragmatic. Many real estate owners have not invested in maintenance and repair, so their buildings are often in poor condition.

Further, we realized that the Nordstadt, and hence the Nordmarkt ward, was a heterogeneous and lively area with a compact mix of residential accommodation, workplaces, and culture and leisure facilities. It is one of the smallest, but by far the most densely populated district in Dortmund. We noticed a plethora of small- and medium-sized enterprises, especially connected with the service industry and retail trades, of which

Figure 11.2. Nordmarkt, Dortmund. Photo by Mbdortmund (2007). Available at Wikimedia Commons "Dortmund, Nordmarkt" by Mbdortmund is licensed under CC BY-SA 2.5.

Figure 11.3. Nordmarkt, Dortmund. Photo by Kevin Hillen (2014).

a large part caters to the needs of different ethnic groups (like specialized groceries, tea rooms and restaurants, Internet and telephone shops, travel agencies, etc.).

This reflects the fact that, from its early days, the Nordstadt has been a working-class and immigrants' quarter. During the heyday of steel and mining, workers were attracted, especially from Poland. In the postwar period, foreign workers from southeast Europe, Turkey, and the Maghreb settled in the area. In the 1980s and 1990s, many late repatriates from Central and Eastern European countries and the CIS states, as well as asylum seekers from central Africa, came in. Over the last years, the area has seen an increased influx from Bulgaria and Romania, but also from Iraq, Lebanon, and Syria. The Nordstadt, with its affordable rents and its established social-support networks, has thus always been an "arrival district." Today about 65 percent of the approximately 53,000 (registered) Nordstadt inhabitants have a migration background.

At the same time, the consequences of the decline of the heavy industries since the 1970s, and the resulting far-reaching structural changes in the economy and society have struck a hard blow to the residents of the Nordstadt. In particular, unskilled workers and immigrants are having severe difficulties on the labor market. Their children are facing serious problems in the education system, as high rates of school dropouts testify. As a consequence, the area is characterized by long-term unemployment, low qualifications, socioeconomic deprivation, and environmental degradation. Signs of poverty are evident, and child poverty is disturbingly high. While the Nordstadt was always an outsider in relation to the established rest of Dortmund, and especially the "bourgeois" southern parts of the city, with increasing sociospatial polarization, its stigmatization as a neglected and dirty "low-status area" has dramatically intensified in recent years (Caesperlein and Gliemann, 1999: 115; May, 2003).

We were taught that the Nordmarkt was, and still is, a place that illustrates the different faces and perceptions of the Nordstadt very well. Twice a week, the large public square hosts a rich and colorful farmers' market. On these days, the Nordmarkt presents itself as a vivid gathering place for a multitude of social and ethnic groups. Its international flair plays a crucial role in the city's marketing strategy to attract people from further away. On other days, however, it serves as a long-established meeting point for alcoholics and other drug addicts, endowed with a special infrastructure like a kiosk and street social workers. The square's occupation by these groups is widely debated in the media and in the area. It is a thorn in the side of many politicians, but also of numerous neighbors who complain about feeling uncomfortable and being pushed out of a central public space.

In Search of Encouragement

However, from the scholarly literature, I was also aware that alarming statistics and negative external perceptions of a deprived neighborhood very often differ from the internal perspectives of the residents. In many cases, the bad image has little to do with the everyday experience of living in a disadvantaged neighborhood. Keil (2006: 349) shows that this holds true of the Nordstadt. It was therefore disconcerting that, of all people, our potential new neighbors so strongly cautioned against the area.

The same day, I called up an official of the City of Dortmund's school administration. I explained my concerns and asked how he would assess the situation and the quality of the local schools in the Nordstadt. He enthusiastically started to sing the praises of the area's primary schools, which were ambitiously and successfully developing innovative integration concepts to tackle the challenge of the difficult social and ethnic class make-up in the schools. With audible pride, he called my attention to the fact that just a week ago, one primary school had been awarded the prestigious title "Best German School" in a nationwide competition. He talked about the city's long-lasting efforts to improve the Nordstadt's quality of life by numerous area-based initiatives, attempting to achieve "a better social mix" by making it more attractive for middle-class families—for people like us, as he constantly emphasized—and he stressed the key role of education and schools in this process. I confronted him with the result of our previous evening's survey and asked him if he would recommend us to move into our dream house. He was silent for a moment. Then he answered: "Are you asking me as a civil servant or as a father of two?"

My last endeavor to find reliable persons to ask about our plan to settle in the Nordstadt led me to my future place of work, the School of Spatial Planning. Some of my future colleagues had done research on the area and knew it very well. They described in great detail the manifold efforts of the EU URBAN II Community Initiative (2000–2006) to improve the quality of the physical urban environment, especially public spaces, to support the local economy, to prevent social exclusion, and to stimulate grassroots initiatives and local inhabitants' networks. They agreed that this regeneration program had contributed a lot to enhance the overall situation in the neighborhood. Nonetheless, even in this well-informed group that looked at the Nordstadt and its residents with sympathy, no one cheered us up by suggesting that everyday life in this quarter was better than its reputation or that we could enroll our children in the local schools without severe reservations.

At this point, our courage left us. We said farewell to our urban dream house and moved instead into a semi-detached dwelling in one of the conventional, suburban-like middle-class residential areas in the "respectable" south, ten walking minutes from my workplace.

The Personal is Political

This experience puzzled us a lot. It was obvious to us that our housing choice was not just a personal matter, but had a political dimension as well. We had liked to think of ourselves as open-minded, tolerant people. Coming from low-status families, we had both ascended to a stable middle-class position via our education. So far, we had rarely sensed any fear of contact with people from other backgrounds, and we had always lived in socially and ethnically diverse neighborhoods. We were critical of contemporary trends in neoliberal urban policy, and I, in particular, detested the German education system—not least because of its crucial role in the reproduction of social inequality. Hence, we would have been the ideal candidates for planners' efforts to attract middle-class families to disadvantaged neighborhoods in order to achieve a more balanced social mix, especially in the schools. However, as a result of worries about our children's safety and their educational prospects, we preferred to enter the safe haven of a more bourgeois area, and turned our backs on Dortmund's greatest challenges. Embarrassed, we asked ourselves: if, when it comes to showing one's colors, even people like us avoid living and learning among and with the marginalized and poor, whom could we expect to decide otherwise? Who, if not us?

These considerations marked the beginning of a new research project: middle-class families in the cities. For some years now, I have explored the housing choices of middle-class families who have found their place of residence within the administrative borders of a city (and not in suburban or rural areas)—and how, in turn, their housing decisions impact on and change the social and spatial structures of the city. My special focus is on families who have settled in socially more or less homogeneous areas (or in areas which are about to become middle-class dominated, like gentrifying neighborhoods). I am particularly interested in how these families explain their choice with regard to the cities' growing inequalities (polarization, school segregation, etc.). Do they see and reflect on their own role in these processes? Are they aware that their microlevel household decisions affect the city's macrostructures? And if so, how do they ponder over their choices with regard to the ideal of a socially more equitable, cohesive, and sustainable urban society? The analytical background of these questions is the assumption that the housing choices of the upper and middle classes, and not of the lower strata of society, are the main driving forces of current processes of social segregation.

My Field is Everywhere

As you can see, my first entry into this field of research was deeply personal. Nonetheless, I never thought of it as being "just personal." In my short autoethnographic account, I have therefore, tried to combine the personal, the political, and the scholarly (Burnier, 2006: 412; Schlichtman and Patch, 2014). This approach also informs an important part of my research. The fact that I have firsthand experience with what I am investigating helps me to gain access to other parents. If you like, my field is everywhere. I constantly meet other parents in my daily life, at home and at work: in the kindergarten, in the schoolyard, at parents' evenings, in sports clubs, in the neighborhood, and in the corridors, offices, and canteens of my university. Conversations arise easily. My experience is that housing choices, and how we locate ourselves with regard to the city's sociospatial fabric, are topics that most parents talk about easily and frankly. Increasingly, such discussions also take place at professional meetings or conferences: when I report on my research, colleagues or auditors often feel motivated to contribute their own experiences and opinions. As a consequence, a large part of my empirical data originates from my personal circles and from informal sources.

I strive to balance this bias with more formal and distanced approaches. Together with my colleague, Joachim Scheiner, and a group of students, I have conducted a standardized full population survey on housing choices and patterns of everyday life in four new housing developments for families in Dortmund, to which I will refer below. And, of course, I permanently relate my findings to the scholarly literature. It is crucial to be aware of academic discussions on the role and relevance of middle-class families in current urban restructuring processes, often referred to as reurbanization and (family) gentrification.

Exploring the New Single-Family Developments in the South of the City

As the urban contexts described in the literature are very different, I will restrict my account to the Dortmund case. Like many other cities, over the past decade the moderately shrinking city of Dortmund has done a lot to attract the much-coveted group of middle-class families to the city, or to hold them within its administrative borders. To this effect, city officials have been advised by planners and private consultants to satisfy the demand for single-family homes in the city. What is more, the latter recommend not only stepping up efforts to create family-friendly housing, but tailoring whole neighborhoods to the special needs of parents and children, which involves developing entire residential areas for families. As a result, new developments, most of them heavily reminiscent of traditional suburbia, are mushrooming.[1] They are dispersed throughout the whole of the municipal area, but the Dortmund planning office recognizes that the demand in the better-off south is much higher than in the less well-reputed northern parts of the city.

My particular area of research, defined by the catchment area of the elementary school, are the wards of Eichlinghofen, Menglinghausen, and Salingen, south of Dortmund University of Technology, where about 11,200 people live. Privately owned homes mark the overall appearance, albeit multiple dwelling units can also be found. Here, some of the newly-built single-family developments adjoin older developments erected in the postwar reconstruction period (like the one we have moved into). Due to the almost complete destruction of the inner city in the war, many people escaped to the outskirts. In addition, returning soldiers and refugees had to be provided with suitable housing. Pursuant to the political philosophy of that time, priority was given to the development of small areas characterized by what, from today's point of view, can be described as modest owner-occupied one- or two-family homes, with big fruit and vegetable gardens and sheds for small animal husbandry (today used mostly as garages), designed to encourage self-sufficiency. The environment is still rural. In many respects, these mature single-family housing estates of the 1950s, 1960s, and 1970s no longer meet today's requirements, for example in terms of living space, energy standards, or architectural tastes. It strikes the eye that in recent years many homeowners have modernized, converted, or extended their homes to meet their changing needs.

The old residential developments in the south of Dortmund are now complemented by new ones, erected primarily on industrial and urban wastelands. They vary in terms of style, furnishings, and price. However, they are all basically conventional, as is the whole area, so that it is home to down-to-earth fractions of the middle classes. Those with more ambitious, more fashionable, or more sophisticated housing tastes will not easily find what they want here. Nonetheless, not least because of its closeness to the university and its good connection to several motorways, it is one of the most sought-after residential areas in Dortmund, which results in comparatively high buying and rental prices.

It is important to note that, although fairly homogeneous as regards social structure, the area is very diverse in other respects, notably race and ethnicity. Precisely because of this diversity, it is a magnet, especially for educated and upwardly mobile migrant families in search of a "good" learning environment for their children. At the primary school, about half of the children have at least one parent with a migration background.

The Attraction of a Homogeneous Environment

Having children is fundamental to putting down roots, and purchasing a house is making a commitment. Therefore, the question where to settle is crucial. In the above-mentioned representative survey of four newly-built family enclaves, we asked people which areas they considered when looking for a place to live. The overwhelming majority of the interviewed households said they searched only in the southern parts of Dortmund. Not a single respondent said they looked in the Nordstadt district. On the contrary, along with the large housing estate of Scharnhorst, the Nordstadt is the only borough excluded as a potential place to live by each and every informant.

This is fully in line with the results of my informal talks with other parents, which help to shed light on the reasons for this avoidance. Most of our interviewees said that they actively sought a relatively homogenous middle-class residential environment. Many studies, including our

Figure 11.4. Eichlinghofen, Dortmund. Photo by Susanne Frank (2014).

Figure 11.5. Eichlinghofen, Dortmund. Photo by Susanne Frank (2014).

own, testify to the fact that the enormous interest in stable, more or less secluded middle-class family housing areas is fueled by various factors. Highly pragmatic considerations combine with economic, social, socio-psychological, and cultural motives to form a complex and often contradictory mélange (Frank, 2013). Among the many reasons given, two stand out. The first is social networks. The vast majority of middle-class families do not adhere to a traditional gendered division of labor, but both partners work.[2] Thus, they face the Herculean task of balancing career and family. Well-functioning social networks are resources of existential importance that working parents depend on in managing their everyday life. Neighborhood relationships play a key role in this respect. To live among "their own kind" is very important to middle-class parents, because they are aware that smoothly functioning and reliable networks, which for this reason are most suitable for everyday life, thrive in a socially and culturally homogenous environment with shared values. One interviewee put it succinctly: "I cannot entrust my children to neighbors who let them drink Coca Cola and watch RTL II!" (RTL II is a commercial broadcaster, notorious for trash TV.) Hence, they wish to have neighbors who share the same social background and are in a comparable phase of family life. New developments, where the residents all move in at the same time, are particularly well suited to achieving this.

That "social class" or "social composition," advancing to become the key decision-making criterion in choice of residential location, has another, harsher side to it. As we have known for some time now, education and location are closely related (Butler and Robson, 2003: 146). The second important reason for the tendency of middle-class parents to opt for socially homogenous areas, is their serious concern for the socialization of their children, and especially the quality of early childhood education, school, and later education. This applies not only to the acquisition of formal certificates, like the German "Abitur" certificate that qualifies a student for university studies. At least as important to parents is to be sure that their children acquire a specific attitude to education and work. In residential areas dominated by families with similar backgrounds, lifestyles, resources, values, and aspirations, parents expect to be able to find schools where their children will meet peers of their own social group. This is considered indispensable for developing the specific "habitus of education" that is required to successfully compete in the career market later on (Bude, 2011: 22). Neighborhoods with a large number of socially vulnerable and educationally deprived families are considered to be a very disadvantageous environment in this respect. As a consequence, middle-class parents mobilize their economic, social, and cultural capital in order to be sure that their children will not go to schools with a large number of those children. In large, increasingly segregated German cities like Dortmund, one of the most effective ways to ensure this is to choose to live in the more bourgeois residential areas. "The battleground is for education as much as for housing," says Chris Hamnett (2003: 2422).

Urban Enclavism: A Manifestation of Eroding Solidarity?

Many scholars consider the obvious trend of the middle classes to choose to live in established or newly built middle-class enclaves as a manifestation and a catalyst of deepening social cleavages. Some conclude that these cleavages stand for a "society marked by fragmentation and eroding solidarity where there is no longer room for social responsibility, justice, and tolerance of others" (Tilman Harlander, cited in Kortmann, 2011; translated from German). The German news magazine *Der Spiegel* interprets them as an expression of a more comprehensive trend in which the "elites dissociate themselves" from the rest of society, and hence as "symptoms" of an emerging "two-tier society" (Neubacher and Schmidt, 2008; translated from German). In view of international developments, Rowland Atkinson, in a well-known formulation, describes the formation of enclaves as a manifestation of progressive "middle-class disaffiliation" (2006).

There are not really many objections that one can raise against these interpretations. But, with regard to the question of the consequences for urban social sustainability, can we really assume that middle-class families are happy to retreat to their residential islands and regard the resulting increase in the segregation of the poor unaffectedly and indifferently? My experience shows that very many (albeit not all) of them deplore the unequal social and spatial development of the city, and regard their own contribution to this phenomenon with mixed feelings; more than a few even say that they feel torn. Among the latter are especially those interested in politics; I would class them in the bourgeois-liberal and the more leftist green-alternative milieus. On the one hand, they worry about the social sustainability and cohesion of urban society, and on the other, about the future of their children. The dilemma they face is that, under the condition of current urban social development, these two concerns do not seem to be reconcilable. Forced to make a choice, they do not hesitate to opt for the latter.

Many of the people I interviewed said they had earlier lived in more heterogeneous areas, for example as students. Looking back, they have positive memories of the liveliness of their neighborhood, the international make-up of its population, the diversity of lifestyles, and the wide variety of cultural offerings. A widespread view is that living in such areas is inspiring and stimulating—provided one has no children. Having children makes a world of difference: the moment they enter the stage, the perception and meaning of social mix changes from desirable to menacing. There is one remark that I have heard—with variations—many times: "I cannot live out my social (or, alternatively, multicultural) ambitions at the expense of my children."

The same ambivalence characterizes the field of education. What I find particularly striking is that parents establish connections between their professional experience and their educational aspirations for their children. Many say that they are under considerable stress in their everyday working life as the result of ever-mounting competitive pressures, the relentless imperative of self-optimization, extremely high demands on performance, and expectations of being permanently available and mobile, both socially and spatially. More than a few interviewees, both male and female, complain that they feel deeply exhausted. Against this background, they lament the fact that the sphere of school and education is increasingly defined today by competition, polarization, and selection, in the same way the working world is. School thus prepares their children for a (working) world that they themselves view with skepticism, if not disapproval. Much more desirable, in their opinion, would be a harmonious and humane everyday school life that is appropriate to the needs of all children. At the same time, and since such a turnaround is not in sight, they want to ensure that their children come out on the winning side of educational competition, fit for the harsh world of "really existing capitalism."

To this is added a general feeling of living in times of uncertainty. The global economic and financial crisis, in particular, has opened the eyes of many to the vulnerability of their jobs. Here are just two stories. A mechatronic engineer, father of two, independent entrepreneur, told me that in 2008 he had received such a low number of orders that his business was severely threatened. His wife had a part-time, fixed-term contract as an administrative officer at the university and was not able to compensate for his loss of income. Their nightmare was to have to sell their house and leave the neighborhood. In the meantime, his business has recovered, but not fully. In the second example, the father is a specialized engineer who travels around the world as a plant constructor for a German automobile group. The mother is a part-time project manager for a well-known IT company. They have two children. The global economic crisis hit them hard: he was placed on short-time leave, and she lost her job. For a long, anxious time they felt they were faced with ruin. Today, he is working normal hours again, but she has had to accept a new job far below her qualification level. She comments: "We are still suffering from the shock of 2008."

For these people, as for many others, it is obvious that the postwar society marked by the promise of social advancement has come to an end. Diverse studies document that the winners of globalization and economic transformation frequently experience their own social situation as unstable and insecure. To use the apt phrase, coined by the German sociologist Heinz Bude, they see themselves as "relatively privileged, but also as relatively vulnerable" (cited in Feddersen and Unfried, 2011; translated from German). Status anxiety is widespread. With regard to their children's future, this concern is not about advancing up the social ladder anymore. Maintaining the social status achieved is already a big enough challenge. That this can be accomplished only via education, is deeply rooted in middle-class consciousness.

Family Enclaves as Coping Strategy

Adapting the ideas of Butler and Robson (2003), I propose to interpret the perpetuation of old family enclaves and the emergence of new ones as a sociospatial coping strategy of middle-class parents, who, although successful in the global economy, nonetheless tend to feel challenged and often overwhelmed and insecure in light of the demands this places on them. First, homogeneous neighborhoods are important for coming to terms with the challenges entailed by changing gender roles, since they are most helpful for knitting dependable support networks in close spatial proximity, which, in turn, are indispensable for mastering all the many daily difficulties working parents are confronted with. Second, in a working world marked by permanent insecurity, parents in particular face the challenge of how to provide a social and spatial framework for their children that ensures the degree of reliability, security, and stability that they consider indispensable for child-rearing, and childhood itself. The greater the uncertainty and pressure to adapt in the working world, the greater the wish for a "safe basis" in an urban-suburban neighborhood— especially on the part of parents who grew up and were socialized in small and medium-sized towns or suburbs, and who gained some urban experience during their years of study. Secluded residential communities characterized by home ownership, a fairly high continuity of residents in the neighborhood, and the sociocultural hegemony of the middle-class, promise to provide such an anchor of stability. And in residential areas dominated by families with similar backgrounds, lifestyles, resources, values, and aspirations, they expect to be able to find schools where their children will meet peers of their own social group.

The emergence of middle-class enclaves in the inner cities can thus be interpreted as a collective spatial coping strategy of family households to compensate the demands and impositions of a flexible economy and pave the way toward as secure a future as possible for their children. What becomes clear is that the sociospatial seclusion and distantiation must be grasped as a key element of the middle class's strategy of reproduction (Butler and Robson, 2003: 164; Helbrecht, 2009: 14; Frank, 2013).

What does all this mean for the question of (urban) social sustainability? NIMBY (not in my back yard) is in fact an appropriate term to describe this attitude of middle-class parents. Yet I do not think that we should too hastily jump to the conclusion that withdrawal to middle-class family residential areas represents a fundamental trend toward intolerance and abandonment of solidarity. On the basis of my data and field experience, I have come to view middle-class enclavism as the result and expression of the contradictions and ambivalences characteristic of the attitudes and actions of middle-class parents. Very often these parents function well in the working world of flexible capitalism, and gain self-confidence from this, but since they literally sense its enormous destructiveness with their own bodies, they are worried about the rapid economization of all spheres of life. They wish to safeguard their children from this dog-eat-dog society, but at the same time they want to make sure they become fit for it. They love the urban world in all its colors, but at the same time they strive to demarcate themselves from it. They support claims for greater social mix and a more social and just society, but with their residential and school choices they knowingly contribute to the intensification of social and spatial inequalities. They see and reflect on all these contradictions and suffer from them, but they believe themselves to be inextricably caught up in them.

NIMBY—But Not Abandonment of Solidarity in Principle

In light of these field results and personal experiences, I have become hesitant to interpret urban middle-class family housing developments as a manifestation of the cold-hearted abandonment of solidarity with more socially or educationally deprived social groups. Just as little would I agree with those colleagues who, from the outset, denounce the housing choices of the middle classes as "separatist" or "revanchist." I hope to have demonstrated that it is helpful to try to better understand the mechanisms and motives that push and pull middle-class families to settle in fairly homogeneous better-off areas. (And I wish to underline that the term "understand" in the sociological context of qualitative research methods is not equivalent to "sympathize with"!) Growing status insecurity and concern for the prospects of their children in an uncertain future nourishes the desire to keep a distance, both socially and spatially, from the uncertainties, tensions, and problems that are present in large cities. But behind this, there is normally no aggressive wish to draw boundaries between themselves and those below them on the social ladder; rather, many seem to regret that such social and spatial middle-class seclusion and closure is necessary. This impression is confirmed by the observation that a good number of the middle-class family members work with underprivileged or deprived social groups, either as professionals (social workers, for instance) or spare-time volunteers. Two mothers support a nonprofit department store (*Sozialkaufhaus*) in the Nordstadt. One couple has been responsible for supporting a young binational family with multiple problems (including poverty, violence, lack of prospects) for years. Others are active in church-based social initiatives and projects (such as aid for refugees). Although these people have opted (albeit with some regret, as in my own case) for middle-class homogeneity in their residential and school environment, and thus in one key area of social life, they are attempting to build bridges between different classes and cultures in other areas (Frank and Weck, 2018). "In essence the middle-class is not neoliberal," said the political scientist Franz Walter

(2010, translated from German), commenting on the widespread desire for social fairness.

How can we deal with these contradictions? The obvious solution would be to collectively attack the ongoing subjection of all fields of life to neoliberal market principles, since it continuously makes us agents and accomplices of a system that most of us basically do not want. However, as Marc Fisher has observed, these days "it is easier to imagine the end of the world than the end of capitalism" (2009). As long as this is true, middle-class parents will continue to form enclaves and avoid too-close personal contact with the life worlds of the socially vulnerable and marginalized. This seems to be an important prerequisite for people who are otherwise sensitive and supportive toward those affected by the social inequalities and injustices of contemporary urban development, and who see the importance of solidarity at the level of the city as a whole. Various studies have found a high local potential for monetary solidarity, particularly among privileged urban populations, which is reflected in their approval of local redistribution policies. A clear majority of our better-off respondents support giving financial priority to underprivileged areas, even in times of tight budgets, and declare themselves willing to pay city-wide "solidarity surtaxes" to improve living conditions in disadvantaged neighborhoods, should such a tax be introduced. It further fits the picture that there is common approval of demands to provide more funds or hire more personnel for schools in underprivileged areas, or schools with a difficult population make-up.

These results suggest that the middle classes are indeed aware that schools and neighborhoods like the Dortmund Nordstadt perform an important function in terms of social integration for the city and society as a whole—an integration to which they themselves contribute little, if anything at all, not least because of their retreat to middle-class enclaves. "We always look down at the Nordstadt. We find it unsettling there. But, if we are honest, we are happy that they do all the necessary social work that we are not willing to do," comments a mother of two. The willingness to provide a financial contribution signifies the inner conflict of the middle strata particularly well. One might be inclined to interpret it along the lines of an "indulgence payment" or "buying a clear conscience"—an attempt to assuage a sense of guilt. There is certainly more than a grain of truth in this interpretation. However, it can also be understood as an expression of the resigned but realistic insight of middle-class parents that, given the enormous sociopolitical impact of the issues at stake, private initiative is of little avail here and (local) political action would be required instead. Redistribution policies are often held to be one possible approach. However, beyond this, many middle-class parents subscribe to claims for "more progressive, socially just, emancipatory and sustainable formations for urban life" (Brenner, Marcuse, and Mayer, 2009: 179). Under the prevailing circumstances, their solidarity is very distant indeed. It's time to change these circumstances.

Notes

1. This is why I argue that the spreading of new middle-class family developments represents a strong trend toward inner-city suburbanism (Frank 2013, 2016).

2. In our survey of "new family housing developments," only 3.7 percent of the interviewees said they were a housewife; 0.6 percent said they were a househusband.

References

Atkinson, R. (2006). Padding the bunker: Strategies of middle-class disaffiliation and colonisation in the city. *Urban Studies*, 43(4), pp. 819–832.

Brenner, N., Marcuse, P., and Mayer, M. (2009). Cities for people, not for profit: Introduction. *Cities*, 13(2–3), pp. 176–184.

Bude, H. (2011). *Bildungspanik: Was unsere Gesellschaft spaltet*. München: Hanser.

Burnier, D. L. (2006). Encounters with the self in social science research: A political scientist looks at autoethnography. *Journal of Contemporary Ethnography*, 35(4), pp. 410–418.

Butler, T., and Robson, G. (2003). *London calling—The middle class and the remaking of inner London*. Oxford, New York: Berg.

Caesperlein, G., and Gliemann, K. (1999). *Migration ohne Ortswechsel?—Die Perspektive Einheimischer im Zuwanderungsstadtteil: Konsequenzen für Integrationsprozesse und die räumliche Planung*. Dortmund: IRPUD.

Feddersen, J., and Unfried, P. (2011). Prenzlauer Berg ist Apartheid. *taz.die tageszeitung*. Available at: www.taz.de/!81738 [Accessed 3 Sept. 2016]

Fisher, M. (2009). *Capitalist realism: Is there no alternative?* Winchester, Washington: Zero Books.

Frank, S. (2013). Innere Suburbanisierung? Mittelschichteltern in den neuen innerstädtischen Familienenklaven. In: M. Kronauer and W. Siebel, eds., *Polarisierte Städte. Soziale Ungleichheit als Herausforderung für die Stadtpolitik*, 1st ed. Frankfurt, New York: Campus, pp. 69–89.

Frank, S. (2016). Inner-city suburbanization—No contradiction in terms. Middle-class family enclaves are spreading in the cities. *Raumforschung und Raumordnung*, 76(2), pp. 123–132.

Frank, S., and Weck, S. (2018). Being good parents or being good citizens: Dilemmas and contradictions of urban families in middle-class enclaves and mixed neighbourhoods in Germany. *International Journal of Urban and Regional Research*, 42(1), pp. 20–35.

Hamnett, C. (2003). Gentrification and the middle-class remaking of inner London, 1961–2001. *Urban Studies*, 40(12), pp. 2401–2426.

Helbrecht, I. (2009). "Stadt der Enklaven"—Neue Herausforderungen der Städte in der globalen Wissensgesellschaft. *Neues Archiv für Niedersachsen. Zeitschrift für Stadt-, Regional- und Landesentwicklung*, (2), pp. 2–17.

Keil, A. (2006). New urban governance processes on the level of neighbourhoods. *European Planning Studies*, 14(3), pp. 335–364.

Kortmann, K. (2011). Gated communities: Im Luxus eingemauert. *Focus Online*. Available at: www.focus.de/wissen/bild-der-wissenschaft/tid-22334/gated-communities-urbanismus-light_aid_627768.html [Accessed 3 Sept. 2016]

May, D. (2003). *The struggle of becoming established in a deprived inner-city neighbourhood*. 1st ed. [pdf] Aalborg, Milan: The Fondazione Eni Enrico Mattei. Available at: www.feem.it/userfiles/attach/Publication/NDL2003/NDL2003-101.pdf [Accessed 3 Sept. 2016]

Neubacher, A., and Schmidt, C. (2008). Die Flucht der Elite. *Der Spiegel*, (17), pp. 28–31.

Schlichtman, J. J., and Patch, J. (2014). Gentrifier? Who, me? Interrogating the gentrifier in the mirror. *International Journal of Urban and Regional Research*, 38(4), pp. 1491–1508.

Walter, F. (2010). Suche nach Sicherheit—Was die Mitte wirklich will. *Die Welt*. Available at: www.welt.de/debatte/kommentare/article6569936/Suche-nach-Sicherheit-Was-die-Mitte-wirklich-will.html [Accessed 3 Sept. 2016]

Chapter 12

A Conclusion?

Or: Toward a New Beginning?

ROBERT KRUEGER, TIM FREYTAG, AND SAMUEL MÖSSNER

We learned in the opening chapters that *sustainability* is both a word used to describe behaviors and conditions as well as a normative concept implying a set of principles for the economy, society, and ecology. We have seen that sustainable development and sustainability have a long history in human development. Over the centuries, sustainability has been a guiding concept that has traveled around the world and received buy-in across many diverse constituencies, from governments at all spatial scales, to large and small businesses, private actors, and environmental and social justice groups. How these groups organize around different pieces of the concept has real implications for how it is expressed in policy and practice. And this is where the political challenges lie—in the implementation of sustainability as a guiding principle. It's not that decisions are being made in smoky back rooms with fat-cat elites doing the decision making. Arguably, decisions are being made right out in the open, for all of us to see, and we sometimes seem surprised that the implications of sustainability have such an uneven effect across places and social groups.

Reflecting on the field trips, we learned that there are different and controversial rhetorics and practices that have been implemented in the name of sustainability. We have referred to this as the "sustainability consensus." Thus, for analytical purposes, the entry point of analysis is no longer who is *for* or *against* sustainability. We learned, in fact, that it is very hard to find someone who is not in favor of sustainability. We then focused on the actors and groups and other forces that shape these perspectives and frame sustainability consensus:

- A local politician in China may understand sustainable urbanism as a suitable approach to work for a better living for future generations, to strengthen the city's position in the inter-urban competitiveness, or to push forward his or her ideas of urban development with the support of the community and the voters.

- For a real estate developer in Luxembourg, sustainable urbanism may appear more like an economic resource or a tool to increase market value.

- Civil society in Christchurch, New Zealand, may understand sustainable urbanism primarily as an approach to express and put into practice their ideas and to strengthen their role as participants in the ongoing transformation of their neighborhood.

- Activists in New York or Vancouver may see sustainable urbanism as an alternative to resist neoliberal capitalism and to foster postgrowth or degrowth initiatives.

Let us explore the concept of sustainability consensus more thoroughly.

The Green City, Sustainability, and Consensual Planning

Let's return to our Introduction, where we briefly presented Campbell's typology of resource conflicts in planning (Campbell, 1996). In the center of Campbell's tripartite approach is the green city, like many of the cities presented in the field trips. All lines of conflict are equally handled, and all advocates for the more extreme positions (economy first ecology first, social justice first) could agree on an optimal solution. Campbell's (1996) idea entails a significant and rather underestimated blind spot: The field trips illustrated that planning is not a rational balancing of divergent objectives in urban planning. Consensus is neither made by listening to all voices in society, nor is it a rational balancing of all possibilities. The field trips shed light on the political conditions under which the content and ideas of what actually is economic prosperity, ecological protection, or social justice are constructed. There are hegemonic ideas of sustainable development that dominate and superimpose other understandings of economic growth and environmental protection of social justice.

The French philosopher Jacques Rancière (2002) has argued that consensus is hardly possible since a rational debate is often not possible, simply because people do not understand each other. Conflicts are not between one saying "green" and the other one saying "economy." More often, all participants say "green" but mean very different things by it. Rancière (2002) calls this "disagreement," the nonagreement about the same words filled with different meanings. If a consensus is made, he argues further, it is based on those voices who understand the same meaning by the same word; other meanings are not negotiated but excluded from consensus. From this perspective, consensual planning is a rather contested concept and needs critical questioning.

Consensus is often constructed by arguments that are ostensibly clear and unquestionable to everybody. In our world, it is not the monarch's word anymore, but scientific indicators and academic expertise. The geographer Erik Swyngedouw writes that "environmental politics is a politics legitimated by a scientific consensus which, in turn, translates into a political consensus" (2009: 602). He further explains that environmental politics is often "reduced to the administration and management of processes whose parameters are defined by consensual socio-scientific knowledges" (Swyngedouw, 2009: 602). The *best* solution in the center of Campbell's (1996) triangle is therefore often evaluated based on knowledge that seems not open for discussion.

Given these complexities, it is not hard to imagine that after nearly two decades of sustainable urban development we are no closer to sustainability than we were, especially if we look beyond the upper and middle classes. Similar to how the environment was a sink for flushing the unwanted effects of industrial production for so many generations, now the working poor, those most vulnerable in society, have become the negative externalities of sustainable urbanism.

So, how might we approach these complex milieu conceptually, as scholars, and in practice, as technicians, in order to better understand what they expose about society?

To try to accomplish these, we will do something unconventional in the conclusion of the book. We will introduce not only a new concept that can be used to explore this question but a process in which to do it. In other words, we seek to add to the scholarly analytical rigor that we introduced as well as introduce a rigorous approach for those engaged in planning policy and practice. To assist in this, we introduce the concept of ideology that, for us, is the baseline from where everything and everyone is perceived and valued. This is the baseline for observing the differences and similarities attendant to people, places, and institutions. Going back to the notion of social constructivism in chapter 1, this is the process where a *normal* condition from which we evaluate difference. Following a social constructivist approach, we believe that these positions are not fixed but socially produced and individually constructed every day and in every very moment. While theoretically this could lead to an infinite number of different positions that change every minute, these positions are in fact relatively stable patterns. Therefore, we can identify different sets of similar opinions, perspectives, and imaginations that *structure* and *order* our society. The field trips have highlighted these patterns, particularly in those moments when one had to decide between two directions to follow: economic growth or social justice. This decision was then often legitimized by saying "you cannot have social justice without economic prosperity" or "there is no funding for social activities," and so on.

Accordingly, these sets of positions can be grouped around political ideologies that Michael Freeden defines as a "set of ideas, beliefs, opinions, and values that exhibit a recurring pattern, are held in significant groups, compete over providing and controlling plans for public policy, and do so with the aim of justifying, contesting or changing social and political arrangements and processes of a political community" (2003: 32). The term "ideology" has witnessed many criticisms over time from different philosophical and political strands. Marx and Engels were criticizing the term, yet using it by developing a critique of ideology aiming to unmask social dominion and power. Italian thinker Antonio Gramsci was going further. He observed that there are antagonistic positions in society that are competing for hegemony. Rebuilding the inner city of Christchurch under the dogma of economic growth is a hegemonic position that is not only maintained and defended by police forces and military services, but also by what Gramsci called a "produced consensus" that unifies and subjugates other ideas and perceptions under an umbrella of an ostensible consensus. What makes Gramsci's concept a truly powerful idea is that every hegemony is contrasted by counter-hegemonies. Barcelona's smart city strategy is contrasted by resistant groups producing alternative visions for the city. Montepellier's green city agenda could have been challenged by those who highlight the contradiction of this political agenda. Showcasing the contradictions of Calgary's absurd green oil politics creates awareness for alternative possibilities in society. Even the reflections of individual contradictions, as in the Dortmund field trip, create awareness for the structural hegemonies individuals are embedded in.

And now here is the contribution of this book and the experience it has provided: we have presented a critical lens to the different perspectives and logics that are intertwined with the notion of sustainability. While we could have focused on capitalist consumption, global production chains, or any other example, we believe that sustainable urbanism better unfolds the ideological contradictions of sustainability as a metaconsensual strategy. We used field trips as instruments to extract the different logics and perspectives that come along with sustainability in order to stimulate critical thinking about alternative ways and forms to create a more sustainable world.

This has set up the conceptual exit point from this book looking forward. We now offer a more practical approach for those engaged in policy and practice.

How Things Work is Universal, but in More Ways than One . . . Or, "Critique in the Name of What?"

Wetlands provide ecological services, such as storm water sequestration and water-quality improvements through their filtering process. Engineers can measure the value of a wetland by determining its "replacement value," that is, what it costs to build a water treatment plant, for example, to remove contaminants from gray and black water. Architects can design zero emission developments (ZEDs) and high-performance green buildings that use fewer electrons and/or rely on renewable forms of distributed generation. Planners can design developments that have high-population densities, are close to public transport, have bike-share programs, and house an organic market on the ground floor. Based on climate, biodiversity, and growth rates, urban foresters can determine optimal canopy cover to sequester carbon in our cities. Bankers can create financial instruments to support the development of green retrofits and new green construction. Each of these projects represent technical, managerial, and organizational approaches (or fixes) to sustainable urbanism. These activities epitomize "good" sustainable urbanism. Yet, despite the efforts we witnessed in chapter 2, sustainable urbanism is a complex, highly technical, and contested process. Its operant moniker "sustainable" should not enable projects to go forward without at least questioning who the winners and losers are.

In this final section, we introduce the concept of "engaged pluralism" in an effort to see our way forward. Like Barnes and Sheppard (2010), we see engaged pluralism as a normative approach—it should be "universal." This may sound like a contradiction to our argument about the universality of ideology and techno-centrism in decision making, but it is not. Following William James, the father of American Pragmatism, we advocate for an engaged pluralism that "involves resolving that however much we are committed to our styles of thinking, we are willing to listen to others without suppressing the otherness of the other" (Barnes and Sheppard, 2010: 194). This doesn't mean holding hands and singing "kumbaya." Rather, the task is to learn to "grasp the other's position in the strongest possible light . . . not as an adversary, but as a conversational partner" (Bernstein, 1988: 17). In the remainder of this chapter we will explore these ideas in the context of sustainable urbanism.

Engaged Pluralism and the Sustainability Consensus

Sometimes to understand the present, one needs to study the past.

—Chinese fortune cookie[1]

We are shaped by, and continue to be shaped by, the past. We belong to traditions that we no longer have to think about because we are so ensconced in them. To this point in the book, we have developed a narrative of sustainable development, in general, and sustainable urbanism, in particular. Yet, sustainable urbanism is not an isolated tradition. As we have seen, sustainable development has its own narrative but is also part of other narratives. These include the ideologies of rationalism, capitalism, and related technocratic decision making. Each of these have implications for how sustainable urbanism becomes manifest in the landscape. Each of these ideologies are part of a broader ideology of "foundationalism," which argues that humans have a special faculty of insight that enables us to know the fixed foundations of knowledge. Bernstein (1988) uses the example of "scientism" to illustrate this point. Scientism, Bernstein (1988: 7) argues, is the "conviction that science and science alone is the standard for determining what counts as legitimate knowledge and for determining what is 'real.'" We have shown that foundationalism, and its operant scientism, are pervasive in the planning context. Indeed, it is this pervasiveness that can make planning such a contentious process. It is contentious because of the (false) binary created by its foundational tradition: rational and irrational thought. No matter whether planning is a postpolitical act, a rational process, or catalyzed by city elites, this binary is reproduced. As Chantal Mouffe puts it: "creation of a unity in a context of conflict and diversity is always concerned with an 'us' versus 'them'" (2000: 15). It is this binary that engaged pluralism seeks to overcome.

Engaged pluralism seeks to end the notion that there are absolute beginnings or endings to philosophical questions. It is useful here because it illustrates the effort to create "absolute" certainties in planning decisions. Philosopher John Dewey once referred to searches for the absolute as the "spectator theory of knowledge." Applied to sustainable urbanism, it's easy for many actors to develop "optimal" and "certain" sustainable solutions, plans, and projects, when they can exclude those traditions that are outside the fold of rationalism. Think back to our example of the size of park benches in London in our Introduction. Notions of the nuclear family were so firmly established in English, and Western society in general, that excludes other traditions (that is, they were not even considered) in the park design. This is a simple example, to be sure, but it illustrates the point. Also consider William James's point that a pluralist recognition of the "real world" depends on where one starts.

Feminist philosophers of science have also taken up this point through concepts of situatedness, standpoint, or positionality. Donna Haraway (1989) has argued, for example, that the situatedness of Western scientific knowledge is highly gendered, reflecting the social characteristics of primarily white male scientists who carry it out in practice. Following Barnes and Sheppard (2010: 198), "Nevertheless, the essential point remains: difference is an inescapable and unavoidable aspect of pluralism [of life], and the peripheralization of knowledge or exclusion of potential voices from science distorts the knowledge that is produced." Feminist theory has also illuminated that pluralism is more than getting everyone around the table to achieve "consensus." It is also concerned with the norms governing communication. Erstwhile, marginalized groups must be empowered and given the opportunity to veto decisions. For Barnes and Sheppard (2010: 198), deliberation should be a "ceaseless even-handed debate among different approaches." To ground this point, they cite Longino (2002), who suggests that a plurality of knowledge can be produced if

- recognized public forums for criticism of evidence, methods, assumptions and reasoning are created;

- criticism is taken seriously, with claims adjusted in the face of adequate criticism;

- the existence of public standards for evaluating knowledge claims is acknowledged; and

- equality of intellectual authority among all participants is maintained.

Mouffe adds to this that the "prime task . . . is not to eliminate passions from the sphere of the public . . . but to mobilize those passions toward democratic designs" (2000: 16). The task in science, as in sustainable urbanism, is to engage the plurality of knowledge without marginalizing the different groups that produce it.

Several times in the book we have invited you to be active participants in engaging and critiquing current forms of sustainable urbanism. We have called on you to develop creative ideas and solutions within the context of the field trips you have taken. Following Bernstein (1988: 6), we agree that: "We can best appreciate the vitality and diversity of . . . tradition when we approach it as an ongoing engaged conversation consisting of distinctive—sometimes competing voices." We hope that you enjoyed getting into the field, and that you will continue to explore via your own adventures in sustainable urbanism.

Note

1. The quote is attributable to several sources. Our reference is to a fortune that philosopher Hans-Georg Gadamer received inside a cookie during a dinner with colleague Richard Bernstein.

References

Barnes, T. J., and Sheppard, E. (2010). "Nothing includes everything": Towards engaged pluralism in Anglophone economic geography. *Progress in Human Geography*, 34(2), pp. 193–214.

Bernstein, R. J. (1988). Pragmatism, pluralism, and the healing of wounds. *Proceedings and Addresses of the American Philosophical Association*, 63(3), pp. 5–18.

Bernstein, R. J. (1992). *The new constellation: The ethical-political horizons of modernity/postmodernity*. Cambridge, MA: MIT Press.

Campbell, S. (1996). Green cities, growing cities, just cities? Urban planning and the contradictions of sustainable development. *Journal of the American Planning Association*, 62(3), pp. 296–312.

Haraway, D. J. (1989). *Primate visions: Gender, race, and nature in the world of modern science*. Hove: Psychology Press.

Longino, H. E. (2002). *The fate of knowledge*. Princeton, NJ: Princeton University Press.

Mouffe, C. (2000). For an agonistic model of democracy. In: N. O'Sullivan, ed., *Political Theory in Transition*, 1st ed. London, New York: Routledge, pp. 113–129.

Rancière, J. (2002). *Das Unvernehmen. Politik und Philosophie*. Frankfurt: Suhrkamp.

Swyngedouw, E. (2009). The antinomies of the postpolitical city: In search of a democratic politics of environmental production. *International Journal of Urban and Regional Research*, 33(3), pp. 601–620.

Contributors

Tim Baird is a PhD candidate at the University of Canterbury in Christchurch, New Zealand. He also holds a master's of commerce with first class honours degree from this institution. Tim has published in the areas of sustainability, biosecurity, innovation, and wine tourism, with a particular focus on these issues within the New Zealand wine industry.

Constance Carr is a senior research associate at the Institute of Geography and Spatial Planning, University of Luxembourg. Her research interests focus on sustainable development policy, urban planning, and comparative urban geography, particularly with respect to small states. She holds a master's of environmental studies degree from York University, in Toronto, and a PhD in urban sociology from Humboldt University, in Berlin. She has published in various journals, including *Regional Studies*, *Local Environment*, *International Journal of Urban and Regional Research*, and *Planning Theory & Practice*.

I-Chun Catherine Chang is an assistant professor in the department of geography at Macalester College, United States. Her research interests include global urbanism, urban sustainability, policy circulation, and the political economy of East Asia. She is currently examining the urban sustainability movement of building new eco-friendly and low carbon emission towns across Asia. Her work contextualizes how these new town initiatives manifest on the ground, and also traces how their genealogical connectivities reshape the international circulation of sustainable planning knowledge and practices.

Winifred Curran, an associate professor of geography at DePaul University in Chicago, is an urban geographer who specializes in gentrification and urban policy, especially in terms of urban change, labor, race and gender. Recently, Curran's work has focused on gentrification and community resistance in Pilsen.

Susanne Frank is a professor of urban and regional sociology in the school of spatial planning at Dortmund University of Technology, Germany. As a sociologist, she specializes in Western urban development processes. Her current research and publications focus on contemporary transformations of urban and regional settlement structures, especially on suburbanization, reurbanization, and gentrification. She pays particular attention to the role of the middle classes and the importance of changing family and gender arrangements in these processes. She is fascinated by the role of "nature" in the material and symbolic reinvention of postindustrial landscapes.

Tim Freytag is a professor of human geography at the University of Freiburg, Germany. His research interests include tourism and mobility studies, social and cultural geography, geography of education, urban studies, and metropolitan research.

David Giband is a professor of geography and urban planning at the University of Perpignan and director of the center of research ART-DEV (universities of Montpellier and Perpignan, CNRS, CIRAD). As a social geographer, his research mainly concerns the social dimensions of cities with a focus on urban topics such as housing, poverty, segregation, and education. He has recently worked on social policies in disadvantaged neighborhoods ("la banlieue") in some southern French cities and their effects on spatial fragmentation. He is also interested in sustainable urban politics and planning in French and Spanish Mediterranean cities.

C. Michael Hall is a professor in the department of management, marketing and entrepreneurship at the University of Canterbury, Christchurch, New Zealand and visiting professor, Linnaeus University, Kalmar, Sweden. Current research focuses on issues of tourism and regional development, resilience, and environmental change.

Trina Hamilton is an associate professor of geography at State University of New York in Buffalo. Her work focuses on issues of corporate social and environmental responsibility, and both global and localized governance struggles. She is particularly interested in new forms of politics (including the overlapping of marketplace and traditional political spheres), and the impact of new governance mechanisms on trade and economic development patterns at a variety of scales.

Mike Kohout is a professor of geography at California State University, San Bernardino. He is broadly interested in cultural and social geography, immigration, the US–Mexico border, and southern California. He has written on economic development, labor geography, and immigration politics. His current interest is the cultural geography of California deserts and borderlands.

Freya Kristensen was a PhD candidate in the department of geography at Simon Fraser University from 2008 to 2013, during which time her contribution to this book was written. Her dissertation work looked at how cities construct policy related to the social dimension of sustainability, with a particular focus on the role that municipal sustainability networks play in influencing these policies. Freya holds an MA in International Development from the University of Northern British Columbia. She is currently working as an independent researcher and lives in Vancouver, Canada.

Rob Krueger is an associate professor at Worcester Polytechnic Institute. He has edited a book on the politics of urban sustainable development and published dozens of articles on urban development, urban sustainability, and urban politics. His current interest is on the politics of degrowth in the global north and diverse economies in the global south.

Samuel Mössner is a professor in the department of geography at the University of Münster, Germany. He is the author of a book on urban social policy and governance and several papers on urban politics.

Marit Rosol holds a Canada Research Chair in Global Urban Studies and is an associate professor in the department of geography at the University of Calgary, Canada. She received a PhD in geography from Humboldt-Universität zu Berlin (2006) and an MA equivalent in urban and regional planning from Technical University Berlin (2001). Her Habilitation (advanced postdoctoral degree, 2012) research project on "governing through community participation" was based on her empirical work in Vancouver, Canada. In her research and teaching, Marit connects processes of urban restructuring with wider social theory, particularly political economy, theories of neoliberalism, governmentality, and hegemony. Her work covers such areas as urban (environmental) politics, critical urban food studies, housing, urban gardening, and civic participation.

Cristina Temenos is an urban studies postdoctoral research fellow in geography and the Manchester Urban Institute at the University of Manchester. Her work examines the relationships between social justice and the mobilization of social, health, and drug policies across cities in the global north and global south. Her work has examined social movement mobilization for drug policy reform, the importation and implementation of urban sustainability frameworks, low carbon mobility transitions, and the mobilization of austerity programs and their effects on access to public health services. She is an editorial board member for Environment and Planning C: Politics and Space and Geography Compass. Her work on urban policy mobilities has been published in the *Transactions of the Institute of British Geographers, Environment and Planning A,* and the *International Journal of Urban and Regional Research,* among others.

Index